Ann Petry's Short Fiction

Recent Titles in
Contributions in Afro-American and African Studies

Black Leadership for Social Change
Jacob U. Gordon

Mythatypes: Signatures and Signs of African/Diaspora and Black
Goddesses
Alexis Brooks De Vita

African Visions: Literary Images, Political Change, and Social Struggle in
Contemporary Africa
Cheryl B. Mwaria, Silvia Federici, and Joseph McLaren, editors

Voices of the Fugitives: Runaway Slave Stories and Their Fictions of Self-
Creation
Sterling Lecater Bland, Jr.

Meditations on African Literature
Dubem Okafor

Achebe the Orator: The Art of Persuasion in Chinua Achebe's Novels
Chinwe Christiana Okechukwu

Rethinking the Slave Narrative: Slave Marriage and the Narratives of
Henry Bibb and William and Ellen Craft
Charles J. Heglar

The Harlem Group of Negro Writers
Melvin B. Tolson
Edward J. Mullen, editor

Rereading the Harlem Renaissance: Race, Class and Gender in the Fiction
of Jessie Fauset, Zora Neale Hurston, and Dorothy West
Sharon L. Jones

Critical Essays on Bessie Head
Maxine Sample, editor

Reproduction and Social Context in Sub-Saharan Africa: A Collection of
Micro-Demographic Studies
Samuel Agyei-Mensah and John B. Casterline, editors

"Color Struck" Under the Gaze: Ethnicity and the Pathology of Being in
the Plays of Johnson, Hurston, Childress, Hansberry, and Kennedy
Martha Gilman Bower

Ann Petry's Short Fiction

Critical Essays
Edited by Hazel Arnett Ervin and Hilary Holladay

Contributions in Afro-American and African Studies,
Number 209

Westport, Connecticut
London

Library of Congress Cataloging-in-Publication Data

Ann Petry's short fiction : critical essays / edited by Hazel Arnett Ervin and Hilary Holladay.

  p. cm.—(Contributions in Afro-American and African Studies, ISSN 0069–9624 ; no. 209)

  Includes bibliographical references (p.) and index.

  ISBN 0–313–32291–0

  1. Petry, Ann Lane, 1911– —Criticism and interpretation. 2. Women and literature—United States—History—20th century. 3. African Americans in literature. 4. New England—in literature. 5. Short story. I. Ervin, Hazel Arnett. II. Holladay, Hilary. III. Series.

PS3531.E933Z54 2004

813'.54—dc22   2004000646

British Library Cataloguing in Publication Data is available.

Library of Congress Catalog Card Number: 2004000646
ISBN: 0–313–32291–0
ISSN: 0069–9624

First published in 2004

Praeger Publishers, 88 Post Road West, Westport, CT 06881
An imprint of Greenwood Publishing Group, Inc.
www.praeger.com

Printed in the United States of America

∞™

The paper used in this book complies with the Permanent Paper Standard issued by the National Information Standards Organization (Z39.48–1984).

10 9 8 7 6 5 4 3 2 1

Copyright Acknowledgments

The editors and publisher gratefully acknowledge permission to reprint the following:

George R. Adams. "Riot as Ritual: Ann Petry's 'In Darkness and Confusion.'" *Black American Literature Forum* 6.2 (Summer 1972): 54–58. Reprinted by permission.

Reprinted by permission of the publisher from "Jazz/Blues Structure in Ann Petry's *Solo on the Drums*" in *Liberating Voices: Oral Tradition in African American Literature* by Gayl Jones, pp. 90–98, Cambridge, Mass.: Harvard University Press, Copyright 1991 by Gayl Jones.

Nora Ruth Roberts. "Artistic Discourse in Three Short Stories by Ann Petry." *Women and Language* 22.1 (1999): 29–36. Reprinted by permission.

Gladys J. Washington. "A World Made Cunningly: A Closer Look at Ann Petry's Short Fiction." *CLA Journal* 30.1 (Sept. 1986): 14–29. Reprinted by permission of The College Language Association.

Ann Petry excerpts. Reprinted by the permission of Russell & Volkening as agents for the author. Copyright © 1944 by Ann Petry, renewed 1972 by Ann Petry. Originally appeared in *Phylon*, 1944.

To

Patrick and Hazel McDonald of St. Joseph Parish, Barbados

and

SallyAnn Ferguson, Jennifer Jordan, Ann Kelly, Trudier Harris, and Linda Wagner-Martin, *teachers and scholars extraordinaire*

Contents

Introduction

Hazel Arnett Ervin and Hilary Holladay

In a 1950 essay titled "The Novel as Social Criticism," Ann Petry wrote, "Most of what I have learned about writing I learned the hard way, through trial and error and rejection slips. I set out to be a writer of short stories and somehow ended up as a novelist—possibly because there simply wasn't room enough within the framework of a short story to do the sort of thing I wanted to do." Petry went on to admit, ruefully, "I have collected enough rejection slips for my short stories to paper four or five good sized rooms" ("Novel" 1118).

The suggestion here is that the particular demands of the short story stymied this native of Old Saybrook, Connecticut, who had begun her professional life as a pharmacist who wrote fiction in her spare time. The success of her first novel, *The Street* (1946), would seem to bear out her self-evaluation. *The Street*, a tragic tale of Lutie Johnson and her fellow tenement dwellers on Harlem's 116th Street, won Petry a Houghton Mifflin fellowship and established her as a best-selling novelist. Petry is the first African American woman to achieve such a distinction, and she is the only black female novelist of her generation whose fame approaches that of male counterparts Richard Wright, Ralph Ellison, and James Baldwin. With a debut novel in 1946 that has sold more than a million and a half copies to date and has never been out of print, Petry is a force to be reckoned with, both within and beyond the realm of African American literature.

By the time Petry published *Country Place* (1947), her second novel, she had moved back to Old Saybrook. Along with her husband, George Petry (1907–2000), who was newly discharged from the army in 1947, she settled in a historic home on Old Boston Post Road in her hometown. After nine years in New York City, Petry seemed poised to write many more novels, further burnishing her reputation in that genre. Yet, despite living a long life that afforded her the opportunity to write at her leisure, Petry published only one other novel, *The Narrows* (1953). While *Country Place* and *The Narrows* received very favorable reviews, it is *Miss Muriel and Other Stories* (1971), Petry's sole volume of short fiction, that comes closest to equaling *The Street* in lasting significance.

The inclusion of stories from *Miss Muriel* in college textbooks such as *The Norton Anthology of African American Literature*, *Call and Response: The Riverside Anthology of the African American Literary Tradition*, and the *Heath Anthology of American Literature* means that many students are getting to know Ann Petry primarily as a short-story writer. This is not without irony, given Petry's belief, at least in 1950, that she was more naturally suited to the novel. Still, Petry's stories, though few in number, are excellent examples of a demanding genre and are fine ways to get to know the writer.

Petry broke into print as a writer with "Marie of the Cabin Club," a racy little crime story published under the pseudonym Arnold Petri in 1939 in Baltimore's *Afro-American*. For this story, Petry received five dollars. "I was tempted," she wrote, "to frame the check but I didn't" ("Ann Petry" 264). Four years passed before her next story was published. During this period, Petry was living in New York City and working at a variety of jobs that she believed would help her as a fiction writer. She also took a creative-writing class, which she credited with increasing her confidence and enabling her to accomplish her goal as a fiction writer.

"On Saturday the Siren Sounds at Noon" appeared under her own name in a 1943 issue of the *Crisis*. "On Saturday" points toward Petry's later, more mature fiction. It is the story of a black man whose unhappy wife leaves their children untended while she goes out with her boyfriend. In her absence, their locked tenement apartment catches fire, and one of the children dies. Once he realizes her culpability, the enraged protagonist kills his wife and later jumps to his death in front of an onrushing train.

Though betraying the melodramatic tendencies of a writer still finding her way with potent material, "On Saturday" drew the attention of an editor at Houghton Mifflin, the venerable publishing company in Boston. The editor asked if Petry was writing a novel she could enter in Houghton Mifflin's literary fellowship competition. "I said no, I wasn't, but perhaps by the following year I would be" ("Ann Petry" 264). With the editor's encouragement in mind, Petry set about writing *The Street*. Winning the coveted $2,400 fellowship allowed her to complete her first novel without financial worry. In 1946, a gala reception at the Hotel Biltmore in New York celebrated the book's publication. Houghton Mifflin knew it had a best-seller on its hands, and Petry, the struggling short-story writer, knew that all of her efforts leading up to "On Saturday the Siren Sounds at Noon" had something to do with what appeared to be her meteoric success.

What had turned the key for Petry? Scholars of Petry's writing have long been familiar with the name of Mabel Louise Robinson, the Columbia University fiction-writing instructor to whom Petry dedicated *The Narrows*. In essays and interviews, Petry always singled out Robinson as the person whose motivational teaching helped her achieve success. Other than Miss Robinson, Petry had little instruction in creative writing. Although one of her high-school English teachers had predicted that Petry could become a professional writer, Petry did not go to college with that goal in mind.

Instead, Petry took the safe and familiar course charted by her father and maternal aunt, successful pharmacists for whom she had worked during her high-school years. At the Connecticut College of Pharmacy in New Haven, Petry studied "physics, chemistry, mathematics—everything to make me a pharmacist" (Greene 78). Practical though it was, this was clearly a default option for an extremely creative young woman who had started elementary school at age four and done well academically ever since. In addition to being a very good student, Petry was an expert seamstress and baker who sold cakes and curtains to her neighbors. These skills suggest that she could have followed in the footsteps of her mother, Bertha James Lane, an entrepreneur of diverse talents who was a "chiropodist, hairdresser, licensed barber, manufacturer of hair tonic, creator of a liquid cleaner for use in the bathroom," and founder of a business called "Beautiful Linens for Beautiful Homes" ("Ann Petry" 260). But in this middle-class family, a college degree was expected of Ann Lane before she entered the business world full-time. A high-school graduate at 15, she waited 2 years before continuing her education, perhaps partly because she was so young and partly because her parents were already paying for her older sister's education at Pembroke College, the female division of Brown University. "[F]inally they said to me, 'Why don't you try to go to pharmacy school?' So I said 'Sure. When?'" (Mrtek 79–80).

Ann Petry's early labors in the family business had not exactly endeared the profession to her. She had spent her teenage years helping out at her family's Old Saybrook pharmacy and, after her college education, she worked at their store in Old Lyme. While still in high school, she had toiled in the pharmacy seven days a week. "The only time that drugstore was closed was on Christmas in the afternoon and Thanksgiving in the afternoon," she once said, with an uncharacteristic note of resentment, adding that "if it weren't for that experience I would probably have tried to become licensed as a pharmacist when I lived in New York City" (Mrtek 84). The pharmacy profession's loss was literature's gain.

New York was, of course, a startlingly different world from Old Saybook. For the first time in her life, Petry was not part of a racial minority. In and around Harlem, she was one of a great many black people walking down the sidewalk, attending a movie, or riding the subway. Intent on developing herself as a writer and citizen, she worked for two Harlem newspapers, first selling advertising copy and later as a reporter and columnist; studied painting and piano; tried her hand at acting; cofounded a consumer-education group for black women; and taught in an after-school program for children similar to Bub, the eight-year-old boy so poignantly portrayed in *The Street*. During her apprentice years, before she had published "Marie of the Cabin Club," Petry turned to the autobiographies of writers for inspiration and practical advice. Among those she read was *My Day in Court* (1939) by Arthur Train, a Boston-born lawyer and prolific author of crime novels and mysteries. While reading Train's autobiography, she came across a passage that spoke directly to her:

[Train] said that if he were a beginning writer one of the things that he would do would be to enter Mabel L. Robinson's course in the short story at Columbia University. Needless to say I promptly applied for admission to the class.

I spent a year in Miss Robinson's short story class. And during another year I was a member of the workshop that she conduct[ed] at Columbia. What I didn't learn through trial and error I learned from Miss Robinson. She taught me to criticize what I had written and to read other people's creative efforts with a critical eye. Perhaps of even greater importance she made me believe in myself. ("The Novel as Social Criticism" 1119)

Nearly 40 years later, Petry still recalled her instructor with gratitude. In an autobiographical essay published in 1988, she described her class with Miss Robinson: "It was a great experience. She made me believe in myself. She said, 'You have all the necessary qualifications: imagination, command of the language. Whether or not you become a writer is entirely up to you. Plough to the end of the furrow'" ("Ann Petry" 264). And plow Petry did. Her experience in Miss Robinson's class provided her with the skills and confidence she needed in order to embark on a critically acclaimed and lucrative career.

The stories in *Miss Muriel* evince an integrity of style and theme no longer common in American fiction. Their compassionate characterization and sense of location are equally rare today. To understand how Petry approached the writing of these well-crafted stories, we can turn to Mabel Robinson's own guidelines that appear in her coedited text (with Helen Hull), *The Art of Writing Prose* (1930). In a chapter called "Fictitious Narrative," Robinson and Hull give a short course in fiction writing, complete with exercises in characterization, theme, and other essential elements. Although Petry had probably heard the adage commonly repeated to fledgling writers, "Write what you know," some specific guidelines were needed. In "Fictitious Narrative," Robinson and Hull fill in the blanks, gently ridiculing the apprentice writer who would set a story in a remote, exotic location rather than on familiar turf:

When you work with your own first-hand material, you remove a serious handicap. In simple terms, this means that you should write about the kind of towns you know best, the types of people with whom you are most familiar, the kinds of emotional experiences you have felt. The fact that Siam seems more interesting to you because you have never been there does not mean that your story about Siam would be more interesting to the reader. He would prefer a story about Salt Lake City, if you know that town. Your imagination is your ability to make new combinations of pieces of your own experience. You need first of all, then, to believe in your material and to search that for your stories. (394–95)

Miss Muriel and Petry's three novels show careful adherence to this advice. *The Street* is set in New York City, where Petry was living at the time she wrote the book. Her other two novels are both set in fictional Connecticut towns: *Country Place* in Lennox, a small seaside town clearly based on Old Saybrook, and *The Narrows* in Monmouth, which seems loosely based on Hartford. Five of the stories in *Miss Muriel* take place in New York City. Five other stories are set in Wheeling, another fictional stand-in for Old Saybrook. The remaining three are set in New England's Berkshire Mountains, Boston, and Essex, Connecticut, yet another fictional village probably based on Old Saybrook or a nearby town.

With Miss Robinson's words echoing in her head, Petry apparently felt that she had to ground her fiction in locales she knew intimately. Although she spent a year as a visiting professor at the University of Hawaii, Petry chose to live most of her 88 years in her native Old Saybrook—a quaint, and still pervasively white, seaside town. Fiercely protective of her professional identity and her privacy, she must have sincerely believed that "a trip around the world [had] not in itself the possibility of better stories than a walk down the main street of your home town. . . . Your family is an experience, or many experiences; your friends, your own feelings, the stages through which you have passed as you grew out of childhood. All of these have the universal human elements out of which a writer builds his stories" (Robinson and Hull 395).

Ironically, Miss Robinson's words of wisdom may have contributed to the smallness of her protégée's body of work. Petry seems to have run out of things to say about the places she knew best. No doubt she expected inspiration to find her in Honolulu, but there is no published evidence that it did. Maybe she should have set aside Miss Robinson's insistence on writing about familiar people in familiar settings. Why not set a story in Bangkok?

The answer is simple: That was not Ann Petry's way. She was a chronicler of the world she knew, and that provided sufficient adventure for her. Like her southern counterpart Eudora Welty, who wrote, "A sheltered life can be a daring life as well. For all serious daring starts from within" (Welty 104), Petry knew that for her, being a writer was in itself a bold act. As a female writer of color, she viewed herself "as a survivor and a gambler" who had beaten nearly insurmountable odds ("Ann Petry" 253). "I once figured out that black writers (authors of fiction and poetry) constitute about .000000005 percent of the American population—and that's a generous figure. There isn't a book maker or an odds taker who would have been willing to bet on my ever becoming a published writer" ("Ann Petry" 257).

This volume, in the tradition of Petry's "firsts," is the first collection of critical essays focusing solely on one book of short fiction by an African American woman. The fact that *Miss Muriel*'s 13 stories could generate such a volume is a tribute to Petry's range, complexity, and staying power. This book's first three essays—Gladys Washington's "A World Made Cunningly: A Closer Look at Ann Petry's Short Fiction"; Sheikh Kamarah's "Ann Petry and African Poetics: A Review of 'Solo on the Drums'"; and Gladys Washington's "Folk Traditions in the Short Fiction of Ann Petry"— provide an overview of *Miss Muriel*'s stories and their cultural, historical, and aesthetic dimensions. While Washington, in her two essays, looks at the artistry and folk history that inform the entire collection, Kamarah uses "Solo on the Drums" as a case study, demonstrating Petry's linguistic and literary appropriation of African oral delivery and storytelling techniques.

The volume's second section examines stories that Petry wrote in the 1940s, her most prolific decade. These essays point us toward recurring themes and conflicts in Petry's short fiction, and they expand on some of the larger claims made in the book's opening essays. Drawing on their diverse backgrounds in philosophy, music, anthropology, and literary studies, the authors of these essays offer insights and analysis that will be invaluable to anyone teaching the stories in *Miss Muriel*. Nora Ruth Roberts takes on "Mother Africa," "Olaf and His Girl Friend," and "Solo on the Drums" in "Artistic Discourse in Three Short Stories by Ann Petry." And the novelist and critic Gayl Jones explores the musical backdrop in "Jazz/Blues Structure in 'Solo on the Drums.'" Paul Wiebe gives us a Blakean reading in "'Miss Muriel': Rewriting Innocence into Experience," while Keith Clark looks at the portrayal of male characters in "'From a Thousand Different Points of View': The Multiple Masculinities of Ann Petry's 'Miss Muriel.'" In "Riot as Ritual: Ann Petry's 'In Darkness and Confusion,'" George Adams finds archetypal patterns and rites of passage in one of *Miss Muriel*'s most powerful stories. Placing this story within the context of Farrah Jasmine Griffin's *"Who Set You Flowin'?" The African-American Migration Narrative*, Deirdre Raynor presents "'Ain't No Room for Us Anywhere': Reading Ann Petry's 'In Darkness and Confusion' as a Migration Narrative." In "Apartheid among the Dead; Or, on Christian Laughter in Ann Petry's 'The Bones of Louella Brown,'" Gene Fendt shows how a theological perspective can illuminate a disarmingly comical story. Amy Lee in "The Narrator as Feminist Ally in Ann Petry's 'The Bones of Louella Brown' " reads the same short story from a feminist point of view with specific attention given to its silences.

Moving forward to the 1950s, theater-arts scholar Barbara Lewis recounts the history of the cakewalk, a unique African American dance form, and explains how Petry contextualizes this tradition in "Taking the Cake: Ann Petry's 'Has Anybody Seen Miss Dora Dean?'" The last two essays deal with the "The Witness," a searing story, first published in 1971, in which racism intertwines with sexual violence. Carol Henderson shows how this historical legacy of racial oppression debilitates the story's protagonist in "'The Man Who Cried I Am': Reading Race, Class, and Gender in Ann Petry's 'The Witness,'" while Eva Tettenborn applies trauma theory in "Traumatic Reenactment and the Impossibility of African American Testimony in Ann Petry's 'Like a Winding Sheet' and 'The Witness.'"

Arthur P. Davis once wrote that Petry's short stories would "stand up best after the critical years [had] passed judgment" on all of her work (197). Though Petry's novels, especially *The Street*, continue to invite close scrutiny, it is time to give her stories their due. As editors, we hope that this book will serve as a helpful companion to *Miss Muriel and Others Stories* and in other ways will prove also that Petry was not, as she once supposed, an inadequate short-story writer who needed to become a novelist but, rather, a writer equally adept at both genres.

WORKS CITED

Davis, Arthur P. *From the Dark Tower: Afro-American Writers, 1900 to 1960*. Washington, DC: Howard University Press, 1974.

Greene, Marjorie. "Ann Petry Planned to Write." *Opportunity* 24.2 (April–June 1946): 78–79.

Mrtek, Robert. "A Visit with Ann Petry, May 16, 1984." *Ann Petry: A Bio-Bibliography*. Ed. Hazel Arnett Ervin. New York: G. K. Hall, 1993. 77–88.

Petry, Ann. "Ann Petry." *Contemporary Authors: Autobiography Series*. Ed. Adele Sarkissian. Vol. 6. Detroit: Gale Research, 1988.

———. *Miss Muriel and Other Stories*. 1971. Boston: Beacon Press, 1989.

———. "The Novel as Social Criticism." *Call and Response: The Riverside Anthology of the African American Literary Tradition*. Ed. Patricia Liggins Hill. Boston: Houghton Mifflin, 1998. 1114–19.

Robinson, Mabel Louise, and Helen Hull. "Fictitious Narrative." *The Art of Writing Prose*. Ed. Roger Sherman Loomis et al. New York: Richard R. Smith, 1930. 392–433.
Welty, Eudora. *One Writer's Beginnings*. Cambridge, MA: Harvard University Press, 1984.

Chronology

1908	Born Ann Lane, October 12, in Old Saybrook, Connecticut, to Peter Clark Lane Jr. and Bertha James Lane. The youngest of two daughters.
1912	Enters Old Saybrook Elementary School.
1922	Begins to write short stories.
1925	Graduates from Old Saybrook High School
1931	Earns Ph.G. degree from Connecticut College of Pharmacy in New Haven (now School of Pharmacy at the University of Connecticut, Storrs).
1938	Marries George D. Petry of New Iberia, Louisiana, on February 22. Resides at 2 East 129th Street, New York, until 1946. Works until 1941 as salesperson and as journalist for New York's *Amsterdam News*.
1939	Using the pseudonym Arnold Petri, publishes first short story, "Marie of the Cabin Club," in the *Afro-American* (Baltimore).
1940	Joins American Negro Theatre in New York and, for over a year, performs as Tillie Petunia in *On Striver's Row* at the Schomburg Center for Research in Black Culture.

1941   Works as editor of the woman's page and reporter for New York's *People's Voice* until 1944. From 1942 to 1943, is columnist of weekly "The Lighter Side." Studies drawing and painting at New York's Harlem Art Center.

1942   Attends Mabel Louise Robinson's creative-writing workshop and course at Columbia University. Helps found the Negro Women, Inc., a consumer's watch group. Prepares skits and programs for the educational office of the Laundry Workers Joint Board.

1943   Publishes short story "On Saturday the Siren Sounds at Noon." Receives invitation from an editor to enter Houghton Mifflin's Literary Fellowship competition. Serves as publicity director of the National Association of Colored Graduate Nurses. Serves as recreation specialist of Harlem's Play Schools Association Project at New York's Public School No. 10, located at St. Nicholas Avenue and 116th Street.

1944   Publishes short story "Doby's Gone." Submits an outline and several chapters of *The Street* to Houghton Mifflin's Literary Fellowship in fiction.

1945   Wins Houghton Mifflin's Literary Fellowship Award in fiction; receives a stipend in the amount of $2,400 and the publication of *The Street*. Publishes short stories "Like a Winding Sheet" and "Olaf and His Girl Friend."

1946   Publishes *The Street* and dedicates the novel to her mother. Is included in *The Best American Short Stories, 1946* for "Like a Winding Sheet." The collection is dedicated to Ann Petry. The New York Women's City Club honors her for her "exceptional contributions to the life of New York City."

1947   Publishes short stories "The Bones of Louella Brown," "In Darkness and Confusion," "The Necessary Knocking on the Door," and "Solo on the Drums." Publishes *Country Place* and dedicates the novel to her father and husband. Relocates with husband to Old Boston Post Road in Old Saybrook, Connecticut.

1949   Birth of daughter, Elisabeth Ann Petry. Death of father. Publishes first book for children, *The Drugstore Cat*, and dedicates it to relatives Anna Houston Bush and Anna Louise James.

1953   Publishes *The Narrows* and dedicates the novel to Mabel Louise Robinson.

1955   Publishes *Harriet Tubman, Conductor on the Underground Railroad* and dedicates it to her daughter, Elisabeth Ann.

1956   Death of mother.

1958   Publishes short story "Has Anybody Seen Miss Dora Dean?" Works as a writer for Columbia Pictures in Hollywood on screenplay for Kim Novak's *That Hill Girl.*

1960   *Harriet Tubman, Conductor on the Underground Railroad* is transposed into braille for the Library of Congress.

1963   Publishes short story "Miss Muriel."

1964   Publishes *Tituba of Salem Village* and dedicates it to uncle Frank P. Chisholm. Under the auspices of the Library of Congress, *Tituba* is transposed into braille.

1965   Publishes the short story "The New Mirror."

1967   Publishes the short story "The Migraine Workers."

1970   Publishes *Legends of the Saints* and dedicates it to sister Helen L. Bush.

1971   Publishes short story "The Witness." Publishes *Miss Muriel and Other Stories* collection and dedicates it to brother-in-law Walter J. Petry. Publishes short story "Mother Africa" in *Miss Muriel* collection.

1972   Lectures in English at the Miami University of Ohio.

1973   Delivers at Suffolk University a lecture on her life and works: "This Unforgettable Passage."

1974   Serves as visiting professor in English at the University of Hawaii. Biography is entered into *Who's Who of American Women.*

1976   Publishes poems "Noo York City 1," "Noo York City 2," and "Noo York City 3" in *Weid: The Sensibility Revue* (Bicentennial Issue II, American Women Poets).

1977   Biography is entered in *Who's Who Among Black Americans.*

1978   The National Endowment for the Arts awards her a creative-writing grant.

1981   Publishes the poems "A Purely Black Stone" and "A Real Boss Black Cat" in *A View from the Top of a Mountain.*

1982   Delivers the Fourth Annual Richard Wright Lecture at Yale University.

1983   Receives Doctor of Letters from Suffolk University.

1984   Receives "Black Women of Connecticut: Achievement against the Odds," an award for literature from the Connecticut Historical Society.

1985   Receives citation for literary achievements from the City of Philadelphia, April 9. *The Street* is reprinted by Beacon Press (Black Women Writers' Series).

1986   Publishes the short story "The Moses Project" in *Harbor Review* (English Department, University of Massachusetts). Biography is entered in *Great Women in Connecticut History* (Hartford, CT: The Permanent Commission on the Status of Women).

1988   Publishes autobiographical essay "Ann Petry" in *Contemporary Authors: Autobiographical Series*. Receives citation from the United Nations Association of the United States. Receives Doctor of Letters from University of Connecticut. *The Narrows* and *The Drugstore Cat* are reprinted by Beacon Press (Black Women Writers' Series).

1989   Receives the Lifetime Achievement Award at the Fifth Annual Celebration of Black Writers' Conference at the Friends of the Free Library in Philadelphia on February 4. Receives Doctor of Humane Letters from Mount Holyoke College. Biography is entered into *Who's Who in Writers, Editors and Poets*. *Miss Muriel and Other Stories* is reprinted by Beacon Press (Black Women Writers' Series).

1992   Houghton Mifflin reissues *The Street*. Petry receives Connecticut Arts Award from the Connecticut Commission on the Arts in Stamford. Reads from her writings during the 30-minute evening broadcast of "Connecticut Voices" on Connecticut Public Radio in Hartford. Is the first of 13 Connecticut writers invited by The Connecticut Center for the Book and *Northeast* magazine to appear in the November 14 issue of the magazine. Also, Mayor of Hartford declares November 14 "Ann Petry Day." And on November 14, an Ann Petry Conference is held at the Trinity College of Hartford. Author Gloria Naylor reads "Tribute to Ann Petry."

1997   Enters a local convalescent hospital. Death of author on April 28.

A World Made Cunningly: A Closer Look at Ann Petry's Short Fiction

Gladys J. Washington

In the September 1979 issue of the *CLA Journal*, Rita Dandridge calls attention to the fact that the novels of black women have received much less critical attention than those of their male counterparts.[1] She points out that the critics, being mostly male and frequently white, have generally dismissed the novels by black women with merely a perfunctory glance; and on the few occasions when they have deigned to take a closer look, they have approached these works with "apathy, chauvinism, or paternalism." She further asserts that while these approaches differ, they have a pernicious similarity in that each tends to "minimize the worth of the black woman's novels." Professor Dandridge concludes that if any fair and equitable assessment of these novels is to be made, that assessment must be made by a different breed of critic, and she sets guidelines for the new critics to follow. She admonishes them to

examine each novel within the context of the writer's purpose; . . . [to] exhibit an understanding of the conditions under which the novelist has worked and by which her intentions have been molded; . . . and finally , . . . [to] make known the contributions that the black woman's novel has made to Americans generally and Afro-American specifically.[2]

The charges that Professor Dandridge levels at the critics for their failure to make any serious attempt at an evaluation of the fiction written by black women are certainly valid. However, if the novels have fared poorly at the hands of the critics, the short fiction has fared even worse, since the short story traditionally has commanded less attention than the novel. It is not surprising, then, that the short fiction written by black women would fall into a special category of critical neglect. So it is with the fiction of Ann Petry, who, in my opinion, is one of the most important, yet most neglected, black women fiction writers since World War II. In 1945, Miss Petry won the Houghton Mifflin Literary Scholarship, with which she was able to complete the writing of her first novel, *The Street*. This work, published in 1946, brought her to the attention of the literary world and gained for her rather wide recognition as a literary artist. Since this publication, however, she has received little critical attention by either black or white, male or female critics. Despite the fact that Miss Petry's novels have been published consistently by a major publishing company, and despite the fact that many of her short stories have appeared in major anthologies, the critics have remained strangely silent.

To examine the canon of Miss Petry's work is to discover a very talented and versatile artist, one who is possessed of a brilliant wit, a fine sensitivity, and a creative genius of the highest caliber. Even the often extreme negativism of a critic like Robert Bone diminishes as he approaches the work of Ann Petry, whose novel *Country Place* [1947] he considers "one of the finest novels of the post war (World War II) period."[3] Also, David Litttlejohn, in *Black on White*, commends Miss Petry for her "solid, earned, tested intelligence" and for her wisdom—a wisdom, he says, that

reveals itself in a prose that is rich and crisp, and suavely shot with the metallic threads of irony. It is a style of constant surprise and delight, alive and alight on the page. It is so charged with sense and pleasure, you can taste it—and yet never . . . is it mere display.[4]

With the exception, then, of these brief, albeit laudatory, comments, together with some few other scattered bits of criticism, the works of this important writer have been virtually ignored.[5] Further, of the few critics who have treated Miss Petry's fiction, almost none have given more than a brief consideration to the short stories. Being thus convinced that the fiction of Ann Petry, most especially the short fiction, deserves a closer look, I propose here to undertake an examination of her short fiction through a consideration of those short stories contained in the volume entitled *Miss Muriel and Other Stories* [1971], a collection which, I believe, provides a panoramic view of Ms. Petry's world—its topography, its inhabitants, its traditions.

The world of Ann Petry is, to appropriate a phrase from John Donne, "a World made cunningly"—a world crafted with the skill and artistry of a writer intensely aware of her art and very keenly attuned to the nuances of the world about her. Moreover, Petry's world is a world inhabited by real people—good and bad people, warm and loving people, frustrated and angry people, black and white and brown people, natives and foreigners, adults and children. It is also a world of animals and trees and flowers; it is urban and rural, cramped and wide, liberal and prejudiced. Petry's world is microcosm of the real world inhabited by real people coping with real problems and enjoying real pleasures. It is also a world in which the black experience in America is central—sometimes tragic, sometimes joyous, but always intense and personal.

The thirteen stories that comprise *Miss Muriel and Other Stories*, the briefest consideration of which reveals the breadth of Ann Petry's world, fall into two distinctive groups. One group depicts a small-town world of simple people enjoying simple pleasures—people whose lives, on the surface at least, are quiet, serene, and uncomplicated. The other group of stories depicts life in the cities and reflects all the tensions and frustrations that are traditionally associated with the urban scene. Petry's small-town world is a world that is placid and "innocent" and appropriately viewed through the eyes of a child. It is a world of pleasant backyards, with lovely gardens, fragrant cherry trees, and "talking honey bees."

This world begins to take shape in the first two stories, "Miss Muriel" [1963] and "The New Mirror," [1965], which recall incidents in the life of the Layen family, the only black family in Wheeling, New York. Samuel Layen, the town druggist, resides here with his wife, her sister, Sophronia, and the Layen's young daughter, who narrates the stories. Through the eyes of the narrator, the reader is able to experience family gatherings in the Layen backyard—one of her coveted "private places"—where the family sits on summer nights after the drugstore is closed. It is here that

[o]n warm June nights the fireflies come out, and there is a kind of soft summer light, composed of moonlight and starlight. The grass is thick under foot and the air is sweet. Almost every night my mother and father and Aunt Sophronia and I, and sometimes Aunt Ellen and Uncle Johno, sit there in the quiet and in the sweetness and in the curious soft light.[6]

Having grown up in the small town of Old Saybrook, Connecticut, Ann Petry knows quite intimately the scene that she describes here, and she invites the reader into her private place to share her reverie, to experience with her a simple, less-complicated time when one might enjoy the pleasurable sensation of a soft summer night and bask in the warmth of family and friends.

The natural beauty of the landscape occupies a very special place in Petry's memory, for she returns to it again and again in her stories. In "The New Mirror," for instance, the young narrator alludes to the delicate fragrances that come from all of the flowering shrubs—from "the cherry blossoms and from the small plants—violets and daffodils," and to the music of the song sparrows. She recalls, with special fondness, her father, standing beneath the trees, smelling their fragrances and listening to the "talking" honey bees, "holding that one note—E flat below middle C" (61). Intensely moved by the sheer beauty of the scene, she writes:

[I]f I were a maker of perfumes, I would make one and call it "Spring" and it would smell like this cool, sweet early morning air and I would let only beautiful young, brown girls use it, and if I could sing, I would sing like the song sparrow and I would let only the beautiful young brown boys hear me. (61)

With her eye for detail and her keen sensitivity to the sights, the sounds, the smells, the natural beauty of this small town, so similar to the small New England town of Old Saybrook, Connecticut, where she grew up, Petry creates a quiet, peaceful world—a world in which the pressures and frustrations of life seem nonexistent.

While Petry's private world is a world of tranquil and fragrant back-yards, it is also a world of lazy summer days spent lying in the sun, enjoying a favorite fishing spot. In "Miss Muriel," for example, when Johno comes to spend the summer with the Layens, the Layens' daughter, Uncle Johno, and Dottle (a friend of Johno's) take their fishing poles, their lunch, and a thermos bottle filled with lemonade and set out for the creek. The young narrator describes the experience in the following manner:

[I]t was a two-mile walk from where we lived to the creek where we caught crabs ... The water in the creek was so clear I could see big crabs lurking way down on the bottom; I could see little pieces of white shells and beautiful stones. We didn't talk much while we were crabbing. Sometimes I lay flat on my stomach on the bridge and looked down into the water, watching the little eddies and whirl-pools that formed after I threw my line in. (33)

Scenes such as the one described here serve to remind the reader not only of some of the more pleasant aspects of the black experience in America but also of the bittersweet nature of that experience; they are reminders of the fact that the bleakness of life for black Americans has often been relieved by the simple pleasures of life—pleasures that other people enjoy; for as Langston Hughes has observed, "being colored doesn't make me not like the same things other folks like who are other races." This fact, too frequently ignored by black writers, but so very central to black survival, is always evident in the fiction of Ann Petry.

As Petry's small-town world continues to unfold, the reader is invited into some of the homes in Wheeling where the domestic lives of the inhabitants are revealed. The Layens' living quarters above the drugstore, as well as the living quarters of the town cobbler, Mr. Bemish, provide an intimate view of the lives of the people. The Layens' home, consisting of a few rooms above the drugstore and a downstairs parlor, is a very special place for the young narrator of the story. The parlor, she says, is "cozy in winter," and she describes it in minute detail. The "turkey red curtains" at the windows, the deep, soft carpet on the floor, the piano, the "old-fashioned sofa with the carved mahogany frame," and the round stove that occupies the center of the room all combine to create a sense of warmth and friendliness. This same atmosphere is apparent in Mr. Bemish's cobbler shop, "with the high laced shoe" sign above the door, another one of the narrator's favorite places. On the "black iron stove" there is a tea kettle, and "usually there is a stew bubbling in the pot" (5). In the sleeping area is a shiny brass bed with "intricate designs on the headboard and footboard" and a "chest of drawers with a small gold framed mirror." The wash bowl and a pitcher on the dresser are decorated with pink rose buds, and there is a "bit of flowered carpet" in front of the bed. Such careful attention to details is a hallmark of Ms. Petry's distinctive style and is doubtlessly attributable to her work as a journalist during the early period of her literary career.

This small-town world, however, is not entirely a private one; indeed, it is also a more public world that includes the town drugstore, the Wheeling Inn, and the stately houses occupied in season by the wealthy summer people. Several of the stories in *Miss Muriel* have as a focal point the Layen family's drugstore. All of the inhabitants of this town pass through its doors at one time or another. The long wooden steps that stretch across the front of the building provide a good perch from which the young narrator of the stories can observe and eavesdrop unnoticed. With fancy scrollwork on the screen door and the word "druggist" painted on the windows with "the most wonderful curliques and flourishes," it is a favorite haunt of the Layen girl. She is continuously fascinated by the shelves of gleaming bottles and jars inside dark mahogany, glass-enclosed cases—jars which, she fancies, "could have held wool of bat and nose of turk, root of mandrake and dust of toad" (83). She notes that the soda fountain, "in a separate room rather like a porch with a great many windows," has "mouth-watering syrups" and that the "cherry and lemon syrups smelled like a fruitstand on a hot summer day" (64).

Despite her somewhat nostalgic view of small-town life, Ann Petry never allows nostalgia to cloud her vision of some of the harsher realities of such an environment. As she herself points out, this "*seemingly* innocent world contains all the frustrations that are an inseparable part of that [the black] experience."[7] Though essentially tranquil, the day-to-day existence of the townspeople of Wheeling is occasionally shattered by acts of violence. Sometimes these violent acts are a result of seething undercurrents of prejudice, as is the case with Mr. Bemish, whose life is threatened by Dottle Smith and Chink Johnson because they resent the attentions that this white man is paying to Aunt Sophronia, the sister of Mr. Layen. Bemish is forced to leave town in the dead of night while Dottle and Chink stand "watching him like two guards or two sheriffs" (55). When the young narrator, angered and frustrated at seeing her friend, the cobbler, being so badly used, lashes out at her uncle Dottle, he can only reply, "You don't understand."

Additionally, there is one instance of self-inflicted violence in the little town of Wheeling—the mysterious suicide of Forbes, the butler in "Has Anybody Seen Miss Dora Dean?" [1958] Forbes takes care of the summer home of Mrs. Wingate, one of the wealthy summer residents of Wheeling. When his body is found on the railroad track in Shacktown, where all those barefoot foreign women lived with the "red light in the window," speculation and rumors spread rapidly through town. In the midst of rumor and speculation, however, is an expression of the community's genuine concern and sympathy for the Forbes family. Thus, while this world is not totally devoid of problems, it is one in which problems are more manageable and less devastating, perhaps because of the closeness and support of the community.

The urban world of Ann Petry, the setting of the second group of stories in *Miss Muriel,* stands in marked contrast to the small-town world of Wheeling, New York. It is a world of junkyards and tenements, of night-clubs and barrooms, of riots and riffraff; it is a world "in darkness and confusion." In "Mother Africa," [1971], for instance, the reader is intro-duced to the junkyard world of Emanuel "Man" Turner—a world of "dis-order and confusion," of "worn out tires, inner tubes and parts of cars, broken chairs and rickety tables, heaps of clothing and piles of old bot-tles." This junkyard setting of "Mother Africa" is symbolic of the urban scene as Petry perceives it; here is a reflection of its inhabitants, whose lives are, in one way or another, trash heaps of disillusionments, disap-pointment, and frustration. As Petry observes, these city dwellers are "pulled by many more forces, lost more quickly in a rougher shuffle than their small town counterparts. The dirty streets were meaner and dirtier than a Connecticut town's conscience would dare allow."[8]

That the streets are indeed "meaner and dirtier" and that they do reflect the trash heaps of the lives of their inhabitants are two facts that are ap-parent in the story entitled "In Darkness and Confusion." William Jones, his wife, Pink, and their niece, Annie Mae, eke out a bare existence on the top floor of a Harlem tenement. The street on which they live, William realizes

wasn't a good street. . . . Almost half of it on one side consisted of the back of three theaters on 125th Street. . . . There were few trees on the street. Even those were a source of danger, for at night shadowy, vague shapes emerged from the street's darkness, lurking near the trees, dodging behind them. He had never been ac-costed by any of these disembodied figures, but the very stealth of their move-ments revealed a dishonest intent that frightened him. (260)

The only release that William finds from the trash heap of his life in Harlem—the only light in the darkness of his days—is his anticipation of a letter from his only son, Sam, who is in the Army somewhere in Georgia. But even this small light is extinguished when he learns from his son's Army buddy that Sam has been imprisoned for defending himself against an assault from a military policeman. The anger that has been seething within the father from the time that he learns of his son's imprisonment erupts when he witnesses the killing of a black soldier by a white police-man in Harlem barroom on a Sunday morning. Without even realizing it, he leads the barroom crowd into the streets and urges the people to riot. The scene is chaotic: "As the crowd surges into the streets, they are joined by girls in their summer dresses, boys in tight-legged pants, old women dragging kids along by the hands" (285), a man on crutches, a blind man—virtually the entire community venting its rage against the system that keeps them imprisoned in the junkyard that is Harlem.

The scenes of Petry's urban world are depicted as graphically as are the scenes of her small-town world. The writer's ability to infuse her descrip-tions with such clarity and force results from the fact that she was inti-mately acquainted with both worlds. Her life in New York—working as a journalist for two newspapers and covering "everything from teas to fires, with births, deaths and picket lines interspersed"[9]—provided many invaluable experiences. Not only was she able to observe, firsthand, life in Harlem—the streets, the houses, and the living conditions—but she was able to write every day, a fact which, she felt, contributed greatly to her development as a writer.

Miss Petry's newspaper career also brought her into contact with in-dividuals from every stratum of society. As a reporter, she got to know "many of New York's citizens, visited their homes, heard their stories . . . watched their reactions,"[10] and she used them to people her fictional world. It is not by accident, then, that Petry's world is inhabited by a wide variety of people reflecting a multiplicity of tendencies, attitudes, desires, and determinations. They are black, white, and brown; they are rich and poor, young and old.

The nonblack characters in Petry's fictional world, as do their counter-parts in the real world, exhibit a wide range of temperaments. There is, for instance, Mr. Bemish, the kindly shoemaker in "Miss Muriel" who befriends the Layens' daughter, bakes delicious molasses cookies for the children, and pays court to Mrs. Layen's sister, Sophronia. There is also the simpering Mrs. Wingate in "Has Anybody Seen Miss Dora Dean?" who is short, fat, and blond, whose "face looks like the face of a china doll," and who "simply could not live without Forbes," her black butler. Then there are the ludicrous morticians, Whiffle and Peabody, whose in-eptitude is a primary source of humor in "The Bones of Louella Brown" [1947]. There is the bigoted Mrs. Taylor in "The Necessary Knocking on the Door" [1947], whose death is directly related to her bigotry. In "The New Mirror," there is the bright, industrious young Portuguese boy who works in the Layens' drugstore. He develops such an affection for Mr.

Layen that he prefers his employer's household to his own. And, finally, there is Pedro Gonzales, the gas station owner in "The Migraine Workers" [1967], whose humanitarian nature is expressed in his compassion for a group of migrant workers huddled together, like animals, in the back of a truck driven by a most unsympathetic black man.

The blacks who inhabit Petry's world are both native and foreign, and they, too, display a wide range of attitudes and behaviors. Perhaps the most despicable black character in any of the works in *Miss Muriel* is the truck driver alluded to earlier. This man arrives at Pedro's gas station with a truckload of men, women, and children who are "ragged and filthy, their dark skins covered with sores and . . . [with] burrs and straw in their matted hair." In response to Gonzales' questions regarding the conditions under which these people are being transported, the driver says, bowing and smiling ingratiatingly,

Well, folks don't usually see'em, . . . we run'em through at night and don't stop nowhere; nobody sees 'em and nobody gets upset by 'em. This time the truck broke down . . . then I took the wrong turn and that's how I came to your place. Pure accident, boss, pure accident. (118–19)

In addition to this unsavory truck driver, many other types of black people inhabit Petry's world. There is Aunt Frank, the rum-soaked cook in "Miss Muriel"; Forbes, the stereotypical butler in "Miss Dora Dean?" who quietly commits suicide on the railroad tracks of Shacktown; Emanuel Turner, the junkman whose pride is restored by the gift of a nude statue that he erroneously names "Mother Africa," and Johnson, the machine shop laborer in "Like a Winding Sheet" [1945], whose monotonous days in a restrictive environment and unbearable nights in a dead-end job threaten to strangle him, creating an explosive situation that erupts in unbridled violence. Returning home after a night of frustrating experiences on the job, in a coffee shop, and on the subway, Johnson strikes out viciously at his wife, who is trying to tease him out of his somber mood:

[H]e kept striking her. . . . He had lost all control over his hands. And he grasped for a word, a phrase, something to describe what this was like and he thought it was like being enmeshed in a winding sheet. . . . And even as the thought framed in his mind, his hands reached for her face again, and yet again. (210)

In contrast to Johnson, however, is the West Indian dock hand in "Olaf and His Girlfriend" [*sic*] [1945] whose love and fidelity for Belle Rose drive him literally to travel the world over in search of her, determined that they shall be united and confident that time and distance have not diminished their love.

Petry's world also includes children. They are small black children such as Sue Johnson in "Doby's Gone" [1944] skipping to school holding tightly to the hands of her imaginary playmate, Doby—loving school and teacher, seeking acceptance by her white classmates, and smarting from their cruel rejection. In contrast, there are the teen-age white delinquents in "The Witness" [1971], testing the fortitude of Charles Woodruff and ultimately forcing him to leave this town that he had hoped to make his home. These youngsters, with their heavy black jackets, he thinks,

could pass for the seven dark bastard sons of some old devil twelfth century king. Of course they weren't all dark. . . . All of them were white. But there was about them an aura of something so evil, so dark, so suggestive of the far reaches of the night, of the black horror of nightmares, that he shivered deep inside himself when he saw them. (218)

Looking at them, Woodruff has a foreboding of the inherent evil that will result in an act so violent and humiliating that he finds himself unable to remain in this town, fleeing it under the cover of darkness.

Not only do Ann Petry's characters exhibit a variety of personalities: they also represent a variety of occupations—domestics, industrial workers, craftsmen, professionals, and entertainers. The teacher, for example, appears frequently in the stories in this collection. In the title story, "Miss Muriel," Uncle Johno's friend, Dottle Smith, teaches English at a school for black people in Georgia; and he gives lectures and readings during the summer to supplement his income (30). Charles Woodruff, in "The Witness," is an English teacher who has retired from the University of Virginia and is presently teaching in the small town of Wheeling, New York. "The Necessary Knocking on the Door" depicts an incident in the life of Alice Knight, a Washington, D.C., teacher attending a conference in the Berkshires—a conference that promises escape from "years of suffocating heat that started in June and did not end until October; years of trying to teach grammar to indifferent high school students; years of taking repeated insults that were an integral part of life in the capital" (245). In the final story in the collection, "Doby's Gone," a first-grade teacher, Miss Whittier, endears herself to the young black child, Sue Johnson, on Sue's first day at school. Miss Petry's teachers exhibit sensitivity and dedication; yet, they are very human, subject to human frailties, disappointments, and frustrations.

Entertainers also figure prominently in Ann Petry's world—singers, dancers, musicians—their portraits sometimes fully drawn and at other times merely sketched. Among the sketches are the "Chorus of Sixteen Brown Girls," which appears in "The Creole Show" referred to in "Miss Dora Dean," and Belle Rose, the night club singer in "Olaf and His Girlfriend" [sic]. The full portraits include the itinerant piano player in "Miss Muriel"—the carefree ladies' man, Chink Johnson, who performs at the Wheeling Inn in the summer, playing the "talkin' blues" with "a cigarette dangling from his lower lip . . . a blue-gray, hazy kind of cloud around his face . . . playing some kind of fast, discordant sounding music . . . slapping the floor with his long feet and . . . slapping the keys with his long fingers" (28). They also include Kid Jones, in "Solo on the Drums" [1947], whose drums are an outlet for his pent-up emotions as they echo the myriad disillusionments of his life:

The woman in Chicago who hated him. The girl with the round soft body who had been his wife and who had walked out on him this morning in the rain. The old woman who was his mother, the same one who lived in Chicago and who hated him because he looked like his father, his father who had seduced her and left her, years ago. (240)

Miss Petry's world is indeed a world made cunningly. It is urban and rural; it is cramped and wide; it contains people of various colors with an infinite range of dispositions. The credibility of Petry's world, however, rests not only upon these elements but also upon the skill with which the writer weaves into her stories the realities of the black experience—those traditions, both African and American, that have shaped the lives of black people. Two most important aspects of that tradition, music and dance, have exerted a tremendous influence upon the lives of black people—from the tribal music and dances of Africa to the slave songs and minstrel shows to the blues and jazz rhythms of contemporary America.

In "Olaf and His Girl Friend," for example, Petry focuses upon tribal dance in her description of the "Dance of the Obeah Women," performed by Belle Rose to the insistent beat of the drums. The dance is ritualistic, trance-invoking; it speaks of voodoo and witchcraft:

It was an incantation to some far-off gods. It didn't belong in New York. It didn't belong in any nightclub . . . under the sun. . . . It was a devil dance—a dance that's used to exorcise a spirit. (194)

Again, in "Miss Muriel" and in "Solo on the Drums," Petry uses the piano player, Chink Johnson, and the drummer, Kid Jones, to focus upon the black musical art forms—blues and jazz. In both of these stories she deals not only with the lives of professional musicians but also with the effects of this music upon both the performers and their audiences.

Music has played a significant role in the lives of everyday, ordinary people as well as in the lives of professional musicians, a fact that is clearly evident in the world that Ann Petry creates in her fiction. This fact is exemplified in the very staid and proper butler, Forbes in "Has Anybody Seen Miss Dora Dean?" The title of this work is the title of a song from an 1890s minstrel show entitled "The Creole Show"; and Forbes whistles it continuously as he goes about his daily chores. It is a tune that seems to transport him from the mundane world of day-to-day existence to a glittering, exciting, thoroughly enchanting world of "cake-walks, beautiful brown girls, and ragtime." Another instance of the importance of music in the lives of ordinary black people is seen in William Jones, who appears in "In Darkness and Confusion." Jones is a man who finds that some of the gloom of his life in Harlem is dispelled as he sits in a barroom on a Sunday morning listening to the wail of a jukebox.

Finally, woven into the fabric of most of the stories in the volume—sometimes strident, sometimes subdued but always present, defining character and influencing situation—is the religious or moral element that is the bedrock of the black experience. It is manifested in the presence of the church and the clergy, but it is also apparent in certain moral attitudes exhibited by the people of Petry's world. The religious black folk of Bridgeport, for instance, are "scandalized" by the young Mrs. Forbes "pounding out whore-house music on the piano" (103); and the neighbors of Emanuel Turner, even the neighborhood drunk, Ginny the Baptist, are so disturbed by the naked statue of "Mother Africa" that graces his junkyard that Turner becomes a virtual pariah—the target of their ridicule and vituperation. Further, the mere presence of the church, both in the small towns and in the cities, seems to provide for the characters of Petry's world a sense of well-being and comfort, a ray of hope in an otherwise hopeless existence. And so it is that Pink Jones in "In Darkness and Confusion," despite the drabness and desolation of her life on the top floor of a Harlem tenement, finds herself on Sunday morning dressed and ready for church. It is in the church that she seems to find the strength to endure and to make some sense out of the chaos of her life.

The view that the reader gets of Petry's world, then, is a world that is in perfect balance. It includes the cities, the small towns, and some places in between ("The Migraine Workers"). Its inhabitants are of all colors, shapes, and sizes: they are native and foreign, prejudiced, liberal, compassionate, cruel, indifferent. Her themes are universal; yet she is able to capture the very essence of the black experience in its many and varied complexities. Recognizing prejudice, brutality, and pain as indigenous to the black experience in America, Petry carefully chronicles these horrors; yet she never loses sight of the fact that being black does not mean, nor has it ever meant, the inability to enjoy the simple pleasures of life—such pleasures as can be experienced in a loving, nurturing family.

From having examined *Miss Muriel and Other Stories*, I believe it is evident that Ann Petry is a writer of considerable skill and talent and that her works are certainly deserving of more critical attention than they have heretofore received. She spent many years learning her craft, and she learned it well—a fact to which her works attest. Petry's sensitivity to the world around her, her careful attention to detail, and her distinctive prose style place her among the really fine writers of this century. It has appropriately been said of Ann Petry that

[d]rawing upon her knowledge of country and city, early history and the present day, she writes with an accuracy sharpened by her scientific training and made vivid and dramatic by the ability of a skillful journalist who looks beneath the surface of events . . . to discover where and how those events touch the human heart.[11]

NOTES

1. Since the 1970s, critics have improved their analytical attention to novels and short stories by black women writers.

2. Rita B. Dandridge, "Male Critics/Black Women's Novels." *CLA Journal* 23 (September 1979): 11.

3. Robert Bone, *The Negro Novel in America* (New Haven: Yale University Press, 1958), 180.

4. David Littlejohn, *Black on White: A Critical Survey of Writings by American Negroes* (New York: Viking, 1966), 155.

5. In addition to this collection of criticism, forthcoming criticism of Ann Petry include *An Ann Petry Encyclopedia*, edited by Hazel Arnett Ervin, and *The Critical Response to Ann Petry*, edited by Hazel Arnett Ervin.

6. Ann Petry, *Miss Muriel and Other Stories* (Boston: Houghton Mifflin, 1971), 14–15. Subsequent page references will be to this volume and will be included parenthetically in the text of this paper.

7. Comments in a personal letter from Ann Petry (March 3, 1983).

8. Marjorie Green, "Ann Petry Planned to Write." *Opportunity* 24 (1976): 79.

9. Ibid., 79.

10. Ibid.

11. Richardson, 157.

Ann Petry and African Poetics: A Review of "Solo on the Drums"

Sheikh Umarr Kamarah

The role of the writer, once defined by Ann Petry, is to help the reader to know and to understand the ups and downs and the best and the worst of the experiences of her characters. In other words,

This is what [the character] thought, This is what [the character] hoped, This was his [or her] faith, These were his [or her] difficulties, These his [or her] triumphs.[1]

There is no better example of the writer at work than Petry in "Solo on the Drums" (1947), for the story encourages a closer look at how Petry's creative genius lies in part in her ability to skillfully use oral techniques to generate rich, crisp, intimate, and dramatic prose—prose that enhances understanding of characters, specifically their hopes, difficulties, and triumphs.

For Petry, characterization is "the great strength" of fiction. Writing in "The Novel as Social Criticism,"[2] she adds to the writer's responsibilities:

[Writers] must not manipulate [their] characters to serve [their] interests . . . [or] . . . theme[s]. . . . [As the great strength of fiction,] character[s] must be allowed to battle with themselves to save their souls. . . . Their defeat or their victory is . . . their own. . . . [Otherwise] they lose whatever vitality they had when their creator first thought about them.[3]

So, how does Petry communicate the vitality of her characters? How does she communicate their hopes, difficulties, and triumphs?

Oral literature is an art form that is somewhat distinct from written literature. As Isidore Okpewho reminds us in *African Oral Literature*,[4]

To appreciate the basis for this distinctness[,] it is necessary to remind ourselves
. . . that oral literature is literature delivered by word of mouth before an audience.
This word-of-mouth medium of presentation implies that oral literature makes *its*
appeal first through the sound of the words that reach the ears of the audience and only
secondarily through the meaning or logic contained in those words. (70, emphasis mine)

Writers, on the other hand, Okpewho claims, "are considerably freer" because "they can take as much time as they want in the quiet of their studies
to order their thoughts and presentations in a somewhat different way
from that of oral performers" (70). As underscored in this passage, the
spoken word is a principal and motivating factor in the delivery of an
African oral text—be it a song, story, or poem. In this discussion, Ann
Petry is an African American writer who is influenced in many ways by
an African poetics, heavily dependent upon oral delivery.

This brings us to the devices that will ensure an effective oral delivery
or presentation—that is, to the style and techniques that make oral literature an art form. In *African Oral Literature,* Okpewho lists (and discusses
at length) stylistic devices of oral literature such as repetition, parallelism,
piling and association, tonality, ideophones, digression, imagery, allusion,
and symbolism (70–101). Ann Petry's short story "Solo on the Drums"
reveals the presence of staging, deixis, additive patterning, repetition,
fragments, and parallelism, all of which function to create dramatic effects,
vivid images, and a fullness of expression by and meaning for her
characters.

"Solo on the Drums"[5] is about the celebrated musical artist, Kid Jones,
who is tortured by the impact of a failed relationship. The opening paragraph of the story introduces us to the musician:

The orchestra had a week's engagement at the Randlert Theater at Broadway and
forty-second street. [**] *His name* was picked out in lights on the Marquee. The
name of the Orchestra and then *His name* underneath by itself. (235, emphasis
mine)

Via staging, an oral technique by which a linguistic item is fronted or
topicalized, Petry hints at the intimacy of prose or that she is operating
on the assumption that the audience is at one with the storyteller. The
break in idea (indicated by my double asterisks) between the first and the
second sentences of the opening paragraph violates conventional written
narrative, but fits well in the logic of conversational text. What the storyteller has done is to topicalize the phrase *His name* to introduce the subject
of the story. In oral delivery, this break helps the narrator to present two
different but related themes. First, Petry captures our attention by initi-
ating a conversation with us, the readers, thereby ensuring our participation in the process. Then, using a cataphoric reference, she introduces
her protagonist. The pronoun *his* refers not to an antecedent but to some-

one yet to be mentioned by name. This urges us to read on and sets the stage for the purpose of *saying* the story.

The repetition of the phrase *His name* establishes a pattern that runs throughout the story, aimed at reinforcing stretches of utterances in the narrative by which coherence is achieved. In the paragraph to follow, the narrator gradually but dramatically leads us to the name:

There had been a time when he would have been excited by it. And stopped to let his mind and his eyes linger over it lovingly. Kid Jones. *The name—his name— up there* in lights that danced and winked in the brassy sunlight. (235, emphasis mine)

The name *Kid Jones* itself is a sentence, a theme, and an experience. The reader is forced to pause after the name, for it draws attention to itself by not being subordinated to a larger utterance. By thematizing the name, and by using both name and place deixis in "The name—his name—up there in lights," Petry appeals to our sense of sight as she literally points to the place where the protagonist's name appears. This quotation is just one example of how Ann Petry employs techniques of oral narrative—in this case, fragments, staging, and deixis all at once—to achieve dramatic effects, but, again, these techniques are echoed throughout the story by a storyteller whose words are intentional.

Another feature of Ann Petry's prose is that it is additive rather than subordinative. The pragmatic connector, *and*, is the ingredient of the additive style, a characteristic of orally based expression. In the first and second paragraphs of "Solo on the Drums," Petry uses a total of eight *ands*. *And* is one of the linguistic items that poses a problem for sentence-based theories of grammar. Part of the problem is that this item is not really part of the structure of syntactic units. It has a sequencing function of relating syntactic units and fitting them into a discourse context.[6] Ann Petry very often uses *and* in its additive function as in oral discourse. Witness the following:

It's all there in the trumpet—pain and hate and trouble and peace and quiet and love. (237)

In this passage, *and* functions as a pragmatic connector that reveals how Kid Jones's mind produces and processes the feelings of *hate* and *love*, *peace, trouble, quiet* and *pain*. Through the sequencing of the words in this additive pattern, readers feel the sense of urgency with which the message is conveyed as well as the sharp contrasts in emotions expressed by the words themselves.

Repetition is certainly one of the most fundamental features of oral literature. It has both aesthetic and utilitarian values. One of the specific stylistic values of repetition in Petry's story is to give a certain amount of emphasis to something that needs to be stressed. Sometimes she enacts her repetitions. Witness how she uses repetition to dramatize time reference:

[T]he men in the band turned their heads toward him—a faint astonishment showed in their faces. He ignored them. The drums took him away from them, took him *back,* and *back,* and *back,* in time and space. (239, emphasis mine)

The repetition of the word *back* is used to emphasize how far back in time the protagonist is taken by the drums. The idea that Kid Jones's art is used as a means of escape from his emotional torment is expressed in these lines. But it is Petry's use of repetition that makes the idea of going back in time dramatic and rhythmic. Petry uses this shared way of saying[7] because it is more revealing and dramatic than, perhaps, the expression, "far back in time." The author also repeats phrases that directly reveal the sources of Kid Jones's predicament:

And then it was almost as though the drums were talking about his own life. The woman in Chicago *who hated him.* The girl with the round, soft body *who had been his wife* and *who had walked out on him.* . . . The old woman *who was his mother,* the same woman who lived in Chicago, and *who hated him* because he looked like his father, his father *who had seduced her* and left her years ago. (240, emphasis mine)

The use of repetition for the italicized phrases has a piling effect that enhances the theme of Kid Jones's life being overburdened with a myriad of complexities and disillusionments.

For Petry, fragments are also a source of crisp and dramatic prose; they represent the structure of natural speech. One way that Petry uses fragment is to reveal to her readers a protagonist

[who] hadn't changed any. Same face. No fatter and no thinner. No gray hair. Nothing. (236)

In a chirographic consciousness, these utterances are mere fragments, not sentences. In natural discourse, the utterances are complete in themselves as each addresses a theme and all create the bigger picture of changelessness. This device (fragments) helps Petry to achieve crisp prose. It is precise and elucidating. It also helps the author to achieve realism since fragments enhance drama and revelation. Furthermore, Petry's prose is intimate and not alienating as formal written syntax might be. *She* often uses what I would call serial adjectives as fragments for dramatic and aesthetic effects. They are usually one-word sentences (or fragments as sentences):

Kid Jones kept up the drum accompaniment. *Slow. Careful. Soft.* (236, emphasis mine)

In describing the way Kid Jones plays the drums, Petry uses a series of adjectives, each having a life of its own. Put together, the adjectives create a dramatic effect on the reader. The words help create a mental picture of the action. Using the fragment is much more revealing and dramatic than clustering all of the adjectives in one "correct" but undramatic sentence like "Kid Jones kept up the drum accompaniment in a slow, careful, and soft manner." Petry, therefore, has to dislocate conventional syntax to achieve the desired effect.

The author uses the same method in revealing what goes on in Kid Jones's mind while he plays the drums in the theater:

The sound seemed to come not from the drums but from deep inside himself; it was a sound that was being wrenched out of him—a *violent, raging, roaring* sound. (240, emphasis mine)

The sound described here, which Kid Jones calls "the story of my life" and "the story of my hate" is given a life of its own through the dramatic serialization of the adjectives *violent, raging,* and *roaring.* As Petry often appeals to her readers' senses, this quotation and the one before it appeal to our sense of sound. Readers are called to listen to both "soft" and "roaring" sounds and to contrast Kid Jones's inner turmoil with the gentle sound of the drums (or his art).

A final characteristic of Petry's stylistic prose is parallelism, a narrative device by which the narrator gathers via balanced relationship the ideas and images that may seem independent of one another. In the passage below, Petry uses lexical parallelism to convey the idea of emptiness:

Rain in the street. Heat gone. Food gone. Everything gone because a woman's gone. (237)

In the phrases *heat gone, food gone, Everything gone,* and *a woman's gone,* the syntactic structure is N + V (noun followed by verb). In this case the verb *gone* is kept constant while the nouns vary. Although the nouns may seem independent of one another, by maintaining the syntactic slots of the phrases, they enter into a balanced relationship of ideas and images. The idea of emptiness and the image of nothingness are effectively conveyed by this style.

Petry also employs parallelism for the purpose of contrast:

It's everything you ever *wanted.* . . . It's everything you never *got.* Everything you ever *had,* everything you ever *lost.* It's all there in the trumpet—*pain* and *hate* and *trouble* and *peace* and *quiet* and *love.* (237, emphasis mine)

Parallelism allows the narrator to make the sharp contrast between what is *ever wanted* and what is *never got*, what is *ever had* and what is *ever lost*.

A writer who engages her readers in dialogue, and who appeals to their senses of sight and sound in order to reveal her character's inner turmoil and triumphs, Ann Petry functions in "Solo on the Drums" as an oral performer, or at least as someone who has been influenced by the orality of her African cultural background. In "Solo on the Drums," Petry arrests the attention of her audience by way of the skillful use of the oral techniques staging, deixis, addictive patterning, repetition, fragment, and parallelism. Without these techniques Ann Petry could not have achieved the dramatic and aesthetic effect found in this story. Without these techniques, Petry could not have allowed her character, Kid Jones, his "vitality."

NOTES

1. Ann Petry, "The Novel as Social Criticism," in *African American Literary Criticism, 1773 to 2000,* ed. Hazel Arnett Ervin (New York: Twayne, 1999), 94–98.

2. Ibid., 97.

3. Ibid., 97.

4. Isadore Okpewho, *African Oral Literature* (Bloomington, IN: Indiana University Press, 1992). Subsequent page references to this source will be included parenthetically in the text of this essay.

5. Ann Petry, "Solo on the Drums," in *Miss Muriel and Other Stories* (Boston: Houghton Mifflin, 1971), 235–42. Subsequent page references will be to this volume and will be included parenthetically in the text of this essay.

6. Michael Stubbs, *Discourse Analysis: The Sociolinguistic Analysis of Natural Language* (Oxford: Basic Blackwell, 1983), 77.

7. I borrow the phrase from Karla Holloway, "The Woman's Way of Saying" and "The Oracular Text," in *African American Literary Criticism, 1773 to 2000,* ed. Hazel Arnett Ervin (New York: Twayne, 1999), 332–38.

Folk Traditions in the Short Fiction of Ann Petry

Gladys J. Washington

In *Blues People*, a thought-provoking analysis of African American music in America, LeRoi Jones (Amiri Baraka) observes that only religion and the arts managed to escape being "totally submerged by Euro-American concepts." He continues, "These non-material aspects of the African's culture were almost impossible to eradicate and are the most important legacies of the African past, even to the contemporary Black American" (89). The truth of this statement is reflected, I believe, in the tendency for African American writers to return continually to a wellspring of the black experience—sometimes quite consciously, as with writers Ralph Ellison, James Baldwin, Toni Morrison, and Alice Walker, but sometimes, almost incidentally, as with writer Ann Petry. Despite Petry's New England upbringing (having been born and reared in Old Saybrook, Connecticut), she is, nonetheless, keenly aware of the many nuances of African American folk culture, and she is able, almost effortlessly, to weave these folk traditions into the very fabric of her fiction, enriching the narratives and giving them depth and color.

The briefest examination of Ann Petry's work will reveal the many and varied threads of African American folk culture—sometimes dominant, at other times subdued, but always present and always handled with the adeptness and beauty of the consummate artist. Although certain threads of African American myth and folklore are to be found in much of Petry's fiction, nowhere are they more apparent than in *Miss Muriel and Other Stories* (1971). Of the 13 stories that comprise this volume, a great many incorporate some aspect of African American myth and folklore.

In his now-classic work *The Souls of Black Folk,* W.E.B. Du Bois lists storytelling and music as two of the greatest gifts that African American people have given to America (186). Ironically, it was these very "gifts" that enabled slaves to survive the humiliation and degradation of their abject experience. As one writer puts it, the songs of the slaves enabled them to "transcend their temporal situation," and their folktales enabled them to escape or at least to "control and understand their situation" (Levine 134).

The first gift identified by Du Bois, the art of storytelling, has its inception in the slavery period, and has persisted to this day as an integral part of the African American folk tradition. Just as slaves would sit outside their cabins and tell stories on summer evenings, after slavery, black people across America would sit on their front porches or in their front yards spinning tales for delight and entertainment. Zora Neale Hurston in *Mules and Men* (1937) calls our attention to this practice when she observes, "It was the custom of men folks particularly to gather on the store porch of evenings and swap stories" (4). Then quickly she adds, "Even the womenfolks would stop and break a breath [tell a story] with them at times" (4).

It is out of this tradition of storytelling, then, that the Uncle Johno-Dottle Smith tales emerge in Ann Petry's short story "Miss Muriel" (1963). Every summer, Dottle and Johno take a break from the segregated southern schools where they teach to visit the Layen family, the only black family in the little town of Wheeling, New York. On quiet summer evenings, the Layen family gathers in their backyard to be entertained by the stories of Uncle Johno and Dottle Smith: "Wonderful stories in which animals talk, and there are haunted houses and ghosts and demons, and old black preachers who believe in heaven and hell" (33).

The similarities between these stories and the African folktales are quite striking. In one of the stories told by Uncle Johno, two of the most popular of African folktales are merged. The tale concerns a preacher who tries to outrun an "overly friendly and very talkative rabbit" (35). In the classic African folktale, the rabbit by his status in the animal kingdom is a stock character that is also used to symbolize helplessness. In the African American folktale, the rabbit often symbolizes the condition of the slave. As Arna Bontemps has pointed out, the rabbit is frequently endowed with admirable qualities of "a practical joker, a braggart, a wit, [or] a trickster" (31). Thus, in Johno's story, not only does the rabbit outwit the preacher at every turn, but as in the typical African folk tale, he is a braggart who never misses an opportunity to taunt the preacher with his accomplishments.

The preacher tale, according to Arna Bontemps, is a very ancient type of folktale, combining the religious tales of antiquity and the anecdotes used by Baptist and Methodist ministers to proclaim the gospel to their congregation. These tales, he has noted, were modified and adapted, and "took root in one section of the South or another and became part of the cultural heritage of the local folk" (32). Originally, the preacher's tale, though sometimes humorous, was highly moralistic; however, as it was assimilated into African American folklore, it lost some of the moral tone and didacticism of the earlier stories while retaining much of the humor. Thus, while Johno's tale about the preacher and the rabbit has some superficial moral overtones, its essential ingredient is humor; its primary purpose is entertainment.

In like manner, Dottle Smith's story about the preacher and the talking cats is intended purely to evoke humor. A preacher, seeking refuge from a violent storm, is forced to spend the night in an old, dilapidated house alleged to be haunted. During the night, he encounters by turn, six giant cats—each larger than the other. They sit down beside him, stare menacingly and inquire, "Has Martin got here yet?" Their sizes and their manners are so frightening that the preacher flees the house, feeling that he will be safer outside in the storm (35). While this is the typical ghost story so popular in African American folklore, it incorporates some elements of the other two popular folktales—the preacher tale and the fable.

Among the most interesting type of tales in the canon of African American folklore is the tall tale or the joke, especially one in which a black person or black society is the butt of the joke. Such a tale about the Muriel cigars is Dottle's. According to Dottle, a black man attempted to purchase cigars in a small southern town. When he asked for Muriel cigars, the shopkeeper said, "Nigger, what's the matter with you? Don't you see that picture of that beautiful white woman on the front of the box? When you ask for them cigars, you say Miss Muriel cigars" (34). This story is an example of those private jokes that continue to circulate among black people that help them to cope with the tensions of life in a racist society because laughter, even laughter directed at oneself, is often the best antidote for pain. As Sterling Brown once pointed out, such jokes, as they developed in African American folk culture, often "pled the racial cause" (as does Dottle's joke) or satirized "separate but equal." In either case, the jokes always produced laughter, although that laughter was sometimes bitter (14). However, the laughter was often a way of escaping—for a time, at least—from the harsh realities of daily existence.

Besides humor, entertainment, or escape, storytelling in the folk culture of African Americans also serves a more serious purpose—that of education and instruction. In "Miss Muriel," Ann Petry reveals her understanding of this role, a fact that is evident in her description of the storytelling sessions in the Layen backyard. First, she gives the stories a natural setting, perhaps as a reminder that traditionally African and African American storytelling is an outdoor activity—whether in tribal groups in Africa or outside slave cabins, whether for entertainment or instruction. Even the narrator of her story emphasizes both the beauty and appropriateness of the setting when she says,

I looked around thinking . . . what a wonderful place this is to listen to stories. The sun is warm but there is a breeze and it blows through the long marsh grass which borders the creek. The grass moves, seems to wave. Gulls fly high overhead. The only sound is the occasional cry of a gull and the lapping of water against the piling of the bridge. (35)

Not only are the stories in *Miss Muriel* told in a natural setting, but they are often serious and informative, for the narrator tells how from time to time, Dottle Smith would recite whole acts from *MacBeth* or *Hamlet* or "all of 'The Song of Solomon'" (41). Then, again, she says, he would tell long stories about the South that "had so much fear and terror in them that she would shiver though the air was warm" (41). At these times, Smith takes on the character of the ancient African griot that memorized long histories of his tribe and transmitted them orally to the people of his village for their education and instruction. The horror stories that Dottle recounts for this audience, like the stories of the ancient griot, also contain the history of his people and teach lessons that his people must learn if they are to survive in American society. Indeed, storytelling has always been an important instructional tool in both African and African American societies—a fact to which Melville Herskovitz attests when he recalls the statement of a Dohemean man who said to a white man, "You whites have schools and books for teaching your children[;] we tell stories, for our stories are our books" (Levine 90).

Not only are the stories themselves significant in the African American folk tradition, but so are the storytellers, for they have occupied a very prominent place both as custodians of history as well as entertainers. Over the years, these individuals developed storytelling into a fine art, cultivating a skill in presentation that delighted their audiences, as is the case with the storytellers in "Miss Muriel." Levine points out that nothing was too difficult for a good storyteller to represent: "The chanting sermon of a black preacher and his entire congregation, the sound of a railway engine, the cries of barnyard animals, or the eerie moans of spectral beings" (89). Such dramatic technique endeared these storytellers to their audiences. Apparently, Uncle Johno and Dottle Smith possessed these qualities in abundance, for according to the young narrator, she never tired of their stories:

Though I have heard these stories many, many times, Dottle and Johno never tell them exactly the same. They change their gestures, they vary their facial expressions and the pitch of their voices [so that] we forget the bats swooping over our heads, ignore the mosquitoes that sting our ankles and legs, and sit mesmerized while he [Dottle] declaims "Shall I compare thee to a summer's day?" (40)

The ability of these men to totally mesmerize their audience in this way places them among the great African and African American storytellers.

Another aspect of the African heritage and the second great "gift" of black people to which Du Bois refers is music. From the ritual music of Africa to the work songs and spirituals of the slave plantations to the blues and jazz of modern America, music is central to the African American experience, and indeed to the American experience in general, for it was the enslaved African peoples who gave to America her indigenous folk music. On this point, Alain Locke notes that since folk music always arises from the peasant class of any culture, assigning slaves and freedmen to the peasant class provided them the natural environment in which to create "our national music" (13). Further, while Locke views the spirituals as "true folk classics," he also recognizes the importance of secular music, such as blues and jazz. It is this secular folk music that Ann Petry treats most extensively in her short stories.

In the *Miss Muriel* volume, for example, music and musicians occur quite frequently. In the lead story, "Miss Muriel," Chink Johnson, one of Aunt Sophronia's suitors, is a piano player at the local inn. Every summer, he comes to the small town of Wheeling, New York, to entertain the "summer people." Much attention is given to the style and technique of this musician. Johnson is the quintessential blues player. On one occasion, listening to him play, the narrator says,

[H]e played the piano, or rather, I guess you would say he talked the music. It is a peculiar kind of musical performance. He plays some chords, a series of them, and he says the words of a song—he really doesn't sing, but his voice does change in pitch to, in a sense, match the chords that he is playing, and he does talk to a kind of rhythm which also matches the chords. (29)

In *Blues People*, LeRoi Jones defines the blues as a sequence of chords, noting that in the performance of the blues, the piano is used in a "percussive and vocal fashion" (30). In playing chords and changing the pitch of his voice to "match the chords," Chink is performing in classic blues style, and it fits perfectly Jones's definition of the blues.

If music is central to the African American folk tradition, then the drum is perhaps the single most important instrument in the creation of that music. Writer Mildred Hill-Lubin has said that the dominant characteristic of African American music is rhythm and that "this rhythm begins with the frantic beat of the drum" (177). She further states,

[I]n traditional African society, the life of the people revolved around this instrument. It was used as language; it informed the village of births, death, initiation, rites, weddings. . . . The drummer in the society occupied an important place and was considered the musician par excellence. (177)

Thus, the drum was not only used for entertainment, but it was also used as a communication device in African societies. In Petry's portrayal of character and development of plot in "Solo on the Drums" (1947), she reveals an understanding of the important role that the drum has played in the creation of African American music and in the history of African American people. Kid Jones, the major character in the story, plays drums in a nightclub with a group of musicians. On a particular night after his wife has left him for the piano player, his music is especially plaintive. As he plays, the drums transport him to a time long past—perhaps to some ancestral village. The drums "took him back in time and space. . . . He was sending out the news. Grandma died. . . . The man from across the big water is sleeping with the chief's daughter. . . . The war goes well with the men. . . . It is cool in the deep track of the forest, cool and quiet" (239).

Although Jones is playing for the entertainment of his audience, his reflections are a reminder of the pragmatic use of the drums in African societies, and they serve to establish a connection between him and the drummers of his ancestral past. Here, and in many other places in "Solo on the Drums," the communicative power of this instrument is emphasized, sometimes merely through Petry's use of language. In one place, for example, she says, the drums "respond with a whisper" when struck. At another time, they "talk" to the piano, and at another point, they "answer the phrase played by the horn" (289). Petry's use of words such as "respond," "whisper," "talk," and "answer" seem to endow the drums with human qualities.

Not only are the drums used for communication, they are traditionally used to create a variety of moods. As Kid Jones plays his solo on the drums, the rhythmic beat reaches out into the audience, engulfing and mesmerizing the listeners. The spell that it casts is completely engrossing. "A man sitting near the front shiver[s] and his head jerk[s] to the rhythm; it is so romantic that a sailor puts his arm around the girl sitting beside him and [holds] her face still and press[es] his mouth over hers" (238). The spell is so compelling that a child hearing it "sneak[s] in through a side door and slid[es] into an aisle seat. His mouth [is] wide open; and he clutch[es] his hat with both hands, tight and hard against his chest" (239). Here, as in African societies, the beat of the drum is riveting, intensifying the emotions and liberating the spirit from the temporal bonds that have held them captive.

For the most part, Petry treats the positive aspects of African American music. She does not ignore the fact that for years, African Americans themselves have felt certain kinds of black music, especially the blues, to be inherently inferior. The blues has been considered not only inferior but also sinful. Thus, African Americans often dissociated themselves not only from the music but also from those people who played such music. This attitude can be seen, for instance, in Mr. Layen's instinctive abhorrence for Chink Johnson, the blues piano player in "Miss Muriel." Referring to him as "Lightfoot Jones," "Shake Jones," and "Barrelhouse Jones," Layen expresses his disdain for the character and considers him an unworthy suitor for his sister-in-law Sophronia. He says that this is an individual who "merely beats out his life, beats out his lungs, beats out his liver, on a piano" and because of that, he does not want "his restless feet hangin' around" (21). The use of the term "barrelhouse" immediately labels Chink as inferior or low class, especially since the term originally applied to a rough type of music often heard in brothels and bawdy houses and had come to be associated not only with low-class music but with low-class individuals as well (Jones 146).

This negative attitude by black people toward blues is also evident in the short story "Has Anybody Seen Miss Dora Dean?" (1958). Here, the daughter of a Baptist minister, Sarah Forbes, is described as a "frivolous," "flirtatious," and "fast" one who "likes to play cards, and played pinochle for money" (98). The narrator immediately establishes Sarah Forbes as a person of questionable character, for certainly these were not thought to be qualities of a well-mannered young lady. It is not surprising, then, that Sarah "scandalizes the people in her father's church by playing ragtime on the piano at dances, and parties, and cakewalks" (98). The narrator also recalls having been told by her father that the music Sarah played had always been called "whorehouse music" and that it was difficult for him to understand how it got to be called "ragtime." Statements such as these, taken together with such characterizations as those of Sarah Forbes and Chink Johnson, are indicative of how some black people held this type of African American folk music in low esteem. Also indicated, I believe, is Ann Petry's sensitivity to a peculiar aspect of the African American experience.

Inextricably bound to the tradition of music in African American folk culture is dance—whether it be ritual dances of African societies or the many and varied forms of modern dance in contemporary American society. Alain Locke has attributed the inherent rhythm of black music to African Americans' long association with the dance that he calls the original source of rhythm (14). In *Black Dance*, Lyne Emery has pointed out that dance is a "fundamental element of African American aesthetic expression and that religious as well as secular and recreational dances . . . in one form or another prevailed all of African life" (2). Recognizing the place of dance in the African American experience, Petry gives some attention to the dance—both ritual as well as recreational—in her short stories.

For example, the story "Has Anybody Seen Miss Dora Dean?" takes its title from a song in an all-black minstrel show of the late 1800s called "The Creole Show," which is credited with having revived the dance called the cakewalk. This dance, originated by slaves as a satire on the dance of white plantation owners, became quite popular at festivals that were held during harvest time (Emery 91). Not surprisingly, however, the dance almost completely disappeared after Emancipation until it was modified by Charles Johnson and reintroduced in "The Creole Show." In a brilliant finale to this show, Johnson and Dora Dean performed the cakewalk, dancing to a tune entitled "Has Anybody Seen Miss Dora Dean?" inspired by Johnson's beautiful female partner. After its revival, the cakewalk became quite popular as an "exhibition dance" and appeared in quite a number of musical productions (Emery 208).

It is interesting to note that Petry makes several references to "The Creole Show" and to the cakewalk in her short story "Has Anybody Seen Miss Dora Dean?" Forbes, the butler (and the major character of the story) continually sings or hums the song "Has Anybody Seen Miss Dora Dean?" The song itself had come to be almost synonymous with the cakewalk. Also, at one point in the narrative, Petry gives a very graphic description of the dance called the cakewalk, explaining that although she had never seen it performed, she had often heard it described. This dance, like many other aspects of the African American heritage, had been preserved and handed down by word of mouth from one generation to the next.

In "Olaf and His Girl Friend" (1945), Petry gives some attention to ritual dance and its place in the African American tradition. Olaf, a dockworker in Bridgetown, Barbados, is separated from Belle Rose, whom he wants to marry, by the girl's aunt, who does not consider Olaf a fitting husband for her niece. Belle Rose is sent from the island out of the reach of Olaf. Knowing Olaf's fear of water, the aunt is sure that he will not follow Belle Rose. Despite his fears, however, Olaf does indeed follow Belle Rose around the world, pursuing her relentlessly for years. At last, Olaf finds Belle Rose dancing in a Harlem nightclub. Petry devotes several pages to describing the ritual dance that Belle Rose performs—unaware that Olaf is watching silently from the shadows. The dance, called "The Obeah Woman," mesmerizes the audience and, perhaps, saves Belle Rose's life. It is a dance that is often performed as part of the obeah ceremonies in the West Indies—ceremonies that include "prayers, incantations, and . . . an African dance performed to the inspiring sound of the tom-tom" (Emery 62). The word *obeah* has come to be associated with "evil magic"—a term that accurately describes Belle Rose's performance, for it was "an incantation to some far-off evil gods," a dance that "didn't belong in any nightclub that has existed anywhere under the sun," and "a devil dance that was used to exorcise a spirit" (194–95).

The fact that Belle Rose is thought to be an obeah women only serves to heighten the spellbinding, trance-provoking effect of the dance. As Olaf moves towards her, Belle Rose

reached back into that ancient, complicated African past that belongs to all us and invoked all the gods she knew or that she'd ever heard of. . . . She began to sing in a high, shrill voice. It was the same kind of chant a witch doctor uses when he casts a spell; the same one that the conjure women use and the Obeah women. (198)

Then Belle Rose moves slowly toward Olaf; he lets the knife slip from his fingers and takes Belle Rose in his arms. They walk out of the nightclub hand in hand. This passage, which describes the reunion of Olaf and Belle Rose, underscores not only the beauty but also the power of ritual dance and its importance in African American folk culture.

So far, we have seen how Ann Petry weaves into her short stories threads of the African American folk tradition, especially those that relate to the arts—storytelling, music, and dance. However, if the arts are the major threads of this tradition, then surely, religion is the loom on which these threads are woven, for religion is the foundation of African American folk culture. It is the wellspring from whence flows African peoples' artistic expressions—their stories, their music, and their dance. For African peoples in general, religion is part of their daily living, not merely "something to be attended to on Sundays and forgotten the rest of the week" (Emery 49). Just as religion occurs naturally in African and American societies, it occurs just as naturally in the world of Ann Petry's fiction. Many of the stories in the *Miss Muriel* volume have distinctive religious or moral tones—sometimes strident, more often muted—but always present, defining character and influencing situation.

For example, in the short story, "The Witness" (1971), the religious overtones may not be immediately apparent, since much of the plot revolves around the confrontation between the black high-school teacher, Charles Woodruff, and a group of white juvenile delinquents. The religious implications become clearer, however, when one considers that this conflict arises out of the beneficence of Dr. Shipley, minister of the congregational church. Dr. Shipley asks Woodruff, his only black parishioner and the new teacher in town, to assist him in helping to reform this group of juvenile delinquents. Woodruff agrees because he feels that it is his Christian duty to "make some kind of contribution to the life of this small town that had treated him with genuine friendliness" (214).

Then, of course, there is the patriarch of the Layen household in "Miss Muriel." Mr. Layen is a man of principles and character, qualities that reveal themselves in his manner of conduct both professionally and personally. He is a devout man who attends church every Sunday with his family and uses his "pure lyric tenor voice [to] sing solos in the congregational church choir" (21). He treats everyone who comes into his drugstore with courtesy and respect, and expects no less for his family. For the characters in "Miss Muriel," as with those in "The Witness," religion is essential to their very existence. Religion influences their thoughts and actions; it molds their characters—indeed, it is the basis of their very philosophy of life.

In a work like "In Darkness and Confusion" (1947), on the other hand, the mere presence of the church influences situation and provides a ray of hope to those caught in an otherwise dark and hopeless world. Pink Jones, for example, despite her meager resources and the miserable circumstances of her existence on the top floor of a Harlem tenement, assumes the responsibility of caring for a recalcitrant niece. Although she experiences overwhelming problems—problems that would easily defeat the average individual—she never loses faith in her religion and in the church. For her, the church is a sustaining force—one that enables her to make some sense out of the chaos of her life. Thus, every Sunday without fail, she finds herself "dressed and ready for church." Traditionally, the church has played a vital role in providing African American people emotional relief from the problems of life. As explained by Pink Jones, besieged by mounting difficulties, "[i]t just seem like I can stand by worries better when I go to church" (274).

Having examined briefly the fabric of Ann Petry's fiction, one discovers that the threads of the black folk tradition are many and varied and skillfully interwoven—so interwoven, in fact, that they sometimes almost defy extrication. Nevertheless, the presence of this folk material is undeniable, and it is that presence that gives Petry's narratives substance, depth, and color. Moreover, by including such materials in her fiction, Petry celebrates and helps to preserve what W.E.B. Du Bois has called the three great gifts of black folk: "the gift of story, the gift of music and song, and the gift of spirit [religion]" (186).

By employing folk traditions in her fiction, Petry establishes herself within the mainstream of African American literature and aligns herself with the great writers, both past and present, that have drawn also upon the inexhaustible stock of folk material. As Arna Bontemps has pointed out, writers who utilize folk traditions are "in line with Aristophanes, Shakespeare, and St. Paul, all of whom drew similarly from their folk sources" (36). It is not surprising, then, that black writers such as Ann Petry have found themselves returning again and again to let down their buckets into this deep, rich wellspring of African American folk life and culture.

WORKS CITED

Bontemps, Arna. "Introduction to the Book of Negro Folklore." *Black Expression.* Ed. Addison Gayle. New York: Weybright and Talley, 1969.

Brown, Sterling. *Negro Poetry and Drama.* Washington, DC: The Associates in Negro Folk Education, 1937.

Du Bois, W.E.B. *The Souls of Black Folk.* 1903. New York: Bantam Books, 1989.

Emery, Lyne F. *Black Dance*. Palo Alto, CA: National Press Books, 1969.

Hill-Lubin, Mildred A. "And the Beat Goes On . . . A Continuation of the African Heritage in African American Literature." *CLA Journal* 22 (December 1979): 177.

Hurston, Zora Neale. *Mules and Men*. 1937. New York: HarperCollins, 1990.

Jones, LeRoi. *Blues People: Negro Music in White America*. New York: William and Morrow, 1963.

Levine, Lewis. *Black Culture and Black Consciousness: Afro-American Folk Thought from Slavery to Freedom*. New York: Oxford University Press, 1978.

Locke, Alain. *The Negro and His Music*. Port Washington, NY: Kennikat Press, 1936.

Petry, Ann. *Miss Muriel and Other Stories*. Boston: Houghton Mifflin, 1971.

Artistic Discourse in Three Short Stories by Ann Petry

Nora Ruth Roberts

The work of Ann Petry (1908–1997)[1] falls between that of two major tendencies in African-American literature. Her first novel, *The Street* (1946), was often linked with the "protest novel" tradition developed by Richard Wright. As Paula Giddings notes, Petry's *The Street* was held up as the paradigm of the "most powerful protest novel authored by a Black woman" (137). Petry was not herself of the Communist-Party-affiliated generation of those like Wright and Ellison who came of age during the Depression years of the 1930s. Nonetheless she was, through her short stories, to make the bridge that, as Arthur P. Davis points out, was to abandon the protest tradition, "for a more universal and introspective tone" (qtd. in Giddings 240).

Raised in a middle-class environment as one of two daughters of the Black pharmacist in a small New England nearly all-white town, Petry focuses much of her work on the effects of community on the individual. Not surprisingly, Petry does write autobiographically about assaults by white schoolchildren; sadly, perhaps, she does not write much about lasting friendships with white neighbor children (my own family members included). In fact, she remained an important if somewhat reclusive mainstay of the Old Saybrook, Connecticut, community for the better part of her life. Her one foray into the big-city arena was during World War II, when her husband, George Petry, was in the Army overseas, and Petry began her career as a fiction writer while working with the Harlem press. The publisher's advance on *The Street* allowed George and Ann Petry to buy the house they wanted in Old Saybrook, where they raised a daughter and participated discreetly in community affairs while Ann devoted herself to writing.

That Petry was not immediately popular with a new generation—although her popularity curve has been recently on the rise—may have been due to the fact that initially the predominant themes of her early stories, published in *Miss Muriel and Other Stories* (1971), have to do with the relationship of the African-American community to the imposition of white values as reflected in and perverted by white culture. At the same time, Petry was not a feminist in the way that term has come to be defined. Lutie, the heroine of *The Street*, is certainly a strong female protagonist, but clearly Petry was as interested in male characters as she was in female and she cannot rightly be taken up as a grandmother of the African-American feminist revolution.

One of the reasons for Petry's self-designed distinctiveness from recently discussed African-American concerns may arise from the fact that she was born (in 1908) in a small town in rural Connecticut, where her family were middle-class shopkeepers and where there were some few white families who welcomed her as playmates. After a stint in Harlem during the second world war when she worked as a journalist while her husband was in service, Petry was so appalled by the conditions of poverty and degradation that she had witnessed in the ghetto that she wrote several stories and was signed by Houghton Mifflin to write *The Street*. Proceeds from the sale of this book enabled her and her returning husband to buy a house in her home town in Connecticut, where she remained until her death.[2]

What is remarkable about the three stories discussed here from the *Miss Muriel and Other Stories* collection is not that they were all three written by a woman about men, but that they address the topic of the relationship of artistic discourse to the African-American community in ways that defy ordinary sociological analysis. Key to an understanding of this relationship is the thesis put forward by Henry Louis Gates, Jr., especially as developed in his newer work, *The Signifying Monkey* (1988). In this work, Gates adopts the traditional view that African-American discourse is an answer or a riposte to conditions of oppression and discrimination foisted on the Black community by the white. In analyzing the difference between two tropes, or two distinct sets of troping—white English's predominant mode of signification and Black English's rebellious "signifyin(g)"—Gates argues:

We see here the most subtle and perhaps the most profound trace of an extended engagement between two separate and distinct yet profoundly—even inextricably—related orders of meaning dependent precisely as much for their confrontation on relations of identity, manifested in the signifier, as on their relations of difference, manifested at the level of the signified. We bear witness here to a protracted argument over the nature of the sign itself, with the black vernacular discourse proffering its critique of the sign as the difference that blackness makes within the larger culture and its historical unconscious. (45)

Simultaneously expressive of a community's traditions, culture, and connectedness, African-American Signifyin(g), in Gates's terms, is also an exercise in resistance to oppression. It is a language that, in its virtually organized reluctance to yield to assimilation, "(un) wittingly disrupted the nature of the sign = signified/signifier equation itself" (Gates 46). Furthermore, this "complex act of language Signifies upon both formal language use and its conventions, conventions established, at least officially, by middle-class white people" (Gates 47). Thus, the African-American "Signifyin(g)" tradition that suggests itself as a central motif in the three stories by Ann Petry considered here is a tradition born of oppression and discrimination manifested in a war of discourse more often than of physical battle.

Houston Baker, furthermore, traces the particularly strong hold of African-American discourse to its origins in the practices of early slave traders themselves: "Slaves from the same tribes in West Africa were separated when they arrived in America in order to minimize the chances of rebellion; those on the same small farm or plantation could not communicate with one another until they had developed a lingua franca" (113).

Signifyin(g), then, becomes the dominant mode of language for an oppressed people. This involves inventing and maintaining a language that simultaneously conveys and conceals meaning, that is both a subtle means of communicating emotion rather than mere fact, and a method of deceiving the oppressor. As Baker indicates: "The radically different ethos surrounding the use of language in the black ghetto is as much responsible for its variance from standard English as the employment of black slang words and variant linguistic features by ghetto inhabitants" (113).

An early, often-discussed example of the imperviousness of the oppressor to the muted war cries of the oppressed can be seen in the dispute over the nature of the slave-songs Frederick Douglass notes in his Narrative. As Douglass observed:

I have often been utterly astonished, since I came to the north, to find persons who could speak of the singing, among slaves, as evidence of their contentment and happiness. It is impossible to conceive of a greater mistake. Slaves sing most when they are most unhappy. The songs of the slave represent the sorrows of his heart; and he is relieved by them, only as an aching heart is relieved by its tears. (58)

This war between Signifyin(g) and signification, especially as they are interrelated in the tropes of white artistic discourse and Black communal oral traditions, is very much the meat of Petry's exploration in the three stories analyzed here. The plot of "Mother Africa" (published in the *Miss Muriel* collection for the first time) is unusual in and of itself. Spring has come to Harlem, finding the junkman, Emanuel Turner, called, eponymously, Man, searching for goods to add to his stores. A pair of garbage-disposal men offer to bring him a statue from a rich client's house. When it arrives, it is huge and of some dark, shining metal, and Man dubs it "Mother Africa." The neighbors are not so appreciative, desecrating the statue with brassieres and turbans, but Man is loyal. The presence of the statue causes him to clean up his yard, plant grass, and eventually to clean himself up, too, to the extent that shaved, with clean clothes, he looks like a new man.

The statue and the cleaning up cause him to recall his past life, when he had been married to a wife he loved, who had died in childbirth. Life had seemed worth fighting for then, along with dignity and self-respect. The statue—"Mother Africa"—had brought all that back to him. Then comes the denouement. Climbing up to remove some neighbor's desecration, Man realizes that the statue is not African at all, just a huge white woman made out of dark metal. Devastated, he calls in the scrap metal people and begins to go back to his familiar ways as "Junk," "Rags," "Bottles," the neighborhood's filthy ragpicker. One must be careful not to take this as a story too literally about "Signifyin(g)." Rather, the story does seem to develop some important themes Hilary Holladay, in her new book for Twayne, indicates are vital to an understanding of Petry: Namely, the eponymous hero, Man, is pitted against his community precisely because he chooses a work of art to enshrine. Holladay's sociological view of the story—including her discussion of the statue as an artifact representing gender and race (rather than art qua art)—takes the story out of the realm of Signifyin(g) and places it, as Holladay points out, in the realm of community vs. individual. Signifyin(g) in Gates's and Baker's terms would demand that the Junkman, Man, speak for the community, that the work of art be an act of Signifyin(g) or of preserving Black identity in the face of white man's onslaught. That clearly is not the case in these stories. Complex questions of essentialism, of the figuration of the idea of Mother Africa in the story of that title, and of the native dance in "Olaf," certainly can be fruitfully discussed. However, in the case of all three stories here presented, Petry does not examine how the Black artist Signifies on behalf of the rest of the African-American community. More to the point, especially in the case of Man in "Mother Africa," the black artist must protect himself against especially deleterious forces within the community that may threaten to do him/her in.

In terms of Petry's story, the statue develops a reality both for Man and for his community. A dialogue ensues. Man clears a space for the statue, having in mind a statue in the park. Thinking all the time the statue is

"Mother Africa," he clears a spot and plants grass and puts up a little picket fence. The neighbors' answering salvos are to treat the statue as equally real—as a real oversized naked woman scandalizing the community. At night, they place outrageous clothing on it, making of the statue in Man's eyes something lewd and ludicrous.

Bonnie TuSmith's exploration of ethnicity, language, and community is useful here. By adopting a nondiscursive, non-oral white-man's mode for expression in his harboring of the statue, Man has broken the network of the linguistically-based community; in TuSmith's words, the sharing of "a common language of suffering and the wisdom black people have gleaned from their group historical experience" (79). So long as Man accepted his traditional place in the community (virtually that of a Trickster figure since his buying and selling wove the community together into a common weft) and sang his bittersweet song of poverty and degradation, he was accepted as the artistic expression of the neighborhood's soul. By bringing in the upstart, unfamiliar means of discourse—white man's art (even when he thought it was an African sculpture)—Man violates the tradition of Signifyin(g) and carries it into the terrain of signification—of the oppressor's discourse.

If the discourse of the statue is the discourse of art, Man becomes its protector against the denigrations of the philistine community:

He thought that in a day or two the statue would be forgotten and everything would be just as it has been before. But it wasn't. During the night someone, drunk or sober, male or female, hung a pink brassiere on the metal woman, draping it lewdly across her breasts. It flapped in the wind. The harsh pink of the material was an outrage to the dark beauty of the statue. And Man viewing it, felt harassed. (141)

By desecrating the statue with a blatant sexual innuendo, the community utilizes an act of Signifyin(g) to reject Man's attempt to adopt the dominant culture's norms of general artistic signification by an act of Signifyin(g).

Two songs, one sung by Man in his guise as "Junk," the other chanted by the neighbors in derision at the statue, sum up the disparity in the discourse between Man and his community.

On the spring morning before he is offered the statue, Man goes out into the street: He had a big baritone voice and he let it out as he half talked, half sang the words: "I B-u-y, b-u-y! Ole rags, ole bottles, ole sewin' machines!' His voice went up and down, down and up. It cut through, went over, went under, the other sounds in the street—the hum of traffic, monotonous, regular; the low-pitched voices of passersby . . . No one ever had an old sewing machine to sell or to give away but he liked the sound of the word and his voice lingered on "machines," caressed it, very nearly exhausted the scale on it, as he placed a bit of old metal on his cart. (129)

Thus we are introduced to Man as a being who can appreciate making music in an artistic way, although that music is only an aspect of his ordinary business. The song becomes even more significant as it becomes the only appropriate greeting he can think of to express his joy at having "Mother Africa" in his yard: "He felt like singing. But he had no song, never had heard of any song, suited for such a moment, no melody that could possibly match the feeling of tenderness that suddenly assailed him at the thought that this big dark woman was his" (149). What he does sing is his buying and selling song going "up and down the scale five times on ole sewin' machines" (149).

By contrast, the neighbors, looking out the window at the newly ensconced statue, call out,

Shame! Shame!
Everybody know your dirty black name!
Shame! Shame!
Everybody know your dirty black name! (137)

This establishes a war between Man and his neighbors. Interestingly, the more at odds he is with his neighbors over the question of keeping the statue in his backyard, the more determined he is to clean himself up personally, get a shave and a haircut, indulge memories of his late wife, until he is almost beyond recognition. Repeating the dialectic of the social and the individual, Man allows the statue to isolate him from his immediate associates at the same time that it unifies him with his racial heritage.

It is no wonder then that when that link to his heritage proves to be a fraud—the statue he has dubbed "Mother Africa" does not have Negroid features——he feels betrayed. The "art" that has beguiled him in the person of a statue representing his ethnic pride turns out to be another trick of the white man. The white community has poisoned his life as surely as the white girl in Petry's later novel *The Narrows* (1953) poisons the black community that is the focus of the novel. In retaliation, Man returns to his former ways, and sells the statue for scrap metal. The only artistic discourse he will countenance will be a reprise of his buy and sell song.

Petry wrote "Mother Africa" before the onset of the worst of what Cornel West refers to as "black nihilism." However, by examining the frame structure of the story—Man's start as something like Ellison's "invisible man," his ability to surface, regain optimism and fuel that with returned memory, then his ultimate return to his old "invisible self" as a ragpicker—we can see some of the interdynamic between the nihilism West discusses and the relationship of the insular, self-protective black community to an individualism that Man attempts to achieve before he is cut down by an oppressive external white society. As West explains:

Nihilism is to be understood here not as a philosophic doctrine that there are no rational grounds for legitimate stands or authority; it is, far more, the lived experience of coping with a life of horrifying meaninglessness, hopelessness, and (most important) lovelessness. (40)

Man, in his attempt to become everyman, becomes no man. It is difficult to determine whether Petry is suggesting that the Mother Africa statue leads Man into a false hope and allows him to rebuild his morale and self-respect on false premises. Is she arguing against Black essentialism? The fact that the community is never fooled suggests that Man's discourse of individualism—and its projection onto the statue—is interpreted by the neighborhood as a threat. Community cohesion and continuity outweigh the intrusion of even an artifact of cultural heritage that the community finds foreign to its own practices. Of course, when Man himself sees that the statue is a hoax foisted upon him by the white community—and that thereby all formal artistic discourse, Black or white, may be equally deceptive—he returns to the old invisibility with which the community is comfortable. He returns to his bartering song, the song of the street tradesman—and he returns in his personal aspect to the nihilistic self-destructive life from which he had for a moment seen a way to emerge.

It is difficult to speculate on Petry's own position in this story. What TuSmith points out about John Edgar Wideman would seem to be true of Petry as well: the "experience as an upwardly mobile individual who became an unwitting assimilationist had direct bearing" on her art (86). Thus arises a certain anxiety of influence from cultures outside the ethnic "home" culture. As TuSmith explains:

When European American culture is the norm and other cultures are 'substandard,' wanting to write the best would imply turning one's back on one's ethnic culture. For literature to ring true, however, the writer cannot deny a large part of him- or herself or the community in which this self was nurtured. (86)

While this story is situated in Harlem, a place where Petry only transiently made a home, it expresses through its interest in discourse and artistic tropes, mainstream (white) values as well as those of the ethnic community, and, through examinations of individual interaction with community, many of the concerns that Petry as a Black artist remaining most of her life in white surroundings may have been particularly interested in exploring.

"Olaf and His Girl Friend" [1945] is a story that can also be examined in terms of its relationship to questions of discourse, particularly of the problematic Black discourse of oppression. It is narrated by an interested bystander of indeterminate race and gender but presumably African American male. The result is, in M. M. Bakhtin's concept, a dedication to the study of a verbal art [that] can and must overcome the divorce between an abstract "formal" approach and an equally abstract "ideological" approach. Form and content in discourse are one, once we understand that verbal discourse is a social phenomenon—social throughout its entire range and in each and every of its factors, from the sound image to the furthest reaches of abstract meaning. (259)

Surpassing the dimension of "ideological" art, the dance at the heart of the story creates a meaning for art beyond that of mere enjoyment. As the mysterious narrator tells it, Olaf was a dock worker in Barbados who loved a beautiful native girl, Belle Rose. Belle Rose's grandmother,[3] however, wanted a better mate for the girl and moved her to New York, out of Olaf's reach. Deeply in love, Olaf overcame his fear of the sea and took a ship, which he hoped would wind up in New York. This was during wartime, and Olaf wound up sailing all over the globe.

In an extraordinary tour de force of discourse, the entire merchant marine corps becomes involved in an underground way in Olaf's plight. Messages start with the hail: "Olaf from Barbados is looking for Belle Rose." As the narrator recounts:

The dock worker told a friend, and the story went in to the kitchens and the freight elevators of great hotels. Doormen knew it and cooks and waiters. It traveled all the way from the waterfront to Harlem. People who'd never heard of Belle Rose knew that a man named Olaf was looking for her. (189)

This proves to be a most remarkable underground form of communication. It suggests a unity among African American workers and neighborhood people that has not, for the most part, been plumbed so successfully, except possibly in the work of Ernest J. Gaines. Here, the chain effect is etched in, and no matter how incredulous the audience may be, it seems convincing.

There is a war going on, spies are thwarting each other's attempts to get secret messages through about armaments and deployments. Effortlessly, through the mess kitchens and chains of deck hands, the message gets through to Olaf: "Belle Rose is dancing in New York in a place that is not good. . . . She dances. And it is not a good dance" (187). When one considers the messages that are not getting through, this underground communication among Black (and other) workers is remarkable. It suggests both a cohesion to the African-American community combined with a bond with the white working-class community, and a sense that love, always, takes precedence over war. For the workers on the ships and on the docks, the Germans and Japanese are known, predictable, and not worth talking about. The plight of Olaf, one of theirs, in search of his ladylove warrants an all-out effort that would confound even a James Bond. This underground network suggests a function of discourse only recently addressed by the major theorists—that of forming a bond among a minority population that both circumvents and eludes the dominant sector even while it exists in plain view. As Gates notes, utilizing a quote from Jean Toomer:

If "the Dixie Pike," as Jean Toomer put the matter in Cane, "has grown from a goat path in Africa," then the black vernacular tradition stands as its signpost, at the liminal crossroads of culture contact and ensuing difference at which Africa meets Afro-America. (4)

The story of Olaf and Rose, then, is more than the story of a remarkable network bringing two lovers together; it is an exploration of the entire system of discursive linkage within the African diaspora. It may come as no surprise to modern readers that the goal of the "Dixie Pike" itself, the heart of the entire signification and signifyin(g) system is what some critics refer to as "Black joy," or the act of love. This discovery would seem to be the nexus of this story, as well. The cross-ethnic nature of the interlocking web through which the message is repeatedly passed may presciently contribute to West's proposed cure for nihilism:

Nihilism is not overcome by arguments or analysis; it is tamed by love and care. Any disease of the soul must be conquered by a turning of one's soul. This turning is done by one's own affirmation of one's worth—an affirmation fueled by the concern of others. This is why a love ethic must be at the center of a politics of conversion. (43)

Clearly, in this story, the reason for this retreat to the underground is to protect the central core of love from the ravages of the oppressors—the bosses of the shipping lines, the generals issuing war directives, and even of Belle's own grandmother,[4] who has herself internalized and enforced the standards of the commodification of love that West suggests is at the root of the nihilism he warns against. The tension between true love and commosdified [sic] love, between true joy, and joy perverted to serve the needs of a rapacious white audience persists throughout the story. This is shown when Olaf arrives in New York, ascertains that Belle Rose is the star attraction at a club called the Conga, and determines to bring her home. Actually, he does not at first know what he determines. Belle Rose, dressed in a "native" costume that involves yards of ruffled petticoats and calico and a turban on her head, dances a wild island dance taught her by her obeah grandmother. Half of New York flocks to Harlem to see her. The community, as well, is organized around the expression of sexuality and tribal memory that Belle Rose's dance represents. For its appreciative and wide audience, Belle Rose's dance functions similarly to Olaf's underground message. Surely, some have come to gawk and enjoy vicarious

thrills. But for most the dance binds them in a unity born of tribal identity
and sealed by the universal seam of sexuality that runs through all of us.

Olaf at first does not know what to make of the dance. Has his true love
been desecrated? He takes out a knife; he pulls Belle Rose off the stage.
Will he kill her? The audience holds its breath. The nameless narrator
reports:

> The drums had stopped. Everything had stopped. There wasn't so much as a glass
> clinking or the sound of a cork pulled. It seemed to me that I had stopped breath-
> ing, and that not one in the place was breathing. She began to sing in a high, shrill
> voice. I couldn't understand any of the words. It was the same kind of chant that
> a witch doctor uses when he casts a spell; the same one that the conjure women
> use and the obeah women.
> Her voice stopped suddenly. They must have stared at each other for all of five
> minutes. The knife slipped out of his hand. Clinked on the floor. Suddenly he
> reached out and grabbed her and shook her like a dog would shake a kitten. She
> didn't say anything. Neither did he. And then she was in his arms and he was
> kissing her and putting his very heart into it. (196)

Passion and art are often discussed as related discourses, but the passion addressed is frequently that of the mind rather than of sexuality.
Here, the whole love affair between Olaf and Belle Rose has been enacted
and participated in by a huge cast of messengers and audience, and, it is
safe to assume, will be conveyed to strangers, as the narrator is conveying
it to the reader. In that sense, for the sailors conveying the early messages,
for the audience witnessing the consummation of Olaf's quest, the art of
the combined thrust of folklore and species-old passion are not merely a
discourse conveying an experience. They are the experience. Art has made
its conquest.

If this rapture with which the story climaxes is a particularly Black
version of what Jacques Lacan has referred to as jouissance, then perhaps
the love that lies at the core of this particular community can be seen in
essentialist terms. By including as participants a multiethnic, multiclass
cast of participants and onlookers in this drama, Petry seems to suggest
that all can be liberated from the constraints of dominant-culture Puritan-
ism by a release of the free play of Black jouissance, as occurs in this story
in Belle Rose's obeah dance and the final kiss. As Gina Dent explains in
a valiant attempt to explicate the ineffability of this mode:

> It is a question of love, of ethics, and not of sexual difference, not even of the
> regimes—culture and politics—that accrue value to either side of that difference
> unequally. Jouissance is not the complement to sexual pleasure; it is its supple-
> ment. It is not only oppositional but alternative. (10)

The ultimate gesture in this story—Olaf's grabbing up Belle Rose and
kissing her and eloping with her—represents the ultimate liberation that

perhaps West was to seek: the liberation of eros from its confinement to mammon, the freeing of Black sexuality from commercialization and cooptation in an act that can spread that liberation beyond ethnic perimeters.

The fusion of art and experience is nowhere so evident in Petry's work as in the 1947 story "Solo on the Drums," also included in the *Miss Muriel* collection. The plot is simple—to the degree that there is a plot. Narrated in third person, the story develops that the drummer in a big-band orchestra, Kid Jones, has been told by his wife that she is leaving him in favor of the piano player. What follows is a powerfully mimetic rendition of how the drummer pours his soul into his music. Looking at the piano player, he experiences his hatred. Soft-scaling with brushes, temposetting with the bass, Kid Jones pours his heart and anguish into his performance. The remembered, repeated, refrain of his girlfriend's declaration, "I'm leaving," sets the beat for his music. But the music does more than connect the player with his private anguish:

The drums . . . took him back, and back, and back, in time and space. He built up an illusion. He was sending out the news. Grandma died. The foreigner in the litter has an old disease and will not recover. The man from across the big water is sleeping with the chief's daughter. Kill. Kill. Kill. The war goes well with the men with the bad smell and the loud laugh. It goes badly with the chiefs with the round heads and the peacock's walk. (239)

The effect is almost Jungian in the music's evocation of species trace. As with the statue in the first story here considered, the African heritage is posited as the source of an artistic expression that can reverberate within and uplift the soul of the diaspora African-American who is attuned to respond to it. Like Man Turner, Kid Jones finds expression for his deepest artistry as well as his deepest feelings in the whole racial memory the African motif evokes. As Houston A. Baker, Jr. notes:

Black American culture is partially differentiated from white American culture because one of its most salient characteristics is an index of repudiation. Oral, collectivistic, and repudiative—each of these aspects helps to distinguish black American culture from white American culture. (16)

The discourse of repudiation works in several ways in this story, not the least dialectically. The more Kid Jones hears the refrain of his personal sorrow reverberate through his head, the more he pours that sorrow into his playing—and Petry, it must be noted, does an excellent job of capturing the full range of Jones's pathos in her prose rendition of his playing. Jones is simultaneously pulled inside himself and outside his sorrow with his playing:

He forgot the theater, forgot everything but the drums. He was welded to the drums, sucked inside them. All of him. His pulse beat. He had become part of the drums. They had become part of him. (240)

The experience is so intense, not only for the player, but for the listener and the reader, as to be almost sexual, certainly visceral. In John Dewey's terms, this unity of soul with body with expression constitutes the oneness with nature—man's nature as well as natural phenomena—that is at the core of art. In this piece, as in the other two, memory and desire, soul and racial "trace" blend into a work of art that is unified with nature very much in Dewey's terms.

The dialectic occurs in this piece, as in the other two, in the reception of the audience. Kid Jones has not realized while he was playing that he was actually performing before an audience for pay—he thought he was finding expression for his soul, his sorrow, through his instruments.

When he finally stopped playing, he was trembling; his body was wet with sweat. He was surprised to see that the drums were sitting there in front of him. He hadn't become part of them. He was still himself. Kid Jones. Master of the drums. Greatest drummer in the world. Selling himself a little piece at a time. Every afternoon. Twice every evening. Only this time he had topped all his other performances. This time, playing like this after what had happened in the morning, he had sold all of himself—not just a little piece.

Someone kicked his foot. "Bow, you ape. Whassamatter with you?" (241)

The contrast in discourse between Jones's coming to realize that he has poured out his soul only for a few shekels and the abrupt kick in the shin suggests the same dichotomy between the appreciation that comes from the soul and the philistine surroundings seen in "Mother Africa." Even more than Man Turner, Kid Jones has expressed the highest form of his own personal artistry in his music, only to have that commodified. Like Man Turner singing his rag-picking song to what he thinks is the statue of an African woman, Jones incorporates species mythology, heartfelt pain, and murderous impulse (the piano-player his wife loves is sitting in front of him) into his expression. If Turner gets only derision in return, and Belle Rose's obeah dance is seen as "not nice," Jones finds himself bowing to an estranged audience, "like one of those things you pull the string and its jerks, goes through the motion of dancing." (241)

The particular art form under examination here is that of jazz musicianship. As Ralph Ellison, more contemporaneous with Petry than are some of the modern commentators (and who invoked the same image of the jerking puppet in *Invisible Man*) defined the problem:

There is a cruel contradiction implicit in the art form itself. For true jazz is an art of individual assertion within and against the group. Each true jazz moment (as distinct from the universal commercial performance) springs from a contest in which each artist challenges all the rest, each solo flight, or improvisation represents (like the successive canvases of a painter) a definition of his identity: as individual, as member of the collectivity and as link in the chain of tradition. Thus, because jazz finds its very life in an endless improvisation upon traditional materials, the jazzman must lose his identity even as he finds it. (qtd. in Gates vii)

This would seem to be a perfect exposition of the theme Petry renders into fictive eloquence in Kid Jones's story. Furthermore, all three pieces convey the sense that there is a dialectic at work between artist and audience. In "Mother Africa" Man Turner's increasing appreciation for the statue increasingly estranges him from the neighbors on whom he depends for his goods and sense of well-being. He sees in the statue a racial icon; they see in it a naked hussy. Finally he realizes he has been betrayed; his neighbors have been right. The statue is nothing but a white woman, more white folks' tricks. He gets rid of it, and goes back to his old ways. But he has had the moment while he did believe, when he sang his purest note, recalled a painful love, and got himself cleaned up to the point he is not recognized. The fact that this has all been for a fraud seems to be an authorial statement that art is mere discourse after all. For those who can find the aesthetic sensibility, while they can find it, to appreciate art, a transformation occurs. There is a shift in the reality that goes beyond questions of mere discourse. Man has actually cut his hair and his beard, changed his pants, and allowed himself to think of his dead wife and the love he bore her. A visceral change has come over the beholder, the partaker of the work of art. The fraudulent quality is the discourse quality. Seeing the statue as a white trick, Man is ready to see it the way his neighbors do, as a desecration, a heap of metal, to be sold for junk. He does not even go so far as to see the statue as lewd or vulgar. Torn apart at the scrap metal dealer's, it will bring in money. He is left with a pain, a disillusionment. We must admit that he had a feeling he did not have before. If that feeling is one of having been betrayed, the betrayal was caused by the discourse of art as well as by the white world in general.

It is clear in the Olaf story that Belle Rose's dance is a work of art, and a similar dialectic takes place here. Olaf has been told that Belle Rose is dancing in a way that is "not nice." It is not clear that Belle Rose herself is aware that what seems to her to be a natural but perhaps exotic dance is being sold to attract crowds to pay for an erotic commodity. The description of the costume and the dance itself indicates nothing lewd or sexually suggestive. The power of the dance lies in Belle Rose's conviction that she is conveying a message taught her by her obeah grandmother. Perhaps it is for that reason—the reason that she has not become a whore—that Olaf, when he sees her, does not kill her. The question is, what is the audience getting out of this? The perspicacious narrator recounts the night Olaf entered the club:

The drums started again. And this time I tell you they talked as plainly as though they were alive. Human. They talked danger. They talked hate. They snarled and they sent a chill down my spine. The back of my neck felt cold and I found I was clutching my glass so tightly that my hand hurt.

Belle Rose crouched and walked forward and started singing. It was an incantation to some far-off evil gods. It didn't belong in New York. It didn't belong in any nightclub that has ever existed anywhere under the sun. (194)

Clearly, the audience is getting a vicarious thrill, but is it really unwholesome? The audience wants the obeah experience, the communication with the far-off evil gods. They want to be pulled so far out of themselves that they clutch their glass until it hurts. In that sense they are feeding off Belle Rose in the same way that Kid Jones allows the audience to feed off his personal misery.

Gayatri Chakravorty Spivak's analysis of the gendered subaltern elements of a Third-World novel from her own Indian tradition, Mahasweta Devi's Stanadayini [BreastGiver], suggests a way of putting Belle Rose's dance—and possibly Kid Jones's drum-playing—into perspective. Spivak's effort is to note that the gendered body of a female wetnurse becomes symbolic of the relationship of the subaltern continent to the colonizer. She explores the burden of this metonymical relationship:

As long as there is this hegemonic cultural self-representation of India as a goddess-mother (dissimulating the possibility that this mother is a slave), she will collapse under the burden of the immense expectations that such a self-representation permits. (244)

In much the same way, Belle Rose herself, costumed and displayed, becomes a metonymy for the African diaspora. She shares in common with Man Turner's "Mother Africa" the translation into Otherness of the African heritage. In Belle Rose's case the purpose is to serve the white audience's desire for vicarious consumption. The effect of white gaze on traditions of the African diaspora is to contaminate them—to transform eros or jouissance into pornography. If Spivak's wetnurse becomes emblematic of the relationship between the colonial country and the master country, in the words of a subaltern narrative, Belle Rose's dance, to some extent Man Turner's statue and Kid Jones's playing embody the spirit, the contaminated essence of African diaspora tradition. Belle Rose, in particular, comes closest to resembling the gendered subaltern metonymy Spivak discusses. As Spivak notes:

If only the emancipatory possibilities of the culture of imperialism are taken into account, the *distortions* in the ideals of a national culture when imported into a colonial theater would go *unnoticed*. (245) (italics original)

The distortion here is that through a play on the concept of Black essentialism, related to Black joy or jouissance, African-American eros has been co-opted and corrupted into precisely the act of commodification that translated the African body into the body of the slave. Olaf frees Belle Rose from the white man's gaze through an act of love. (In modern feminist terms, the reader might wonder whether this freeing is a regressive act, forcing Belle Rose out of her place in a self-defined spotlight, however contaminated, and back into the life of an island housewife.) This kiss, the almighty Hollywood metonymy for transcendence of selfhood at the time the story was written, becomes the act of liberation not only from white cultural distortions of the essential African ethos; it becomes, in a very practical sense, an act that will chain Belle Rose to a gendered existence of hard work that will place control of her sexuality not in her own hands (though surely no longer in the hands of the white oppressor) but in the hands of her husband-to-be.

Black essence, or black jouissance, though of course not identical terms, are concepts important to contemporary discussions of diaspora literature. The essentialist argument that Audre Lorde makes connecting women as a group to the "erotic" has been applied as well to the Black subculture. Lorde's case is familiar and goes as follows:

When I speak of the erotic, then, I speak of it as an assertion of the life-force of women; of that creative energy empowered, the knowledge and use of which we are now reclaiming in our language, our history, our dancing, our loving, our work, our lives. (51)

Petry's prescient ability to address the erotic in essentialist terms, as discussed here, transcends gender constructs to locate eros within the Black male as well as female experience. The fact that Belle Rose's naïve ritualistic dance is seen as lewd, as "not nice," the desecration of Man Turner's "Mother Africa" statue by a sexual icon, even Kid Jones's transformation of racially specific erotic pain into commercialized product suggest a moralism that Petry seems to adhere to. This would investigate the morality by which a native tradition—African essentialism or eros—becomes transformed into the white man's pornography. For Petry, unlike later commentators, the answer seems to be to jettison the sexually incriminating act: junk the statue; snatch the dancer off the stage; commiserate with the soul-weary drummer. In all three cases, Black essence has been contaminated, as Spivak has suggested, by the colonizer's codes. As bell hooks puts it:

The contemporary commodification of blackness has become a dynamic part of [the] system of cultural repression. . . . The commodification of blackness strips away that component of cultural genealogy that links living memory and history in ways that subvert and undermine the status quo. (148–149)

Here, hooks seems to suggest not so much an ethnic or racial oppression as a class matter. Calling on "middle-class" Blacks to dissociate from the contamination of the voyeuristic gaze that, as Petry indicates, has trapped Black culture in a painful dialectic of refusal and sub rosa celebration, hooks places the question clearly, in these times, in class terms in a way that would not have been so appropriate during the time when Petry was at the peak of her career. It seems hooks is issuing a manifesto:

The point of raising this question is not to censor but rather to urge critical thought about a cultural marketplace wherein blackness is commodified in such a way that fictive accounts of underclass black life in whatever setting may be more lauded, more marketable, than other visions because mainstream conservative white audiences desire these images. . . . The desire to be "down" has promoted a conservative appropriation of specific aspects of underclass black life, whose reality is dehumanized via a process of commodification wherein no correlation is made between mainstream hedonistic consumerism and the reproduction of a social system that perpetuates and maintains an underclass. (152)

The dynamic of inter-ethnic aspects of the creation of an underclass as opposed to the concern for the Otherness of Black essentialism as a racial quality may be beyond the scope of this discussion of these stories. Certainly that question applies to Petry's two major novels, *The Street*, and *The Narrows*. In these stories the focus is more tightly closed on attention to the relationship between essence and discourse, in that sense between signifier and signified—and signifying. At the same time, the subject matter of communality, of racial trace, inherent in all three of these stories, clearly stretches beyond the bounds of the African American experience. In that regard, and for that reason, Ann Petry undoubtedly speaks to an audience wider than that of her own race. To all who have succumbed to the seductive discourses of art and sensual expression, these stories offer a recognizable—and manifold—meaning. In this way, it becomes possible to place Petry now in the context of the multicultural community that is currently generating so much discussion within aesthetic circles.

NOTES

1. The editors are correcting Ann Petry's date of birth in this essay to 1908.

2. Biographical material on Ann Petry is derived from two interview articles. One is by Garret Condon, "Street Wise," in *Northeast* magazine in *The Hartford Courant*, November 8, 1992. The other article, by Anita Diamant, "A Vision of the Street," appeared in the *Boston Globe Magazine*, February 2, 1992.

3. Editors' Note: It is Belle Rose's aunt and not her grandmother.

4. Editor's Note: Again, the is Belle Rose's aunt, not grandmother.

WORKS CITED

Baker, Houston A., Jr. *Long Black Song: Essays in Black American Literature and Culture.* Charlottesville, VA: University Press of Virginia, 1972.

Bakhtin, M. M. *The Dialogic Imagination.* Austin: University of Texas Press, 1981.

Dent, Gina, ed. *Black Popular Culture: A Project by Michelle Wallace.* Seattle: Bay Press, 1992.

Dewey, John. *Art as Experience.* New York: Perigee, 1980.

Douglass, Frederick. *Narrative of the Life of Frederick Douglass, An American Slave.* New York: Penguin, 1982.

Gates, Henry Louis, Jr. *The Signifying Monkey: A Theory of African American Literary Criticism.* New York: Oxford University Press, 1988.

Giddings, Paula. *When and Where I Enter: The Impact of Black Women on Race and Sex in America.* New York: Bantam, 1984.

Holladay, Hilary. *Ann Petry.* New York: Twayne, 1996.

hooks, bell. *Outlaw Culture: Resisting Representations.* New York: Routledge, 1994.

Lorde, Audre. "Uses of the Erotic: The Erotic as Power." In Marita Golden, editor. *Wild Women Don't Wear No Blues: Black Women Writers on Love, Men and Sex.* New York: Doubleday, 1993, 49–55.

Petry, Ann. *Miss Muriel and Other Stories.* Boston: Houghton Mifflin, 1971.

———. *The Narrows.* Boston: Houghton Mifflin, 1953. Reprint 1988.

———. *The Street.* Boston: Houghton Mifflin, 1946. Reissue 1992.

Spivak, Gayatri Chakravorty. *In Other Words: Essays in Cultural Politics.* New York: Routledge, 1988.

TuSmith, Bonnie. *All My Relatives: Community in Contemporary Ethnic American Literatures.* Ann Arbor: The University of Michigan Press, 1993.

West, Cornel. "Nihilism in Black America," In Gina Dent, ed. *Black Popular Culture.* Seattle: Bay Press, 1992. 37–47.

Jazz/Blues Structure in Ann Petry's "Solo on the Drums"

Gayl Jones

[An] African American writer who has employed techniques from oral tradition to control and liberate the structure of a story, its organization of events, and presentation of character is Ann Petry. "Solo on the Drums" [1947] lacks chronological and sequential dramatic scenes, but the storyline achieves flexibility and intricacy from the musical African American oral traditions of jazz and blues.

Many African American fiction writers and poets acknowledge the superiority of the black musician as artist, and from their early efforts to reshape literature to their own cultural dynamics these writers have made thematic and stylistic references to African American music as guide, with the recognition that the music possesses a greater capacity for complexity and scope. Of course much of the music's refinement is due to its remaining, as an art form and ritual, an unknown though modified continuum of oral tradition, whereas the "writers" (*griots*) had to readjust to written literature in an environment that discouraged or banned such efforts as criminal, from the black codes of slavery to the Jim Crow laws and attitudes of the South (including Louis Simpson's infamous criticism of Gwendolyn Brooks: essentially, that her work would never be important as long as her characters were Negroes). The exchange between Richard Wright and the white woman employer in *Black Boy* crystallizes it all. When she asks him why he's still going to school (he's in the seventh grade), he replies that he wants to be a writer. "For what?" she asks, astonished.

"To write stories," I mumbled defensively.

"You'll never be a writer," she said. "Who on earth put such ideas into your nigger head?"

"Nobody," I said.

"I didn't think anybody ever would," she declared indignantly.[1]

This attitude did not apply to music. During the slave period, though the "talking" drums were banned because of their potential for insurrection, music seen as entertainment was encouraged; as James Baldwin observed, the white listeners often "enjoy it without ever hearing its harsher notes."[2] The meaning underneath the surface sound is seldom heard: "You think it's a happy beat / listen to it closely / ain't you heard something underneath?" (Langston Hughes). Two things seemed to be working in support of the musician as artist: internally, there was the cultural connection with the oral traditions of Africa; externally, music did not hold the same threat to whites as literacy (relegated to folk utterance or performance, it also did not hold the same status), and certainly much of its combative intent went unheard. There were and still are tensions and misjudgments between the Western (European) conceptions of musical art and African American music in regard to harmony, chord structures, rhythms, kinds or uses of instruments, cadences, voice and phrasing, modes of construction, ranges of tones and intonations, presentation and purpose. Likewise some people continue to see differences of orientation as wrong or celebrate the music for the wrong reasons—for instance, Europeans' liking for jazz because of its "raw and savage gaiety" expressive of "an underworld of instinct" which "breathes a simple honest sensuality" and expresses "the mood of childlike happiness."[3] Yet the music continued to flourish because—in spite of the suppressions of the talking drums—there was never the same break in artistic tradition, and the divergences from the Western mainstream that in literature would have triggered rantings of "aberration" could be more readily admitted as innovative and deliberate, even avant-garde. However, again it was easier for Western critics to appreciate the innovations when they were taken up by the European American artists themselves, as in the syntactical aberrations of postmodernist literature and the literary-artistic claims of improvisational technique of certain contemporary Western writers. Yet even here, what African American tradition means by improvisational, that is, something informed by tradition and mastery of its techniques which allows the improvisational riffs, and what European Americans generally mean by it, that is, something "thrown together" or "tossed off," are quite different matters. In fact, much of the structural and thematic integrity of African American art vis-à-vis the West revolves around a problem of meaning.

But to get to the height and depth of structural and psychological complexity of the music, black writers, when they began to experiment with their own artistic traditions, began to look to the music as a significant—

indeed the most significant—extraliterary model. In an interview with Beverly Guy-Sheftall in *Sturdy Black Bridges*, Toni Cade Bambara, speaking of a "fearless and courageous and thoroughgoing" way of "dealing with the complexity of the black experience, the black spirit," says that "music is probably the only mode we have used to speak of that complexity."[4] Such writers recognize the potential for literature to be so used, and we will examine, beginning with Petry, ways in which African American fiction writers have attempted to mine that grand territory. At the same time, African American writers continue to acknowledge and look to the musician as the artistic vanguard and range finder, the most modern and often futuristic artist. Ernest Gaines in an interview with Charles H. Rowell in *Callaloo* made this acknowledgment: "Well, I feel we have expressed ourselves better in our music traditionally than we have done in our writing. The music (blues, jazz and spirituals, for example) is much better than our prose or poetry. I think that we have excelled in music because it is more oral. We are traditionally orally oriented. What I'd like to see in our writing is the presence of our music."[5] And Alice Walker has said: "I am trying to arrive at that place where black music already is; to arrive at that unselfconscious sense of collective oneness, that naturalness, that (even when anguished) grace."[6]

Ann Petry's "Solo on the Drums," then, is also an effort to bring that black musical presence into the writing. No African American writer has yet fully accomplished what the musician has, but it is significant that many black writers see music's potential for modifying the European American fictional forms—in the handling of theme, time, character, dramatic event, and moral-ethical import—differently from even the Europeans who celebrate it, because the black writers hear different things in the music. The European (and European American) is open to only one level of possibility; for the African American the range is pluralistic; jazz frees the imagination; *is* free imagination that is also disciplined, the latter almost always going unheard by the European ear. Michael S. Harper tells it this way in a poem for Miles Davis:

A friend told me
He'd risen above jazz.
I leave him there.[7]

Petry's jazz effort certainly does not mean that she cannot write the traditional short story. She has had, like many American writers, to prove that she can. But like Hairston she makes a deliberate choice here. And unlike the early African American writers, who were double-consciously and continuously working to avoid being considered outrageous or "embarrassing" while proving themselves to white audiences—even to their own people who, like their early European American colonial counterparts, could not imagine a literature written for themselves, and sometimes even about themselves—Petry and other writers of new stories assumed an autonomy over their structures, languages, and characters.

The protagonist of "Solo on the Drums" is a jazz drummer named Kid Jones. Petry not only takes her subject and milieu from the musical oral disciplines of jazz and blues, but combines these in a musical-literary form in the mobility of her narrative, the selection and organization of events, the conflict and resolution.

Petry opens the story in the same way that a jazz musician would introduce major themes: "The orchestra had a week's engagement at the Randlert Theater at Broadway and Forty-second Street. His name was picked out in lights on the marquee. The name of the orchestra and then his name underneath by itself. There would have been a time when he would have been excited by it. And stopped to let his mind and his eyes linger over it lovingly. Kid Jones. The name—his name—up there in lights that danced and winked in the brassy sunlight. . . . He used to eat it up. But not today. Not after what happened this morning."[8] The author gives an inkling of the problem, tells us there has been a transformation. She introduces the theme, welds the musical procedure to the narrative, and as the story progresses the initial situation is repeated, its contexts amplified, its meaning solved or explored through jazz solos and blues-speech interpolations. The motif of blues repetition and the self-assertive motives of blues are expressed in "the name—his name . . . his name . . . his name." Themes of identity and recognition are archetypal in all blues dramas. Blues pulls together and asserts identity (self and other) through clarification and playing back of experiences and meanings. While he "gets his music together" Kid Jones will be "getting himself together." But we still want to know what happened this morning and what has changed.

Next Petry's "music" sounds staccato rhythms and a percussive syntax of the sentences which suggest a reverberating drumbeat solo: "He hit the drums lightly. Regularly. A soft, barely discernible rhythm. A background. A repeated emphasis for the horns and the piano and the violin. The man with the trumpet stood up, and the first notes came out sweet and clear and high. Kid Jones kept up the drum accompaniment. Slow. Careful. Soft." More of the content of the story is revealed: "He wanted to cover his ears with his hands because he kept hearing a voice that whispered the same thing over and over again. The voice was trapped somewhere under the roof caught and held there by the trumpet. 'I'm leaving I'm leaving I'm leaving.'" The indirect monologue combined with drums and repeated blues lyrics suggested by rhythm and syntax continues the musical process and fictional suspense.

As the story unfolds, the past is reiterated and clarified. The equivalents of improvisation on the initial situation become more intricate as more of the story is revealed. Finally, we learn that the piano player has taken

Kid's wife (a revelation that had been foreshadowed through blues double-entendre in the homonyms "marquee-marquis": "the Marquis of Brund" is what they call the piano player.) The conflict is expressed as a musical one, and we discover that the musical-literary structure holds throughout. The jazz-blues lapidary cuts and polishes complication and resolution of the action.

And now—well, he felt as though he were floating up and up and up on that long blue note of the trumpet. He half closed his eyes and rode up on it. It had stopped being music. It was the whispering voice, making him shiver. Hating it and not being able to do anything about it. "I'm leaving it's the guy who plays the piano I'm in love with him and I'm leaving now today." Rain in the street. Heat gone. Food gone. Everything gone because a woman's gone. It's everything you ever wanted, he thought. It's everything you never got. Everything you ever had, everything you ever lost. It's all there in the trumpet—pain and hate and trouble and peace and quiet and love.

His wife's words and Kid Jones's memory of her speech become yet another lyric. The intensity and kinetic pace of that memory is duplicated by the prose. Together with the indirect monologue his thoughts are always expressed in the form of a lyric where the narrative functions as colloquial blues genre. Blues subject matter, meaning, improvised repetitions, slurs and worrying the line, double-edged paradoxes, patterns of light and shadow are clearly evident. In her essay, "The Blues Roots of Contemporary Afro-American Poetry," Sherley A. Williams defines "worrying the line": "Repetition in blues is seldom word for word and the definition of worrying the line includes changes in stress and pitch, the addition of exclamatory phrases, changes in word order, repetitions of phrases within the line itself, and the wordless blues cries which often punctuate the performance of the songs."[9] The substance of the story, like the rhythm of the drums, has "to be listened for . . . insidious, repeated." The flashbacks are never repeated word for word, but with changes in texture, event order, punctuation, and motive.

As we move toward the climax of the story Kid Jones "becomes one" with the drums: "He began to feel as though he were the drums, and the drums were he." In the same way music and literature are joined, and the story itself is a jazz solo on drums. Even so, it does not reach the intricate blending we will find in Amiri Baraka's "The Screamers," where text itself becomes music, where the whole word-sound choreography seems to be the musical composition. This occurs, too, in Leon Forrest's *There is a Tree More Ancient Than Eden* where music and verbal text are one in the paradoxically controlled "free improvisation" of a jazz collage:

Hawk-haunting down the ravaged sleeve of the enveloping raven forest and deep down the whispering flares of light in the distance and spellbound in the powdered dust of the magnolias, swinging scale-like in the breeze and the maypoles of chiaroscuro and fleeing the crowd lord to get back to the old fouled and dawning deed yoking the word into a waxy horror, yes and switching back into the neon cross etched against the moon shaving, oscillating upon the pavement gutters and breaking across a scarecrow plantation, jimmying the locked up bloodhounds leaping over the fencing and deep down the winding woods and the hounds rippling through the high grass and spear-like trees after the shackle-liberated heels; lord yes and clothing patched with ripped-away newspapers and dripping with dreaming long past the whites of their eyes, past the woods and rivers towards the north star swinging sweet and low, where he rode upon a milk-white horse drawing a chariot, in which a rectangular wooden box did rest yes and lord up through dreams of dates and promises and canceled checks, and numbers, and melancholia sliced across the faces, deep to the quick of the aching, weary, troubled bones, as delicate as wings, as prodigious as a ringing hammer, yes and river-wire and lord river-deep. . . . [10]

Actually, there are blues, jazz, spiritual, and sermonic rhythms and imagery all welded here; but it is jazz, I think, that first opened the possibilities of such "sound running" prose and gave directives for a whole verbal form that becomes music. Petry's story provides instead multiple structures within the traditional short-story form; it incorporates jazz and blues solos within a traditionally readable text; and the interface between the musical and literary remains clear. Her story stays a hyphenated mixture where fictional territories (or boundaries) are distinct and recognizable. In the Forrest excerpt there are no such visible junctures; there is a truer welding and a sense of the imaginative heat and power of that achievement.

But Kid Jones is an articulate musician, and the narrative describes and renders the effect of drumming: "The theater throbbed with the excitement of the drums. A man sitting near the front shivered, and his head jerked to the rhythm. A sailor put his arm around the girl sitting beside him, took his hand and held her face still and pressed his mouth close over hers. Close. Close. Close. Until their faces seemed to melt together. Her hat fell off and neither of them moved." The choice of vocabulary provides good musical equivalents: throbbed, shivered, jerked, pressed, melt, moved. The staccato recital suggests the drumbeat, and the vocabulary also fits the passion and ritual movements of the lovers. Their unity is juxtaposed to and reinforces the kinetic energy and unity of Kid Jones and his drums.

The theme of oneness continues with variations, from the drum motif to the patron lovers to Kid Jones's personal reminiscences and the initial predicament of the story recapitulated yet again: "The drummer forgot he was in the theater. There was only he and the drums and they were far way. Long gone. He was holding Lulu, Helen, Susie, Mamie, close in his arms. And all of them—all those girls blended into that one girl who was his wife. The one who said, 'I'm leaving.' She had said it over and over again, this morning, while rain dripped down the window panes." But there is more than repetition. The scenic context—what we see and know of that morning—broadens. As we listen we gain more background and information, for the story's mode of organization is dynamic, fluent, and improvisational. Again, the scenes are not traditionally isolated and dramatic, with extended dialogues and chronological sequences of character revelations and emotional pivotings. Instead, the jazz-fictional scenes are descriptive and lyrical; the drums recreate the emotions, atmosphere, and metaphors of transformation.

The drum solo becomes more fierce in its warring with the piano player: "When he hit the drums again it was with the thought that he was fighting with the piano player. He was choking the Marquis of Brund. He was putting a knife in clean between his ribs. He was slitting his throat with a long straight blade. Take my woman. Take your life. The drums leaped with the fury that was in him." This unity of man and drums in the warring effort is the turning point of the story. From it the past and present, the personal and collective, form adjacent regions and then interpenetrate. The traditional African function of drums as message bearers becomes rhythm and music translated into word and meaning: "The drums took him away from them, took him back, and back, and back, in time and space. He built up an illusion. He was sending out the news. Grandma died. The foreigner in the litter has an old disease and will not recover. The man from across the big water is sleeping with the chief's daughter. Kill. Kill. Kill." The broader social-historical context, significant to the intent of the story, reclaims an aesthetic which reinforces the narrative and dramatic vision of the New World story.

In *Oral Literature in Africa*, Ruth Finnegan discusses drum literature and the drum's historical and ritual uses, noting that "The instruments themselves are regarded as speaking and their messages consist of words."[11] Kid Jones's performance reclaims this kind of communication, but he cannot forget the words he wants to: his wife's "I'm leaving." He is led back from the past, the protean metamorphosis of time/space, to his personal dilemma and his own need for emotional recovery. This collective memory develops Petry's structure and links it to other contexts of oral tradition. Again the drums start talking about his own life; other women are brought in, more details are given. This stuff of the blues and the blues relationships compound the central one of the story—the relationship between Kid Jones and his wife. Finally, Kid Jones forgets everything but the drums: "He was welded to the drums, sucked inside them. All of him. His pulse beat. His heart beat. He had become part of the drums." We are carried further than the incipient unity described earlier. This is the true blues/jazz unity. It is no longer *as if* he were one with the drums; he *is* one with them. Blues paradox arrives in the assertion of what this story—

what all the storytelling—has been about: "The sound seemed to come not from the drums but from deep inside himself; it was a sound that was being wrenched out of him—a violent, raging, roaring sound. As it issued from him he thought, this is the story of my love, this is the story of my hate, this is all there is left of me."

When Kid Jones finally stops playing, the story itself winds down. But the blues experience has contributed to making this the best jazz drum solo he has given. The drumming has functioned as a kind of catharsis, a purgation ritual. Through the music, Kid Jones has done something, said something. He has "killed" the Marquis effectively in a musical ritual, so he won't have to do it in the world; the central confrontations have been transfigured. But the last note of the story, like the last note of a previous trumpet solo, seems to stay up in the air. "Yeah, he thought, you were hot all right. The jitterbugs ate you up and you haven't any place to go. Since this morning you haven't had any place to go . . . Then he stood up and bowed again. And again." The repetition leaves the character suspended; one has the sense of the held note, the blues impulse to action, unresolved.

Although this story does not achieve the complexity and dimensions of experience of the music itself, it provides a direction in modifying the literary text through the use of musical strategies and procedures—the referents of blues and jazz. There are some notable successes, such as Petry's reordering the ways events, character, and motive are presented to the reader, how conflicts are resolved, and how information is given. However, though Petry succeeds in describing Kid Jones's experience, we still wait for a musical-literary structure that could reproduce it, and move us to that territory of complex experience, the territory that Toni Cade Bambara[12] called being liberated by the music.

NOTES

1. Richard Wright, *Black Boy* (1945, rtp. New York: Harper and Row, 1966), 162–163.

2. Houston Baker, Jr., *The Journey Back* (Chicago: The University of Chicago Press, 1980), 88.

3. Alex Aronson, *Music and the Novel* (Totowa, NJ: Rowman and Littlefield, 1980), 132.

4. Roseann P. Bell, Bettye J. Parker, and Beverly Guy-Sheftall, eds., *Sturdy Black Bridges: Visions of Black Women in Literature* (New York: Anchor, 1979), 237.

5. *Callaloo* 3.1 (1978): 46.

6. John O'Brien, ed., *Interviews with Black Writers* (New York: Liveright, 1973), 204.

7. Michael S. Harper, *Dear John, Dear Coltrane* (Pittsburgh: University of Pittsburgh Press, 1970), 5.

8. Ann Petry, "Solo on the Drums," *American Negro Short Stories*, John Henrik Clarke, ed. (New York: Hill and Wang, 1966), 165–169. All quotations from the story are taken from these pages.

9. See Williams's article in *Chant of Saints*, Michael S. Harper and Robert B. Steptoe, eds. (Urbana: University of Illinois Press, 1979), 123–135.

10. This excerpt is quoted from *Giant Talk*, Quincy Troupe and Rainer Schulte, eds. (New York: Vintage, 1975). The novel was published by Random House in 1973.

11. Ruth Finnegan, *Oral Literature in Africa* (London: Oxford University Press, 1970). See "Drum Language and Literature," 481–482.

12. Toni Cade Bambara's short stories "Medley" and "Witchbird" are influenced by jazz improvisation. See Mary Helen Washington's introduction to her work in the anthology *Midnight Birds*, Mary Helen Washington, ed. (New York: Anchor, 1980), 169–171.

"Miss Muriel": Rewriting Innocence into Experience

Paul Wiebe

"Miss Muriel," the opening selection in Ann Petry's collection of short stories, *Miss Muriel and Other Stories* (1971), originally appeared in *Soon One Morning: New Writing by American Negroes, 1940–1962*, a collection that was published in 1963. Along with another short story, "Has Anybody Seen Miss Dora Dean?" (1958), "Miss Muriel" was the only work Petry published during the years when she was occupied primarily with her books for young adults, *Harriet Tubman, Conductor on the Underground Railroad* (1955) and *Tituba of Salem Village* (1964). "Miss Muriel" can be seen as another side of Petry's continuing interest in adolescents during this period. With *Harriet Tubman* and *Tituba*, both historical narratives told from the perspective of an omniscient narrator, Petry attempted to address what she saw as a gap in educational literature for adolescents.[1] In "Miss Muriel," Petry takes a different approach and explores the childhood world from the inside, taking the fictional perspective of an adolescent. The unnamed, first-person narrator in the story is a 12-year-old black girl who lives together with her parents and her Aunt Sophronia in the family-owned drugstore, a situation that obviously recalls Petry's own childhood growing up in Old Saybrook, Connecticut.[2] The narrator records her thoughts and observations during the course of an eventful summer when three men—Dottle Smith, a friend of the family and a teacher at a black college in Atlanta; Chink Johnson, a black piano player; and Mr. Bemish, a white shoemaker—vie with each other in their attempts to court Aunt Sophronia. The story ends in an epiphany for the narrator, who suddenly speaks out against Dottle and Chink when they force Bemish to pack his belongings and leave town. The importance with which Petry accorded

"Miss Muriel" and its coming-of-age tale can be inferred from its position as the opening piece in *Miss Muriel and Other Stories* (and from its prominence in the collection's title); and the fact that the collection ends with another story of a child, "Doby's Gone" (1944), suggests that for Petry, the formative experiences of the child and the adolescent had become the indispensable context for understanding and framing her stories of adults.[3]

Petry's artistic exploration of the young adolescent's world in "Miss Muriel," with its implication that the adult has something to learn from the child's perspective, aligns the work with a literary tradition whose roots can be traced to the Romantics. In particular, William Blake's rendering of the "Two Contrary States of the Human Soul" in *Songs of Innocence and of Experience* has in many ways set the terms that both writers and critics use to discuss the child in literature.[4] Blake's innovation, as Donald Smith argues, is that while "the earlier tradition [of children's religious and moral verse] tried to make adult views understandable and attractive to children (religious and moral verse *for* children), Blake's *Songs*, at least those of *Innocence* did the opposite, being children's verse and views for adults (verse *of* children)" (13). Blake's poems in *Songs of Innocence*, uttered by child speakers, have the quality of what Zohar Shavit, in his study of children's literature, calls the "ambivalent text," a text that seems directed to children and yet has additional layers of complexity that are more likely to be "realized by adults only" (78).[5] Even though children might be able to read the ambivalent text and discern the basic elements of its plot, they will still probably miss "several levels of the text" (78). Thus in the ambivalent text, the "child appears to be much more an excuse [or focal point] for the text, rather than its genuine addressee" (79).

Like Blake's *Songs of Innocence*, "Miss Muriel" has the qualities of an ambivalent text: the first-person narration, the plain style, and the structure of the story, which, as Hilary Holladay notes, has the feel of a diary, mimicking "that form in its loosely episodic, ostensibly artless progression" ("Creative Prejudice" 668) immerse us in a young adolescent's world.[6] In the opening paragraphs of the story, as the young narrator patters on about her close friend Ruth, we might even wonder if we, as adult readers, constitute the genuine addressee. As the narrative continues to unfold, it is tempting to further suspend our critical alertness, for the point of the narrative seems to be to induce in us the pleasure of reliving the innocent way adolescents view the adult world and, at times, to indulge us in the ironic pleasure of knowing more about the motives of the adults that the narrator describes than the narrator can know given her inexperience.

The tables are turned, however, when Petry abruptly closes the story with the narrator's epiphany, a scene that jolts us out of our comfortable position as knowing adult voyeurs in an adolescent's world. The narrator's rejection of Chink and Dottle's expulsion of Mr. Bemish is surprising because the narrator had already implicitly sided with Chink and Dottle when she expressed displeasure earlier in the story that Mr. Bemish, a white man, would venture to court her aunt. Her reaction is also surprising because she considers Dottle her "favorite person in all the world" (3). It is this rejection of her friends' treatment of Bemish that transforms a seemingly simple adolescent's narrative into a complex puzzle difficult for even adult readers to unravel. Moreover, unlike the well-known epiphany in James Joyce's "Araby," an adult voice does not intrude into the narration of "Miss Muriel" to formulate a mature (and obviously retrospective) interpretation of the adolescent's insight.[7] Joyce's narrator already does much of the work for the reader when he simultaneously reveals his boyhood epiphany and expresses it in adult language: "Gazing up into the darkness I saw myself as a creature driven and derided by vanity; and my eyes burned with anguish and anger" (35). On the other hand, Petry's narrator remains in character as she articulates her response to Chink and Dottle, using language that she has heard others use before, along with an adult invective: "You both stink. You stink like dead bats. You and your goddamn Miss Muriel—" (57). The effect of this ending, though not wrapped in adult abstractions, is as powerful as the ending in "Araby"; it sends us back into the text as more critical readers to find evidence that might help us understand how the narrator progresses to her epiphany. And when we unwind "Miss Muriel" from its ending to examine more closely what the epiphany reveals, what we find, I will argue, is that the story is not only concerned with the matter of race and prejudice, which the epiphany stresses; it is also about gender, narratives, and the importance of imitating, revising, and rejecting narratives as a means of struggling out of innocence and into experience. It is as much about the process of gaining experience—and what is not learned in the process—as it is about the final lesson learned.

To understand the complexity of "Miss Muriel," it is useful to refer to two other ambivalent texts from Blake's *Songs of Innocence*, "The Little Black Boy" and "The Chimney Sweeper." Obviously the dissimilarities between the Blake poems and "Miss Muriel" are numerous, but the Blake poems provide a context, in condensed form, for beginning an interpretation of the narrator's epiphany in "Miss Muriel" and for identifying the significance of the step she takes in moving from innocence and into experience. The connection I want to make between the two poems and "Miss Muriel" is the importance each accords to the role of discourse in the world of the innocent. In "Miss Muriel," this emphasis is signified by the title itself, although the importance of the title does not fully manifest itself until the ending. Initially, we might assume that Muriel is the name of the narrator, but it is not until almost halfway through the story that we find out that the name "Miss Muriel" refers to a story that Dottle first tells (and that Chink later revises) about a black man who asks a white shopkeeper for a Muriel cigar, and who is subsequently ordered by the shopkeeper to ask for *Miss* Muriel cigars because of the white woman pictured on the box. The term *Miss Muriel*—at first endowed with mysteriousness in its use as the title of the story, then seemingly deflated to a ordinary commercial term (Muriel cigars), but quickly recharged with racial and gender connotations in Dottle's story and Chink's revision of that story—becomes the site of a struggle over discourse, the struggle of deciding how a term should be coded or recoded and deciding who has the authority to use the term. At the end of the story the narrator enters into this fray and makes a judgment about the term and what she sees as its impact in her world.

The significance of this step taken by the narrator can be highlighted in a comparison of "Miss Muriel" and Blake's poems, for in these poems the child speakers do not successfully engage with the discourse that they find forming their world. The poems thus serve as a reference point for establishing a distinct boundary line between the states of innocence and experience. The innocent speakers in "The Little Black Boy" and "The Chimney Sweeper" will not cross over this line, even when they are confronted with the ugliness of the adult world and presented with narratives that would seem to facilitate their progression into the state of experience. The value of these poems for our analysis of "Miss Muriel" is that they reveal the mechanisms that children deploy to protect themselves and their state of innocence. Their denial of experience helps clarify how the narrator of "Miss Muriel" subtly moves into the realm of experience.[8]

In "The Little Black Boy," Blake is not specific about the setting of the poem, nor does he detail the physical aspects of slavery.[9] What interests him more are the "mental chains" that are formed by a racist discourse. In the first stanza, the black child struggles against the semiotic system constructed by such a discourse:

> My mother bore me in the southern wild,
> And I am black, but O! my soul is white;
> White as an angel is the English child;
> But I am black as if bereav'd of light. (1–4)

The black child feels he is spiritually equal to the English child, but his black skin serves as a contrary sign within the racist discourse system, signifying that he is "as if bereav'd of light." The English child, on the other hand, does not have this contradiction weighing him down because on the outside he is, as the speaker notes, "White as an angel." The black child is trapped in a semiotic system that creates a hierarchical opposition between white and black, coding white with positive spiritual values and black with the negation of those values. Thus the black child feels spiritually equal to the English child, even though his skin color signifies the contrary. This semiotic system has so thoroughly penetrated the black child's thinking that he uses the term "white" to describe his soul, which by definition is incorporeal and therefore not typically associated with a color.

In the next fourth and fifth stanzas, the black child relates a story that his mother has told him, ostensibly to counteract his feelings of racial inferiority. The child reports his mother's narrative as follows:

> And we are put on earth a little space,
> That we may learn to bear the beams of love,
> And these black bodies and this sun-burnt face
> Is but a cloud, and like a shady grove.
>
> For when our souls have learn'd the heat to bear
> The cloud will vanish we shall hear his voice.
> Saying: come out from the grove my love and care,
> And round my golden tent like lambs rejoice. (3–20)

The mother's story is by no means unproblematic, as is evident in the range of interpretations it has elicited from critics. The mother's story has been read, for example, as narrative of comfort and hope; a disturbing recitation of religious quietism in the face of social evil; a covert blending of African religious elements with Christianity; and a confusing, anti-Blakean message that clings to the false doctrine of the body/soul dichotomy.[10] But the precise meaning of the mother's story might be beside the point; what her story offers is an alternative set of discursive terms that are not locked into the rigid hierarchies of the racist discourse that the black child struggles against. The mother recodes black bodies as clouds or a shady grove, minimizing the negative connotations of "black" that the child agonizes over; she also does not explicitly use the other half of the coded opposition, the term "white," to describe the soul. In other words, the mother's story provides an opening for the child, an opportunity to express his sense of self-worth and his desire to be seen as an equal using another discourse that does not automatically fix him in a position of inferiority. This opening, though, to be of any use, requires an act of interpretation, and there is no guarantee that the interpretation will not lead into new and dangerous positions (such as religious quietism). Nevertheless, the mother's story could also serve as a springboard for an interpretation that leads to an assertion of spiritual equality, a state in which the body does not act as an intervening sign, either to hinder the black child or to artificially elevate the white child, and from there, additional acts of interpretation could lead further to an assertion of social equality. The mother has afforded her child a way to begin to pry open the semiotic trap in which he is caught by offering different ways to combine and recode the various terms used in the dominant discourse; the next step is for the child to apply the leverage of interpretation and free himself.

In the last two stanzas, the persona turns to address the English child. Armed with his mother's story, the black child appears poised to unbind himself from the dilemma of the first stanza and to carry the attack to the bearer of the status quo, the English child. The emphasis on "thus" in the transition lines seems to raise our expectations that the argument will be taken to the other camp: "Thus did my mother say and kissed me,/ And thus I say to little English boy" (22–23). At the very least we expect him to repeat the story; at most we expect him to apply the story to his earlier thoughts on the dilemma of reading the body and soul in terms of black and white. But the speaker revises his mother's narrative in an unexpected way:

> When I from black and he from white cloud free,
> And round the tent of God like lambs we joy:
> I'll shade him from the heat till he can bear,
>
> To lean in joy upon our father's knee.
> And then I'll stand and stroke his silver hair,
> And be like him and he will then love me. (23–28)

He begins his revision by taking up the narrative where the mother ends, after the black child and the white child are free from their clouds, but then the black child reenacts the servitude that the racist discourse has engrained in him. He feels he must shade the English child, missing his mother's point that learning to bear God's beams occurs on earth, and thus it is unnecessary to shade one another in heaven. He pictures himself standing while the English child kneels; he feels he must be like the other child (and not himself); and his final desire is not to lean upon God's knee, but to have the English child love him. In the process of interpreting and extending his mother's narrative, the black child has reintroduced his sense of inferiority and reinstated the semiotic hierarchy of white over black that his mother's story had exposed for potential dismantling. Unlike his mother, who studiously avoids the term "white," the black child cannot help using the term. Instead of saying that all bodies are just clouds, he distinguishes between his black cloud and the English child's white cloud, and he imagines himself stroking the English child's silver hair, as if the light-colored hair is something to envy. The striking aspect about the poem is that the black child, in his state of innocence, cannot critique the status quo that is afflicting him. He is assailed by an aggressive racist discourse, but when given a narrative to counteract that discourse, he cannot seize upon it and interpret it in a way that allows him to break through the semiotic structure that encloses him.

The inability of the innocent to critique the status quo is also illustrated in "The Chimney Sweeper." The child sweeper relates how Tom Dacre, a new recruit who is distressed by the woeful conditions of a sweeper's life, has a dream about sweepers who are liberated from their coffins and play in the sunshine, while an angel tells him that if he is good, he will have "God for his father & never want joy" (20). This dream narrative, like the mother's narrative in "The Little Black Boy," is not unproblematic, since the angel can be interpreted as the voice of the status quo whose advice further binds the sweepers to their jobs. But the ambiguity of the dream allows for a variety of interpretations, including those with the potential for critiquing the status quo. In its bluntest terms, the dream is saying that the work of the chimney sweepers will eventually kill them all, for in the dream they are already depicted as being locked in their coffins. The speaker of the poem focuses on the "happy" ending of the dream and reduces the dream to a maxim for the workplace—"So if all do their duty, they need not fear harm" (24)—glossing over the issue of their imminent death and reestablishing the grounds for the status quo.

One conclusion we can draw from these poems is that the narratives in a child's world have a role as important as the experiencing of events. It is typical to associate the process of gaining experience with the firsthand observation of events. The assumption is that unmediated perception is the primary teacher of those who are inexperienced and that it teaches in a way that is more powerful than the way one could teach through language. Thus we have the popular cliché, "Actions speak louder than words." But in order for actions and events to "speak," they must be textualized—that is, they must be transcribed into an explanation or a narrative of the meaning of the actions. For example, in "Miss Muriel," the narrator records that Bemish, after announcing his interest in Sophronia, started showing up at the pharmacy around five o'clock. For the narrator, his appearance at that time is just a fact from which she draws no conclusions. But since we as experienced readers know that someone in love longs to be close to his or her beloved, Mr. Bemish's action "speaks" in the sense of telling us that he is following through on his interest in Sophronia. When Bemish learns from the narrator that Sophronia does not work after five, he starts appearing at the pharmacy at three o'clock, an obvious move from our perspective, but one which the narrator again simply records as a fact, just as she records the fact that Sophronia soon after begins to disappear from the pharmacy at three o'clock to work in the garden. These actions speak of the typical game of pursuit and evasion between a suitor and an uninterested woman, but without this narrative framework to explain these actions, they remain just isolated observations for the narrator.

Not only must innocents who are on the path to experience gather a stock of narratives and explanations to use in transcribing actions and events, but they must also become adept at interpretation, for what the actions finally "speak" is the interpretation that is made of the textualized form of the action. And as Blake's "The Chimney Sweeper" illustrates, degrading conditions can be textualized and interpreted in such a way that there is a denial of seemingly irrefutable facts. When Tom Dacre's head is forcibly shaved, the persona makes that action "speak" in a soothing way: "Hush Tom never mind it, for when your head's bare,/ You know that the soot cannot spoil your white hair" (7–8). What Blake's two poems emphasize is that gaining experience is primarily a matter of gaining experience in constructing and interpreting narratives, and that whatever experience comes from observing actions or from being acted upon is dependent upon how those actions are made to speak. It is not that actions speak louder than words, but that actions speak through words, so that ultimately the opposition that must be considered is not one between actions and words but between one set of words and another, between narratives competing against one another for the right to represent what is happening in the world.

From the Blake poems, we can deduce that there are two types of narratives that the innocent must learn to interpret. One is what we can call the primary narrative. This narrative is the one that structures the world for the child. It supplies the particular stories that explain how the world works, and its terms are the first ones the child turns to when talking about his or her world. This primary narrative is rarely fully stated; it remains mostly implicit, as in "The Chimney Sweeper," for example, where we see its effects, not the explicit rationalization for child labor. Or it reveals itself in fragments, such as in the black child's references to his white soul, the English child's white skin, and his own black skin.

The second type of narrative that Blake's poems call our attention to is what we can call the counternarrative, the narrative that challenges the primary narrative. These are the mother's story in "The Little Black Boy" and the dream in "The Chimney Sweeper." The counternarrative lays out an alternative worldview and reveals, by virtue of its difference from the primary narrative, the semiotic structuring of reality. How a child reacts to a counternarrative (or a primary narrative) becomes, then, one possible gauge of innocence and experience. Blake's interpretation of innocence seems to be that the innocent child reaffirms the primary narrative that he or she has been exposed to. This response is charming when the primary narrative is gentle and benevolent, as in Blake's poem "The Lamb" when the child triumphantly repeats the Christian message to the lamb. But it is frightening when a primary narrative oppresses children and all they can do is reaffirm it, even when they are provided with a counter-narrative that could liberate them. Blake's poems imply that innocent children tend to blame themselves rather than challenge the primary narrative that validates the social structure that is assaulting them. The black child in "The Little Black Boy" imagines that if he could only prove to the English child how well he can serve him—even in the afterlife—then the English child might like him; the sweeper imagines that if he continues to focus on his duty, he will somehow avoid harm. But by doing his duty the sweeper will not alter the fact that his job will kill him, just as the black child will not escape racism by offering himself up to perpetual servitude. As long as the structure (and the narrative that undergirds it) goes unchallenged, it will exert its invisible strength.

In "Miss Muriel," primary narratives and counternarratives are not foregrounded as they are in the Blake poems, but they are both there, nonetheless, operating in the background. In "Miss Muriel" the primary narrative is, as in "The Little Black Boy," a racist narrative. It comes to the fore, for example when Dottle and Uncle Johno tell about their experiences in the South, and it takes a specific form when Dottle tells the Miss Muriel tale. It is also hinted at when Chink first shows up at the drugstore and asks the narrator if she is lost. When the narrator throws the question back at him, he replies, "Yup. All us black folk is lost" (180). After Chink goes inside, the narrator follows because she wants to hear her father and Chink talk about the concept of being lost, which is also implied in her father's game of Stanley and Livingstone: "All black strangers who came into our store were Livingstones—and it was up to the members of the family to find out which lost Mr. Livingstone or which lost Mrs. Living-stone we had encountered in the wilds of the all-white town of Wheeling" (18). Her hopes are dashed, however, because her father dislikes Chink from the beginning, and no discussion materializes on the primary narrative that governs their life in Wheeling.

Although this primary narrative lurks in the background, it does not impinge directly on the narrator as it does on the black child in Blake's poem, nor is it as much of a factor as it is in some of the other stories in *Miss Muriel* collection.[11] Given the larger context set by these other stories, we can assume that the narrator in "Miss Muriel" is occupying, for a brief moment, a place of innocence where the racist narrative does not directly touch her. The concern in "Miss Muriel" seems to lie more with the general counternarrative that has developed in the black characters in response to the racist narrative and that is activated by Bemish's attentions to Sophronia. The narrator senses the presence of this counternarrative when she reflects on why Bemish is not "right" for Sophronia. The question she asks herself is whether she rejects Bemish as a proper suitor of Sophronia because he is old or because he is white. She concludes that it is for both reasons, but this bothers her because rejecting Bemish as a suitor because he is white means that she has "been 'trained' on the subject of race as [she has] been 'trained' to be a Christian" (30). Moreover, this training has been taking place without her being conscious of it: "I know how I was trained to be a Christian—Sunday school, prayers, etc. I do not know exactly how I've been 'trained' on the subject of race" (30). At this stage the counternarrative does not have a specific form; it is not an explicit explanation why a white man should be excluded automatically from courting a black woman. It is only revealed as a feeling that whites should not intrude into the black community. Later, though, a form of this counternarrative will manifest itself in Chink's revision of Dottle's Miss Muriel tale and become the crux of the narrator's epiphany.

The narrator's problem, in contrast to the black child's situation in "The Little Black Boy," is that there are very few explicit narratives for her to react to in the first place. In pondering why she rejects Bemish as a legitimate suitor of her aunt, she stumbles upon the fundamental problem with ideological structures—the fact that they exert considerable force and yet rarely reveal their empowering narratives. Blake's innocents, however, experience no shortage of narratives to confront. Fragments of the primary narratives are revealed to them as well as full versions of counternarratives, but they founder when they attempt to interpret these narratives. The narrator in "Miss Muriel," on the other hand, struggles just to unearth the primary and counternarratives that she senses are out there. She has to wring explanations out of adults, experiment with textualizing events and actions, and learn how to handle narratives. Her epiphany becomes more understandable if we consider that, as a result of her interest in and experimentation with narratives, she has been making subtle progress toward her insight at the end—the insight that if she rejects the actions of Dottle and Chink, then she must also reject the Miss Muriel tale.

Her interest in narratives is one of the reasons she is strongly drawn to Dottle Smith. He immerses her in a world of literature. He tells tall tales, recites poetry, and acts out parts of stories and plays. He impishly connects fictions with her world, grabbing her hair, for example, and saying, "Seize on her Furies, take her to your torments!" (32). In an early scene when the narrator is sent to Bemish's shop to pick up her aunt's shoes, we see her practicing with one of Dottle's narratives. Bemish asks her about the lady who owns the shoes, and taking her cue from the form of Bemish's question, "Who was that lady . . . ?" she repeats one of Dottle's stories: "'Gentlemen, be seated. Mr. Bones, who was that lady I say you with last night?' I lowered the pitch of my voice and said, 'That wasn't no lady. That was my wife'" (3). This response, of course, does not answer Bemish's specific question, for the line is taken out of context. The narrator loves Dottle and his stories, and like any innocent, playful child, seeks to imitate and introduce to others what delights her.

As the story progresses, the narrator becomes more adept at handling narratives and begins to connect narratives and action. The day after Dottle comes to visit for the summer, he, Uncle Johno, and the narrator go crabbing, a relaxing, all-day affair. After lunch, the two men regale the narrator with tall tales and ghost stories. Dottle begins with the Miss Muriel tale, which he "almost always tells" (34). This story is followed by the tale of the black preacher in the haunted house with big cats (the biggest being named Martin), and then a tale about a black preacher who tries to outrun a rabbit that ominously grows larger and larger. At the end of the day when the threesome are returning home, the narrator suddenly runs ahead, and when the two men catch up and Dottle asks why the hurry, she answers, recombining all the stories she has heard: "Miss Muriel, you tell Martin I been here but I've gone and that he ain't *seen* no runnin' yet" (36). Although it is easy to overlook this episode, it represents a significant step for the narrator because she has intuitively created, in miniature, an ideological moment. In other words, she finds herself motivated to act according to the narratives she has heard, and when questioned about her actions, she justifies them by referring to the narratives. It is all a matter of play, of course, and her recombination of the stories results in a confusing jumble of references, but at some level she has made a connection between the stories people tell and the actions people take. The ability to grasp this connection becomes a crucial element in her epiphany.

Just after the trio returns from the crabbing excursion, another important moment occurs that concerns narratives and the narrator's experimentation with them. The narrator finds Chink in the store and introduces him to Dottle and Uncle Johno. When the narrator is alone with Chink, the Miss Muriel story comes up again. The narrator explains that Dottle is from Atlanta, and Chink replies that he knows all about Atlanta—and its racism: "Yeah. 'Nigger read this. Nigger, don't let sundown catch you here. Nigger, if you can't read this, run anyway. If you can't run—then vanish. Just vanish out.' I know the place. I came from there." (36). Taking her cue from Chink's language (and noting that her father isn't nearby), the narrator launches into a section of Dottle's Miss Muriel tale that she heard earlier in the day, the part in which the white shop owner replies to the black man's request for a Muriel cigar: "Nigger, what are you talkin' about you want Muriel cigars. You see this picture of this beautiful red-headed white women, nigger, you say *Miss* Muriel" (73). Unlike the earlier scene with Bemish, the narrator's repetition of Dottle's tale in this context makes sense—or at least it would make sense if the narrator were an experienced adult, for in this case she would be corroborating Chink's experience, saying, as it were, "Yes, the whites down there treat you just like in that Muriel cigar story." But she is not an adult, and Chink chastises her just as her father would—"Little girl, don't you talk that way" (37). The narrator is confused and hurt because she thought they were equals. She has learned the right time to interject a narrative, but has not yet learned that it is not enough just to match words to the occasion. In some cases, she must actually experience what the words talk about in order to qualify her to tell stories.

The scene is also important because it reveals the production of a counternarrative. After Chink chastises the narrator, he notices that she is crying, and he tries to comfort her by explaining why he reacted so harshly:

"Sugar," he said gently, "I don't like that Miss Muriel story. It ought to be told the other way around. A black man should be tellin' a white man, 'White man, you see this picture of this beautiful black woman? *White* man, you say *Miss* Muriel.'" (37)

Having felt the effects of racism, Chink is not content to let such a story slip by. He strikes back at this manifestation of the primary narrative, revising the story so that the values are inverted. It is the white man who should be forced to respect black women, even if it is just their image, not the other way around. He protects himself from the primary racist narrative by taking the offensive and writing his own narrative about how things should be.

At this moment in the story, we do not know what the narrator thinks about Chink's counternarrative. She offers no comments on it, but instead, she proceeds to describe how Chink has managed to maneuver himself into the family circle. It is as if Chink's revision of the Miss Muriel tale is just one more fact that the narrator has recorded. And yet this counternarrative resurfaces in her thoughts at the conclusion when she blurts out her condemnation of Dottle's and Chink's eviction of Bemish: "You both stink. You stink like dead bats. You and your goddamn Miss Muriel—" (57).

The significance of the narrator's epiphany rests squarely on this reference to Miss Muriel. As Hilary Holladay notes, "Chink and Dottle essentially act out the 'Miss Muriel' joke as Chink prefers it: They deny a white man access to a black women, whom they claim as their own property" ("Creative Prejudice" 673).[12] By referring to Miss Muriel, the narrator rejects not only Chink and Dottle's expulsion of Bemish but also the narrative that seemingly motivates their action. To highlight the significance of the narrator's statement, we can refer to Blake's "The Little Black Boy." According to the Blakean model, an innocent child will tell a narrative to reaffirm the state of his or her world, even if it means revising a narrative that critiques the status quo. In the world of the innocent, whatever is, must be right. If the narrator in "Miss Muriel" had remained innocent, we can imagine that she would have rationalized the violence by reiterating Chink's version of the Miss Muriel tale. She would have affirmed somehow that that is the way things stand between the races, and Bemish should have known better. And even if she had heard only Dottle's version, then it would have been only a step—an innocent conclusion, so to speak—to revise it into Chink's version: black men are treated unfairly and violently, so therefore white men should be returned the favor. Her epiphany is striking because it cuts against the grain of what she calls her racial training. In her rejection of the Miss Muriel tale, she has apparently built on what she intuitively grasped earlier in her playful revision of Dottle's and Uncle Johno's tall tales—the fact that the stories one hears (and tells) can influence the actions one takes—and has here seen the insidious connection between the Miss Muriel tale and action in her world. In a moment of revelation, the narrator has glimpsed the subtle machinery of ideology at work and realizes that to disagree with some-one's actions means that the narratives that prompt those actions must also be challenged. Unlike Blake's innocents, who cannot see the structure but only the individual and therefore mistakenly blame themselves for their predicament in a racist and economically cruel world, the narrator sees both the individuals who act ("You . . . ") and the narrative (" . . . and your goddamn Miss Muriel") that shapes their actions.

As remarkable as the narrator's insight is, it is important to recognize as well what her revelation does not resolve. The structure of an epiphany is such that it often prompts one to amplify the significance of the ending, to suggest perhaps, in the case of "Miss Muriel," that the narrator is now an adult. But there are elements in the ending that play down such a reading. First, it must be remembered that the narrator makes her state-ment to her friends as she is running away from them. She is not talking to them face to face, as one adult to another. Also, her statement itself is a mixture of the childish and the adult. She first tells Chink and Dottle that they stink like old bats. This comment harks back to her childish feud with Aunt Frank, the bat attack, and the linguistic associations that come out of that event—the fact the she thinks Aunt Frank's breath stinks like a bat and the fact that Aunt Frank waved her hands at the men and called them "worse than bats" (51). If the story ended with the penultimate sentence about stinking bats, the significance of the epiphany would be considerably less, since she merely would be repeating Aunt Frank's judg-ment, though in regard to different circumstances. We would probably still emphasize the acuteness of the narrator's perception in rejecting what Chink and Dottle did, though we would probably characterize her per-ception as that of a child, not of an adult. The use of the invective (as Holladay notes) and the reference to Miss Muriel do mark the narrator's statement as something more than what a child would say, but her com-ment still occurs within the context of other childish statements.

This mixture of the childish and the adult, even in the narrator's epiph-any, is characteristic of how Petry depicts the narrator throughout the story as she struggles in that gray area between innocence and experience. Petry's argument, we can infer, is that experience does not come in one fell swoop. It comes in increments: through reflection, such as that moment when the narrator muses on the problem of Bemish and his unsuitability for Aunt Sophronia; through linguistic experimentation, such as the time when she is textualizing her thoughts about Chink and notes that he "violates" the piano, and then wonders if this term fits his actions toward Sophronia (39); and through ordinary play, such as those times when she repeats narratives in new situations and recombines narratives to entertain Dottle and Uncle Johno. It is not always clear which moment will be significant in her development, but all is absorbed and stored up to reappear in the future as part of her growing experience. And even though at the conclusion she has grasped a connection between narrative and action and has sensed that the tale of Miss Muriel is flawed because of the behavior it can justify, there is still much left to absorb and to analyze.

Part of what still needs to be sorted out and addressed is the possibility of an alternative or counternarrative to Dottle's and Chink's Miss Muriel tales. If experience is fostered by hearing the narratives produced by those of both genders, then, the narrator's entry in the world of experience is only half accomplished, since she is missing the female perspective on the men's Miss Muriel tales. The issue in both Dottle's and Chink's versions of the tale is masculine power, the power of the male of one race to subjugate a male of the other race, to force him to pay obeisance to the image of the other's woman. Insofar as the narrator rejects Dottle and Chink's treatment of Bemish at the end, she is rejecting this male ritual of dominating males from other races. But saying "no" to the male struggle for racial domination, while a significant step for the narrator, still leaves the issue of gender relations unresolved. The unanswered question is, what is the female perspective on gender relations, especially when it is crossed with the issue of race?

Because of the silence of the women in the story, the narrator has no female version of the Miss Muriel tale to counteract the male version. Neither Sophronia nor the narrator's mother tell a counternarrative. As we track back through the story, we find that Sophronia is taciturn about her own feelings. When Bemish first asks the narrator about Sophronia, the narrator admits, as she reflects on her aunt, that Sophronia is somewhat of a mystery: "I do not know very much about Aunt Sophronia. She works in the store. She fills prescriptions. She does embroidery. She reads a lot. She doesn't pay the piano. She is very neat. . . . She is young but she seems very quiet and sober" (6–7). In the later scene, when Sophronia and the narrator are straightening up Sophronia's bureau, they came across a picture of Sophronia's class at the Pharmacy College. The narrator quickly observes that Sophronia is the only woman in the class of men and that all the men are white. Here once again the issues of race and gender are intermixed, but as the narrator notes, both she and her aunt avoid the obvious topic of race: "I did not say anything about this difference in color and neither did she" (11). The narrator does probe the issue of gender, however. She asks her aunt whether she felt "funny" being around only males, but her aunt dodges the question with the reply, "They were very nice boys" (11). The narrator continues to press her with lawyer-like persistence, but Sophronia refuses to elaborate. When the narrator asks Sophronia one more time, thinking aloud about an instance when a female moth was caught inside the screen door and the male moths gathered on the outside from miles around, and how this seemed rather frightening and how this might be related to her aunt's situation, Sophronia suppresses any further discussion: "You get a broom and a dustpan and begin to sweep in the hall" (12). In other instances, too, Sophronia keeps her feelings inside: after she first meets Chink and does not mention him at the dinner table, or when she hurries inside after hearing Chink drive by with his wagon load of ladies (27; 44). Since Sophronia will not introduce her niece to the world of adult womanhood and its opinions and desires, it is no wonder that the narrator tends to view her aunt with a male gaze, for to her Sophronia is a mystery, and what she hears about Sophronia comes mainly from men. When Bemish says, "dreamily," that Sophronia "looks like a gypsy," the narrator disagrees. To her, Sophronia looks like her mother and her Aunt Ellen, who, according to her father and uncle, "look like Egyptian queens" (6). On the day that Chink first sees Sophronia, the narrator watches Sophronia as she stands by a window, and she describes Sophronia as perhaps a man would—as a beautiful object: "She didn't look real. The sun was shining in the window and . . . she looked golden and rose-colored and lavender, and it was as though there were a rainbow moving in the window" (25). When Chink drives up in a carriage at just this moment and sees Sophronia, we can easily imagine that he is thinking in similar terms. As the narrator notes, he "took a deep breath," and after a quick question about the identity of the woman in the window, he "practically leaped inside the store" (25, 26).

Sophronia's experiences at the Pharmacy College and her ongoing tribulations with her suitors are the raw material for the counternarrative to the men's Miss Muriel tales and to the male perspective in general. Perhaps the most powerful story left untold in "Miss Muriel" is Sophronia's. It is a story that would tell about her courage in attending the all-male, all-white Pharmacy College; her isolation and loneliness in Wheeling, even though she lives with family; her frustration with the silly old white man Bemish as he clumsily courts her; her awakening to sexual desires and the possibility of a social life outside of the family with the attentions of Chink; her delight in discovering the simple joys in life as she learns to dance barefoot in the backyard with Chink; and her bitter disappointment when she realizes that Chink is not, as the narrators says, a "gentleman." But Sophronia keeps this story inside, protecting her feelings even though the narrator presses her for information.

Not only does Sophronia keep her thoughts to herself, but the narrator's mother also enforces a limit on what can be talked about in the house. When the narrator first returns from Bemish's shop with Sophronia's shoes, she mentions that Bemish thought Sophronia looked like a gypsy. Her mother replies, "I wish you wouldn't repeat the things you hear. It just causes trouble" (7). She stops her husband from talking when he works himself into a tirade over Chink and compares Chink to a stallion tracking down a mare (21), and later she puts a halt to her husband's complaint about Sophronia's three suitors not adding up to one man and about Chink being nothing more than a "tramp piano player" (48). The result is a family that is silent on just those issues that affect it the most. The father does not mention Chink to the others when he first shows up at the store (20); Sophronia does not mention her first meeting with Chink (27); and the narrator complains, "I cannot get my mother to talk about him" (38).

The answer to this impulse in the adult world perhaps lies in the ease and frankness of communication found in the world of innocence. Let us unwind the story back even further from the epiphany and return to the first scene in which the narrator describes her friendship with Ruth Davis. It is a scene that is easy to forget because we do not see the narrator among her peers after that point; it seems merely to mark that moment when the narrator leaves behind childhood to begin the gradual transition into the adult world. But if we reconsider this scene after reflecting on the difficulty the narrator faces in trying to coax narratives out of the adult women in the story, one particular fact stands out, and that is that the two girls in the opening scene love to talk. We are not told what they talk about, but that seems less important than that communication is a given in their relationship. The implication of this scene, when we consider it in juxtaposition to what happens in the rest of the story, is that the passage into the world of experience is not entirely what is at issue; what is also important is bringing into the world of experience the frank communication that seems to be an element of innocence. That this element is missing in the adult world is evident in the scene when Bemish violates the sanctity of the family's evening in the backyard. The adults say nothing to him, to the surprise of the narrator. She is the one who confronts Bemish later and explains why he has gone too far: "The yard is a private part of our lives. You don't belong in it. You're not a part of our family" (16).

The introductory scene contains other crucial elements that bear on the issues of gender and race. One easily forgotten fact is that Ruth Davis is white. Initially this difference between the narrator and her friend is starkly foregrounded. The narrator begins by talking about herself and Ruth, how they "like to talk to each other," how they "are very much alike," how they "laugh about the same things" and "are curious about the same things," and how they "even wear [their] hair in the same style" (1)—and then she reveals their one difference: she is black and Ruth is white. In the first scene, Ruth walks with the narrator to her father's store, and then when Sophronia asks the narrator to go to Mr. Bemish's place and pick up her shoes, Ruth says that she should be getting on home, since as she says, "I'm sure my aunt will have things for me to do. Just like your aunt" (2). After this introductory section, Ruth disappears from the narrative. What purpose, then, does she serve? We can draw two plausible conclusions. One is that there is an initial solidarity among women that transcends race. We can contrast this opening scene to Blake's "The Little Black Boy," in which the black child and white child are already at odds at an early age, even though they are too young to really understand the racist doctrine that they have internalized. Although the narrator admits to having been trained to be race conscious, and undoubtedly Ruth has been trained as well, there is no manifestation of this training in their relationship. Their racial difference is a mere exception to an overriding multitude of similarities. The second conclusion that we can draw is that even though Ruth disappears from the narrative, there is a strong suggestion that her experiences as an adolescent girl will parallel the narrator's, not in terms of specific events certainly, but in the sense that she will face the problem of being objectified in male narrative and that she also will have problems finding a female narrative. The fact that Dottle's Miss Muriel tale objectifies white women as an image possessed by the white male indicates that Ruth will face the same problems as the narrator, who is subjected to objectification by such stories as Chink's revision of the Miss Muriel story. Although the narrator and Ruth will be funneled into different worlds because of their race, as women they will nevertheless face parallel struggles against male narratives.

If we use Blake's poems as a gauge of innocence, we can say then that the narrator has taken a significant step beyond innocence in that she has been able to move outside of the structural enclosure of the primary narrative. The persona in Blake's "The Little Black Boy" begins to struggle against the primary narrative because he feels its insidious effects, but since, in his innocence, he knows of no other way to conceive of his world, he tries to argue against the narrative using its own terms and ends up encoding himself into the same position of inferiority. Chink Johnson, reacting against a similar primary narrative, inverts the code that governs the narrative's terms: instead of the black man saying *Miss* Muriel, the white man should say *Miss* Muriel. Certainly from Chink's perspective the primary narrative is effectively sabotaged, but from the narrator's perspective the inverted counternarrative is no different from the primary narrative because it still results in someone being dominated and humiliated.[13] Her revelation is that both these narratives are connected with destructive action, and when she rejects the Miss Muriel tales collectively, she effectively condemns the semiotic system of the primary narrative.

But after rejecting that system, she is left in a void, and this is what the ending does not resolve. In effect, Petry has highlighted an additional obstacle that faces those on the path from innocence to experience, a problem that is gender specific: how are female counternarratives produced and accessed in a society that is dominated by male primary narratives? In Blake's two poems, the production of counternarratives is a given. In "The Little Black Boy," the mother sees her child's dilemma and introduces him to a different explanation of how the world works. In "The Chimney Sweeper," there is no concerned adult to intervene, but the implication is that absent outside help, the unconscious will produce counternarratives in the form of dreams to protect the child. The issue for Blake is that the black child and the chimney sweeper, as innocents, lack the ability to engage in mental warfare, the ability to interpret the counternarratives and turn them against the primary narratives. In "Miss Muriel," the narrator has developed her critical faculty, but since the women in the story have not developed the habit of telling their narratives, she does not yet have a foundation on which to construct an alternative vision of how the world should work.

The ending of the story thus remains open because the narrator is not provided with the content to construct a narrative to replace the male versions of Miss Muriel. Nevertheless, I would argue that there is an answer to this dilemma encoded in the form of "Miss Muriel"—the fact that the narrator is writing herself into adulthood, even though at the moment she has no competing story to set against the male versions of Miss Muriel. Although the narrator is separated, after the first scene, from her childhood friend and from their own conversations, and although she is not furnished with adult women's narratives, she makes up for this void by recording her story as it unfolds. The specific answer to the male versions of Miss Muriel is deferred to the future, but the answer will materialize, the story implies, because the narrator is growing into a woman of experience who writes.

NOTES

I am indebted to Annie Perkins for her insightful comments on an earlier draft of this essay.

1. See "An Interview with Ann Petry" for Petry's explanation of how she became interested in writing the historical biographies (Ervin 98).

2. In "A Visit with Ann Petry, May 16, 1984" and "A MELUS Interview," Petry talks about the real-life counterparts of some of the characters in "Miss Muriel" (Ervin 78, 93).

3. The story that follows "Miss Muriel" in the collection, "The New Mirror," also has an adolescent narrator. As Hilary Holladay points out, the first three stories in the collection are part of a group of five stories that are closely related by their setting in the fictional town of Wheeling. The narrator of "Miss Muriel" seems to appear again as the slightly older narrator in "The New Mirror" and the adult narrator of "Has Anybody Seen Miss Dora Dean?" (Holladay, *Ann Petry* 93–94).

4. Ervin, for example, uses this Blakean terminology when she describes the narrator as a "nameless child who has lived a protected and carefree life in a small New England town [and who] loses this state of innocence when she takes a stand against her uncle and his friend" (3).

5. Richardson notes that Blake's *Songs of Innocence* "does not seem to have been marketed as a children's book [although] it clearly situates itself in the tradition of children's religious poetry and hymns represented by such writers as Watts, Smart, Wesley, and Barbauld" (234).

6. Nevertheless, no one has seemed to confuse the story with children's literature. Petry's works that are typically classified as juvenile or children's literature are *The Drugstore Cat, Harriet Tubman, Conductor on the Underground Railroad, Tituba of Salem Village,* and *Legends of the Saints* (see, for example, Ervin 6–7; "Ann Petry" 269). For a discussion of the nomenclature used to classify children's and young adult literature, see the *Oxford Companion to African American Literature* (Andrews et al. 133–34).

7. L. J. Morrissey argues that the "first-person narrator in 'Araby' is not one character, but three (or better, three moods of a developing adolescent)" (48). These three characters are identified as "simple naïf, a poetic romantic, and a harsh adult censor" (48).

8. One difference that we can note between the poems and "Miss Muriel" is that Blake is interested in innocence and experience as two discrete states. As he announces in the subtitle of his combined *Songs,* he is intent on "Shewing the Two Contrary States of the Human Soul." Petry, on the other hand, situates "Miss Muriel" in what we can characterize as the space between the *Songs of Innocence* and the *Songs of Experience.* The issue for Petry is not how to answer the two questions, "What is innocence?" and "What is experience?" Instead, what interests her in "Miss Muriel" is the means by which one progresses from innocence to experience. Even though there are several paired poems in *Songs of Innocence and Experience*—poems such as "The Lamb" and "The Tiger," the two "Chimney Sweeper" poems, and the two "Holy Thursday" poems—Blake does not consider the issue of how the speaker of the first poem reached the state of the speaker of the second poem. Additionally, one does not get the sense that the speaker of the poem of innocence is the same person as the speaker of the poem of experience.

9. One can speculate that the setting for "The Little Black Boy" is a plantation somewhere within the British empire, or that the black child and his mother have somehow made their way from such a background to England. See Richardson 242.

10. See Leader 110; Hinkel 40–41; Henry 7–8; and Bloom 48–51.

11. See in particular Holladay's discussion of two of the other four Wheeling stories, "The New Mirror" and "Has Anybody Seen Miss Dora Dean?" (*Ann Petry* 101–7).

12. Holladay argues that it is the narrator's "use of invective [that] suggests not only her anger and frustration but also her emancipation from childhood" ("Creative Prejudice" 673). I would agree that the narrator's use of invective is striking because up to this point she has not used such language. But it is what her invective is aimed at—the "goddamn Miss Muriel"—that seems to hold more importance.

13. And that is the "social evil" to be avoided, as Petry explains in "The Novel as Social Criticism," for then "man cannot survive but will become what Cain feared he would become—a wanderer and a vagabond on the face of the earth" (33).

WORKS CITED

Andrews, William, Frances Smith Foster, and Trudier Harris, eds. *Oxford Companion to African American Literature*. New York: Oxford University Press, 1997.

Blake, William. *The Complete Poetry and Prose of William Blake*. Ed. David V. Erdman. Garden City, NY: Anchor, 1982.

Bloom, Harold. *Blake's Apocalypse: A Study in Poetic Argument*. Ithaca, NY: Cornell University Press, 1963.

Ervin, Hazel Arnett. *Ann Petry: A Bio-Bibliography*. New York: G. K. Hall, 1993.

Henry, Lauren. "Sunshine and Shady Groves: What Blake's 'Little Black Boy' Learned from African Writers." *Blake: An Illustrated Quarterly* 29 (1995): 4–11.

Hinkel, Howard H. "From Pivotal Idea to Poetic Ideal: Blake's Theory of Contraries and 'The Little Black Boy.'" *Papers on Language & Literature* 11 (1975): 39–45.

Holladay, Hilary. *Ann Petry*. New York: Twayne, 1996.

———. "Creative Prejudice in Ann Petry's 'Miss Muriel.'" *Studies in Short Fiction* 31 (1994): 667–74.

Joyce, James. *Dubliners: Text, Criticism and Notes*. Eds. Robert Scholes and A. Walton Litz. Harmondsworth: Penguin, 1976.

Leader, Zachary. *Reading Blake's Songs*. Boston: Routledge, 1981.

Morrissey, L. J. "Joyce's Narrative Strategies in 'Araby.'" *Modern Fiction Studies* 28 (1982): 45–52.

Petry, Ann. "Ann Petry." *Contemporary Authors: Autobiography Series*. Ed. Adele Sarkissian. Vol. 6. Detroit: Gale Research, 1988. 253–69.

———. *Miss Muriel and Other Stories*. 1971. Boston: Beacon Press, 1989.

———. "The Novel as Social Criticism." *The Writer's Book*. Ed. Helen Hull. New York: Barnes & Noble, 1956. 31–39; Hazel Arnett Ervin, ed. *African American Literary Criticism, 1773 to 2000*. New York: Twayne, 1999. 94–98.

Richardson, Alan. "Colonialism, Race, and Lyric Irony in Blake's 'The Little Black Boy.'" *Papers on Language & Literature* 26 (1990): 233–48.

Shavit, Zohar. "The Ambivalent Status of Texts: The Case of Children's Literature." *Poetics Today* (1980): 75–86.

Smith, Donald M. "Blake's *Songs of Innocence and Experience* and Eighteenth-Century Religious and Moral Verse for Children." *Essays in Arts and Sciences* 20 (1991): 1–16.

"From a Thousand Different Points of View": The Multiple Masculinities of Ann Petry's "Miss Muriel"

Keith Clark

Interviewer: Are there any black writers that you remember reading either in high school or in your early years as a writer?

Petry: There were two in particular: *Narrative of the Life of Frederick Douglass* and James Weldon Johnson's *Autobiography of an Ex-Colored Man*
—Mark Wilson, MELUS Interview, 1988

The male subject's aspiration to mastery and sufficiency are undermined from many directions . . . by the castration crisis; by sexual, economic, and racial oppression; and by the traumatically inassimilable nature of certain historical events.
—Kaja Silverman, *Male Subjectivity at the Margins*

Whenever I contemplate black women writers' inscriptions of black male subjects, I am reminded of playwright Lorraine Hansberry's belief that black male authors could not imagine complex black women characters. In a 1961 radio round-table discussion that included James Baldwin and Langston Hughes, she declared: "I am altogether certain that in regard to the inner truths of character, the woman character will always partially elude the male writer" (Bigsby 97). It would be disingenuous to extract this statement from its proper literary and cultural contexts: perhaps Hansberry was contesting prototypical representations of black women in the 1940s and 1950s, embodied in Richard Wright's simpering and castrating black women and Ralph Ellison's overbearing black women and their treacherous white counterparts. Indeed, her point is well illustrated by Wright's drunken Bessie Mears in *Native Son* (1940) and his own tyrannical grandmother in *Black Boy* (1945) and by Ellison's smothering

Mary Rambo and sexually predatory Sybil in *Invisible Man* (1952). I would nevertheless question Hansberry's implication that women writers are naturally better at portraying men than men are at portraying women. Indeed, the playwright's own Walter Lee Younger Jr., in *A Raisin in the Sun*, gives us a woman writer's rather facile characterization of a man. Given the difficulty of imaging the world from the opposite sex's point of view, Ann Petry's fictive project becomes an even more stunning achievement, for her nuanced and even startling forays into African American men's interiority accomplish what Hansberry could only allude to.

Still Hansberry's position reflects our tendency to categorize writers within sometimes tendentious gender ideologies. Thus, Wright's entire canon becomes synonymous with the scourge of patriarchy and misogyny, while Alice Walker's emblematizes the deleterious effects of white feminism on black women writers since the 1960s. I myself have not been immune to configuring parochial literary taxonomies based on gender: I have labeled Petry "gynocentric," a designation that may be applicable when interpreting her first novel, *The Street* (1946), but one that fails to consider the scope of her fictive oeuvre.[1] Petry herself bristles at critics' misconceptions about black writers. While acknowledging that she, like most black writers, "write[s] about relationships between black and whites because it's in the very air we breathe," she concludes, "[b]ut we write about it in a thousand different ways from a thousand different points of view" (O'Brien 157). Hence, her work reflects more than a gynocentric or feminist perspective. To be sure, early stories such as the much-anthologized "Like a Winding Sheet" (1946), a harrowing character study of a black man's emotional implosion and attendant physical explosion amidst changing racial and gender roles during World War II (he pummels his wife in an unprovoked attack at the story's conclusion), laid the groundwork for her layered portrayals of black men in "Miss Muriel" (1963).

Indeed, "Miss Muriel" might be considered a companion to "Like a Winding Sheet." In the title story of *Miss Muriel and Other Stories* (1971), Petry dissects black men's Herculean attempts to configure masculinities rooted in socially truncated constructs. Portraying a constellation of men of disparate classes, occupations, geographic milieus, and sexual orientations, "Miss Muriel" explores black men's tendency to valorize culturally sanctioned but emotionally stifling constructions of masculinity. Moreover, she exposes the psychological price these men pay for inculcating terms of masculinity that are anathema to their reality as *racialized* subjects. In effect, the black men who populate the bucolic Wheeling, New York, community—Samuel, the self-made Franklinian man who owns and operates his own drugstore; Chink Jones, the erstwhile southerner whose blues playing and women chasing embody for Samuel an anachronistic and destructive lifestyle; and Dottle Smith, a gay Southerner whom the other men find abhorrent—represent black men's sexual, cultural, and economic liminality and their often misguided response to it. The mosaic Petry creates in "Miss Muriel" depicts black men grappling with subject-hood. Though they often contest the prevailing narrative of masculinity, they still return to debilitating social constructions when conceiving their own identities.

The decade in which Petry first published "Miss Muriel," as well as the genre itself, may account for the scant scholarly attention it has received. Gladys Washington in 1986 admonished critics for being "strangely silent" with respect to Petry's short stories; few critics have investigated them, though *The Street* and Petry's other novels have begun to garner more critical scrutiny.[2] There may be myriad reasons for the critical silence Washington identifies. The year "Miss Muriel" was published, 1963, was the nascent period for the Black Arts Movement, which inaugurated a literary and cultural *shift*. Part of the required exigencies of that shift meant that black writing should be "functional," serving as combination political Molotov cocktail, social manifesto, and community-uplift man-ual. Though Petry was spared the shabby treatment accorded Ellison on college campuses and in print during the 1960s, perhaps works that didn't place white racism at the vortex of black life had little cultural currency. That these were the "politics of literary expression," to invoke the title of Donald Gibson's 1981 landmark study on literary production and recep-tion, harks back to Wright's excoriation of Zora Neale Hurston's folk re-alism in the 1930s, when social protest and naturalism were *de rigueur* modes of artistic expression. Perhaps "Miss Muriel" failed to meet the critical, cultural, and nationalistic criteria for art at this volatile historical moment.

Such protocols of literary production might account for the critical si-lence surrounding "Miss Muriel." Readers and critics expecting sub-sequent works to follow in the "protest" footsteps of *The Street* and its predecessor, *Native Son,* may have been disappointed in and perhaps frus-trated by a story that resists facile categorizations. Reminiscent of her first novel, the story is ostensibly female-centered—key characters include the nameless, perspicacious 12-year-old narrator and her aunt Sophronia, a beautiful pharmacist pursued by both black and white men. Certainly, the title itself, "Miss Muriel," appears to privilege the feminine: it is the punch line to a "joke" that involves white male privilege, black male psychic erasure, and racial and sexual taboos. Still, the story's ostensible gyno-centrism belies the author's foregrounding of the complex ways both black and white men formulate identity and selfhood. Thus, while one could argue that in the story Petry focuses on black female consciousness and writes her most autobiographical fiction (Mobley 357), the text also invites exploration of men's intraracial and interracial relationships and the conflicted dimensions of black male subjectivity.

Critics routinely position Petry as Wright's female counterpart, a disciple of the "Wright school" of literary aesthetics. But while early Petry commentators such as Robert Bone and Carl Milton Hughes as well as more contemporary ones like W. Lawrence Hogue can argue that the literary establishment embraced *The Street*, as it did *Native Son*, because it "approximated the ruling ideological models" (Hogue 31), this assessment does a disservice not only to *The Street*, but also to Petry's subsequent writings.[3] Even though one could read her 1946 magnum opus as a distaff *Native Son*, Petry's novel concomitantly captures male angst and disillusionment in characters such as the building superintendent Williams Jones and the bandleader Boots Smith. Additionally, "Miss Muriel" contains male characters, such as the white Mr. Bemish and black Chink Jones, who share traits with the aforementioned men of *The Street:* Mr. Bemish's sexual malaise and chronic loneliness are as profoundly sad as Jones's, and Chink's attempts to sublimate his racial distemper through music clearly links him to Boots, who also experienced crushing racism. More important, the novel's innovative storytelling apparatus, which decenters character and point of view and instead layers perspectives through a panoply of voices, distinguishes "Miss Muriel." Mark Wilson has called Petry's stories "cinematic," an apt descriptor when considering the narrative technique she employs in "Miss Muriel" (Wilson 78).

Certainly, Petry's panoramic perspective does not privilege any one type of black male. The men of "Miss Muriel" have diverse concerns, with racism being one among many issues they are confronting. Like James Baldwin, Petry avoids characterizing black men as one-dimensional victims of racism. Instead, her black men are more likely to be victimizers than victims. "Miss Muriel" critiques the Wrightian hero perpetually eviscerated by white racism while it also contests contemporary, 1960s-based definitions of black masculinity, often derived from its Anglo-American patriarchal counterpart.

This essay's first epigraph, in which Petry conveys her indebtedness to Douglass's *Narrative* and Johnson's *Autobiography*, informs my "masculinist" reading of her 1963 short story. These primordial texts foreground issues of agency and the negotiation of black male subjecthood, two topics of great importance to Petry. Perhaps more so than her male contemporaries—with the important exception of Baldwin—Petry grasped the multidimensionality of black maleness. In all of her fictions, even in the protofeminist *The Street*, she dislodges putative notions of masculinity by exploring its Otherness—those factors, along with race, that come into play when fictionalizing black male subjects.[4] The observations of Nigel Edley and Margaret Wetherell are pertinent here:

Manliness, in other words, is a contested territory; it is an ideological battlefield. And what is more, if we look back in time, not only do we see that, at certain points in history, one specific discourse of masculinity has dominated over all of the other alternatives (i.e., it has been the most popular way of thinking about men), but we also find that the efforts to control the meaning of masculinity have played a central role in the struggle for power between various social groupings including classes, "races," nations as well as men and women. (106, emphasis added)

Manliness in Petry's discourse is similarly contested territory, a social battleground on which countless personal and social jousts are fought. However, manhood in American literature, let alone in African American fiction, has been synonymous with domination and a distinctly gendered authority that men interpret as a sort of Darwinian natural selection. A glance at Anglo-American and African American literary heroes—Natty Bumpo, Nick Adams, Bigger Thomas—underscores this point. More often than not, black men, especially during the period in which Petry produced most of her fiction, valorized the culturally sanctioned and sacrosanct narrative of masculinity: Bigger Thomas's embittered sighting of an airplane, when he laments that he is not able to fly like the "white boys," becomes a cardinal moment, akin to Douglass's beating of Covey and his cosmic evolution from "slave" to "man." Thus, Petry broadens the discursive treatment of masculinity by dramatizing the many spaces where black men attempt to re-center themselves as subjects and the potential perils they face when embracing deformed and deforming constructions of masculinity. Contrasting sharply with the naturalist's mono-visual perspective, "Miss Muriel's" poly-visual sight lines—the multiple masculinities it showcases—dismantles the notion that black men define themselves solely by a benchmark of white patriarchal masculinity. Petry exposes different forms of erasure—geographic, cultural, sexual, self— and black men's constructive and destructive responses to them.

Appropriately enough, the author's critique of enshrined constructions of masculinity begins with the story's lone father, Samuel. The first black man we encounter, he is presented from the perspective of his daughter, the story's narrator: "I have noticed that my father narrows his eyes a little when he looks at Mr. Bemish" (11). Samuel, like the other black men in the story, accepts some archaic and pejorative facets of masculinity that black men have both embodied and paradoxically challenged. His is contemptuous of all of Sophronia's suitors—Bemish, Chink, and Dottle—each of whom invades the family's personal space. Bemish and Chink are especially notorious, for both trespass upon the family's drugstore, home, and yard, which occupy the same space. The narrator conveys the depth of violation when she describes the two men's respective intrusions. First, she ruminates about Bemish's "visits":

If Mr. Bemish had known this, he might have dropped in on the [on Samuel's] birthday celebration, even though he hadn't been invited. After all, he had sidled into our back yard without being invited and our yard is completely enclosed by a tight board fence, and there is a gate that you have to open to get in the yard, so that entering our yard is like walking into our living room. It is a very private place. *Mr. Bemish is the only person that I know of who has come into our yard without being invited, and he keeps coming, too.* (22, emphasis added)

This passage is also intertextually insinuative, for it recalls both Robert Frost's "Mending Wall" and Gwendolyn Brooks's "A Song in the Front Yard," poems that treat the importance of boundaries as well as the distinction between public and private personae. Recall the former poem's austere injunction that "good fences make good neighbors." Similarly Brooks, Petry's literary contemporary who also abrogated the boundaries of gender in poems dramatizing black men's struggles ("Negro Hero," "Way-Out Morgan"), uses spatial metaphors to suggest the sexual freedom and agency available to women in the "back yard"; alternatively, the publicly visible "front yard" represents a confining space where women's behaviors are proscribed by sexist mores and prohibitions.

Similarly, Petry imbues physical space with personal and psychosocial ramifications. One can only imagine Samuel's sense of personal violation when Bemish intrudes. Described throughout the story as a slightly schoolmarmish, sexually repressed man, Bemish (B*lemish?*) nevertheless moves unrestrictedly in both white and black spaces because of race and gender privilege. Using personal space as a site for social and gender conflict, Petry illustrates the actual power and authority available to even the most unmasculine, effete white male; race clearly trumps gender here. Ironically, setting is crucial as well, for Samuel has insulated his family in a bucolic enclave of New York, a state to which countless black Southerners fled from slavery through the Great Migration of the twentieth century. Still, living in the North again does not buffer blacks from white men's racial and sexual sense of entitlement. Bemish avails himself of both the family's home turf and Sophronia's company—spaces historically susceptible to white male incursion and conquest.

Chink's behavior is just as brazen as Bemish's: "Now Chink Johnson has become a part of the family circle, and he used the same method that Mr. Bemish used. He just walked into the yard and into the house" (27–28). With the addition of Dottle to this assemblage, Samuel cannot help losing his temper:

I shouldn't have let him [Bemish] hang around here all these months. I can't leave this store for five minutes that I don't find one of these no-goods hangin' around when I come back. Not one of 'em worth the powder and shot to blow 'em to hell and back. That piano player pawin' the ground and this old white man jumpin' up in the air, and that friend of Johno's, that poet or whatever he is, all he needs are some starched petticoats and a bonnet and he'd make a woman—he's practically one now—and he's tee-heein' around, and *if they were all put together in one piece, it still wouldn't be a whole man.* (47, emphasis added)

Samuel's outburst demonstrates again how masculinity is contested, his language revealing a fragmented, amorphous manhood that renders "wholeness" illusive. Moreover, the word "piece" clearly connotes a sort of sexual inadequacy, further exposing modern masculinity as tenuous and *pha*llible. That his vituperation is filtered through his daughter's voice buttresses Samuel's sense of powerlessness. Not only does a 12-year-old girl speak for him inasmuch as she, not he, narrates the story; she also visits Bemish's shop with the same ease that he visits her family's store. Each time, she launches bon mots about his intrusive visits and courtship of Sophronia, who is quite a bit younger than he is. In effect, she has license to utter what society prohibits her father from uttering. Samuel's preadolescent daughter possesses the voice and agency that elude a black male adult entrepreneur in the North.

Certainly, Samuel's treatment of Sophronia might be construed as paternalistic, which Hilary Holladay points out: "Although Sophronia is an adult capable of making her own choices, he is extremely protective of her" (96). As Holladay further suggests, Samuel himself might surreptitiously desire his sister-in-law and resent such fierce competition. However, Petry both critiques and complicates what can be interpreted as black men's mimicking of white patriarchal authority. For instance, Samuel's preoccupation with his family's domestic sovereignty counters standard representations of black men as physically and emotionally disengaged from their families. African American men's literature (like white men's writing) abounds with characters who view family/community as a roadblock on the path to self-discovery and subject status. Bigger Thomas, the Invisible Man, and Richard Wright himself most acutely demonstrate the view that family is anathema to black men's abiding quest for wholeness and selfhood. Writing about black men from a cultural and historical perspective, Leland Hall articulates the prevailing representations of black male protagonists: "The American culture and its subsocieties do not expect the Black male to exhibit emotions and feelings about his family or his family's situation and the dire impact that society may have on him when he tries to live up to these unrealistic expectations" (162). Though certainly not the first to do so, Petry nevertheless performs a qualitative literary reinscription by depicting a black male who values and esteems family. Indeed, this narrative situation reflects the profound influence of men such as her father in her personal development.[5]

Samuel's concern with his family's domestic space raises questions about social proscriptions governing race, gender, and sexuality. In the denouement of *The Street*, for instance, family and community are not grounding forces in Lutie Johnson's life but impediments: in behavior more often associated with male protagonists, she commits murder, abandons her son in Harlem, and flees to Chicago, Bigger Thomas's geo-psychic tomb. All of this illustrates the mutability of gender roles and concomitantly challenges a black masculinist discourse that often represents black women as agency-less victims whose lives are encased by white men, white women, black men, and intractable external forces. Samuel's occupation of one space throughout most of the text—his drugstore-home—turns these socially binding gender roles inside out. Typically, domestic/interior spaces have been women's domains while outdoor places have belonged to the men. However, Petry inscribes a black man for whom the domestic site maintains value; it is not an emasculating zone that native sons must fear and flee. Her (re)gendering of space recalls bell hooks's comments on the liberating qualities of "homeplace":

Throughout out history, African-Americans have recognized the subversive value of homeplace, of having access to private space where we do not directly encounter white racist aggression. Whatever the shape and direction of black liberation struggle (civil rights reform or black power movement), domestic space has been a crucial site for organizing, for forming political solidarity. Homeplace has been a site of resistance. (47)

In this context, Bemish's action becomes even more insidious. Ultimately, homeplace becomes another colonized territory, a space where Bemish usurps Samuel's familial authority and independence. The pharmacy-home serves as a tenuous sanctuary, though Samuel's familial investment decidedly counters literary and social representations of black men.

Samuel's characterization epitomizes black male characters' tortured attempts to renegotiate the conditions of masculinity. A variation on Samuel's flawed desire for agency is Chink's life, which reifies the dialectical situation black men face. Courting Sophronia vigorously while unashamedly carousing with several black maids, Chink seems to embody the most objectionable facets of patriarchal masculinity. This point is made achingly clear—both figuratively and literally—when he pinches the narrator's arm in his zeal to acquire information about her aunt; he then orders her to "Shut up" when she objects (26). On the surface, Chink's infliction of bodily pain is the cornerstone of male privilege and echoes Samuel's chauvinistic view of Sophronia. However, Petry shows how pain is the manifestation of black men's historical deformation.

Elaine Scarry's seminal exploration of the historical and psychosocial dimensions of pain allows us to extrapolate the depth of black male pain Petry fictionalizes. Scarry writes, "Physical pain has no voice, but when it at last finds a voice, it begins to tell a story" (3). The pain that Chink so callously metes out reveals the depth of black male liminality and voicelessness. In fact, one of the first phrases he utters to the narrator, "All us black folks is lost" (18), bespeaks his social, physical, and psychic dislocation and disembodiment. That Chink is a blues pianist-singer who lands a job at the local inn resonates culturally and literarily. In one of the story's most plangent passages, Petry captures the essence of the archetypal nomadic black bluesman:

Chink was sitting at the piano. He had a cigarette dangling from his lower lip, and the smoke from the cigarette was like a cloud—a blue-gray, hazy kind of cloud around his face, his eyes, his beard—so that you could only catch glimpses of them through the smoke. He was playing some kind of fast, discordant-sounding music and he was slapping the floor with one of his long feet and he was slapping the keys with his long fingers. (28)

This scene captures the chaos and violence—the Ellisonian "jagged grain"—that lurk beneath the pathos of the blues. Blues, as it has for many African American artists, functions as a musical language through which they can utter an otherwise voiceless pain, which contains a quality of "unshareability" that is exacerbated by pain's "resistance to language" (Scarry 4). The blues in Petry's story specifically and in African American literature generally becomes a means to destabilize and diminish pain's unshareability, for it speaks to and for a people who have been rendered agency-less and silent throughout time and space. Petry situates Chink within a coterie of angst-ridden blues characters—Hughes's "moaning" piano player in "The Weary Blues," Ellison's singer–story weaver Jim Trueblood, and Baldwin's eponymous jazz pianist-prophet in "Sonny's Blues" all come to mind. Each of these characters embodies the regenerative and liberating potential of the blues.

However, what I consider the strange link between Chink and Samuel surfaces after their initial encounter. Responding to his wife's inquiry about Chink, Samuel launches into an apoplectic tirade in which he renames his new acquaintance:

"Shake Jones," he repeated. "Rhythm in his feet. Rhythm in his blood. Rhythm in his feet. Rhythm in his blood. Beats out his life, beats out his lungs, beats out his liver, on a piano," and he began a different and louder rhythm with his foot. "On a pian-o. On a pi-an-o. On a pi—" (21)

Samuel's verbal eruption itself represents a miniature blues performance, indicated by the repetitive and rhythmic cadence of his diction.[6] His blues-tinged *anti*-blues tirade proceeds:

I am talkin' about Tremblin' Shakefoot Jones. The piano player. The piano player who can't sit still and comes in here lookin' around and lookin' around, prancin'

and stampin' his hoofs, and sniffin' the air. Just like a stallion who smells a mare—
a stallion who—(21)

Though his wife interrupts and admonishes him for using salacious language in front of their daughter, Samuel's psychic disequilibrium and
anxiety surrounding his own masculinity are agonizingly exposed.

Samuel's devaluative interpretation of Chink's body approximates the
dominant society's distorted view of black men. He hypersexualizes another black man, showing that he has absorbed Anglo America's cultural
"fiction" of black men as sexually predatory and feral. Certainly, one could
argue that Samuel's disdain stems solely from his frail sense of masculine
identity. After all, he is confined spatially throughout the story, and he
may be harboring a desire for his sister-in-law, a desire that is morally
and socially prohibited. Stated plainly, Chink's palpable and sentient vi-
rility exposes Samuel's relative domestication, which is anathema to the
"socially correct" figuration of masculinity rooted in male sexual domination. However, I would contend that Samuel's verbal paroxysm stems
from his self-abnegating acceptance of society's concept of black men, a
debased social construction he has sought to counter by adhering to such
sacrosanct American values of hard work and economic independence.
Unfortunately, Samuel, whose blackness automatically marks him as
Other, in turn adopts hegemonic cultural values and thereby reduces another black to the same socially confining space. Reminiscent of poet and
cultural critic Audre Lorde's prescient and oft-cited observation, "the master's tools will never dismantle the master's house" (112), Samuel appro-
priates the master's tools—the dehumanizing gaze usually trained on
black men—in order to bolster his identity according to valorized constructions of masculinity and subjectivity. This negating act becomes the
apogee of both self and racial diminution.

Chink's despondent declaration, "All us black folks is lost," contrasts
sharply with Samuel's dogged attempts to define himself according to the
dictates of the American Dream. Still, notwithstanding their marked differences, Samuel and Chink are ultimately mimetic doubles. While Samuel challenges cultural restrictions about black men in relation to family,
he still subscribes to demeaning and anachronistic beliefs about black life
and its cultural traditions. Similarly, though Chink perpetuates the empowering legacy of black oral/vernacular culture through the blues, he
lamentably uses black people—men, women, and children—as means to
his personal ends. These men's symbiotic relationship exposes the vaga-
ries and contradictions embedded in black men's desire for subject status
and how deeply contested masculinity is.

In discussing Petry's exploration of black men within familial and communal settings, I am by no means suggesting that she is the first writer to
do to. Earlier novels such as Charles Chesnutt's *The Marrow of Tradition*

(1901) and plays such as Lorraine Hansberry's *A Raisin in the Sun* (1959) revolve around black male protagonists' pressing anxieties for masculinity within similar contexts. Yet Petry's interest in black men's interiority and/or domesticity takes many intriguing forms in "Miss Muriel." In addition to portraying Samuel in relation to family, Petry offers a variation on the patriarchal and heteronormative family structure through the character Dottle Smith and his relationship with the narrator and her uncle, Johno Ecckles. Though the story doesn't specify the basis of Johno's relationship to the family, it does make clear Dottle's homosexuality and his protracted friendship with Johno; that Johno's wife leaves town when Dottle makes his annual northern visit raises further questions about whether the two men, who attended the same southern college, ever engaged in sexual relationship. Both are described as "race-conscious" men who could easily pass but, refusing to do so, defy categorization. During their southern travels, both blacks and whites respond to them with shock and disdain, for they are frequently mistaken for white. They are bound by, according to Dottle, a "cultivated and developed and carefully nourished hatred of white men" (30), an ironic declaration given his subsequent mimicking of behavior historically associated with heterosexual white men.

Aside from their sexually enigmatic relationship, Johno and Dottle also represent the intersection of cultural, personal, and geographic space in black male subject formation. The precocious narrator relates an important event, a crabbing trip she takes with both men. Her description of the "outing" abounds with vital information about their identities and overall roles in the narrative:

Before we ate our lunch, we went wading in the creek. Johno and Dottle rolled up the legs of their pants, and their legs were so white I wondered if they were that white all over, and if they were, how they could be called black. We sat on the bank of the creek and ate our lunch. Afterward Dottle and Johno told stories, wonderful stories in which animals talk, and there are haunted houses and ghosts and demons, and old black preachers who believe in heaven and hell.

They always started off the same way. Dottle would say to Johno, "Mr. Bones, be seated."

Though I have heard some of these stories many, many times, Dottle and Johno never tell them exactly the same. They change their gestures; they vary their facial expressions and the pitch of their voices. (33–34)

Even as we witness the flowering of the narrator's racial self, her observations about her mentor's roles contribute to Petry's overall portrayal of black male characters.

The ebullient narrator's description of the men's stories recalls what Livia Polanyi identifies as the ritualistic dimensions of storytelling: "The talk ... moves out of the here and now of the conversation into the sto-

ryworld: another time, often another location, populated by other participants" (15). The storyworld Dottle and Johno embroider is the fabric of
black folk/performance culture—black beast fables, preacher tales, and
minstrelsy. The men's southern imagination is buttressed by geography:
The narrator reveals that Dottle "teaches English and elocution and dra-
matics at a school for black people in Georgia," while Johno is "the chief
fund-raising agent for a black school in Georgia" (30). Thus, Dottle and
Johno's storytelling acumen links them inextricably to a southern past and
a vernacular culture—a culture that Samuel has tried to efface. In fact,
Dottle and Johno form with Chink a male creative community, one that
esteems oracy and performance. Dottle and Johno's role as story weavers
elucidates the necessity of maintaining and transporting black southern
culture—of its enduring emotional and spiritual value—regardless of
whether blacks originate from there. Like the storytellers who populate
Zora Neale Hurston's folk-centric tales, Dottle and Johno attest to the
power of performance and ritual in the formation of black subjectivity. In
Hurstonian fashion, Petry dramatizes the incontrovertible southernness
of the black self, even when that self has relocated to the North.[7]

Expanding upon the link between physical and personal space, I would
also note the significance of the idyllic creek at this key juncture in the
narrator's rite of passage. This newly configured, sepia Eden is apropos,
given how blacks have historically envisioned the North as a refuge. Petry's characters creatively respond to what J. Lee Greene in *Blacks in Eden*
calls the archetypal invocation of the paradise motif in Anglo-American
literature and culture:

Building upon the image of America as a New Eden, Anglo-Americans from the
colonial period onward appropriated, transformed, and conflated passages from
the Judeo-Christian Bible to justify their exclusion of Africans and descendants of
Africans from the American family. The biblical stories of the Garden of Eden and
of Man's Fall provided the nucleus around which they formulated tropological
images of American society and subjects—what I call the Eden trope. As social
theorists and literary artists in America have (re)inscribed and employed it over
the centuries, the Eden trope is not confined to the biblical narratives of the Creation and of the Fall. (1–2)

Founding a black "New Eden" in the North, Dottle, Johno, and the narrator represent a variation on the Edenic myth, which excluded all
blacks—men, women, and children. Just as Jim and Huck create an alternative American family on their hallowed and tropological raft, Petry's
triumvirate signifies on standard figurations of the heterosexual Anglo-
American family that excludes homosexuals as well. With Dottle and
Johno positioned symbolically as the narrator's surrogate parents, this
reconfigured family represents a radical re-envisioning of the heterosexist

and exclusionary Edenic myth, which elevates white men, demonizes women, and banishes blacks in Canaanite-like fashion. Comparable to Twain's inclusive vision of the American family, Petry proffers a re-envisioned *African* American family, and in doing so, articulates new ways for black men to resituate themselves as subjects by having them demolish dominant fictions of American identity, masculinity, sexuality, and family.

In reassessing Petry's discursive relationship to Wright, I often reassociate her with Ellison and Baldwin. Dottle's representation as a black gay character is especially striking, given the fiercely heterocentric representations of black men in literature. Charles Nero's identification of Baldwin's iconoclastic role as chronicler of gay men's lives—"although he did not always avoid the old stereotypes, he nevertheless presented complex characters in a positive light" (312)—also applies to Petry's rendering of black men in "Miss Muriel." On the one hand, her portrayal in her 1953 novel *The Narrows* of an effeminate and ostensibly straight white male character who harbored a blatant sexual interest in his young black male employee is stereotypically reminiscent of "Young Emerson" and his overtly sexual interest in the neophyte Invisible Man. But the more interesting character of Dottle both recalls and counters such hackneyed depictions. Superficially, Dottle epitomizes the standard image of a fey homosexual: the narrator describes his "long hair" and "buttery voice" (31); she then notes that Dottle "has a very fat bottom and he sort of sways from side to side as he walks," to which Chink replies, "He seems kind of ladylike" (36); and Samuel disparages him by proclaiming, "all he needs are some starched petticoats and a bonnet and he'd make a woman—he's practically one now—and he's tee-heein' around" (47). These belittling descriptions become even more antigay once the narrator's corroborates Dottle's sexual orientation: "Sometimes he brings a young man with him. These young men look very much alike—they are always slender, rather shy, have big dark eyes and very smooth skin just about the color of bamboo" (31). The cumulative effect of these comments would appear to substantiate Nero's assessment of black gay characters: "In the most virulent homophobic work gays are effeminate, sarcastic males who lead meaningless lives; they disrupt families, are misogynists, and are marginal to black communities and institutions" (312).

Yet Petry exposes the very stereotypes she appears to perpetuate. Dottle, as the narrator's androgynous surrogate parent, plays a core role in the precocious 12-year-old's budding views not only on sexuality, but on race as well. She says that "I believe that my attitude towards Mr. Bemish stems from Dottle Smith" (31). This combines with Dottle's telling of the racially and sexually tinged Muriel cigar joke. In the old joke, the white male shopkeeper is angry that a black man would request Muriel cigars without saying "Miss" Muriel. The point is that even in the most innocuous situations, black men must still adhere to "southern principles," which prohibit them from addressing whites by their first names. By having Dottle tell this story, Petry contests the notion that gayness is a totalizing and isolating identity, one that relegates black gay men to a no-man's-land devoid of black people. Dottle's homosexuality is but a singular facet of his layered, heterogeneous characterization, a representation that demonstrates that black male subjectivity is multifarious and encompasses race, gender, sexuality, geo-psychic space, and voice.

If Dottle and Johno's quasi marriage enables Petry to explore constructions of masculinity and gender, then the story's denouement introduces yet another coupling that is equally revelatory. Though Chink denigrates the overtly feminized Dottle while himself displaying facets of patriarchal masculinity, the story's conclusion links them in a provocative if disconcerting way. Recall Chink's bleak summarization of what he deems blacks' deracinated existence—"all us black folks is lost." This nihilistic view dovetails with what Dottle called his "cultivated and developed" hatred of whites, evidenced in the Muriel cigar anecdote he and Johno recollect for the narrator. In this context, then, Chink and Dottle's act of aggression against the story's lone white male figure, Bemish, seems understandable though deplorable. To summarize briefly, a sea of bats floods the drugstore and descends upon the inhabitants. While Chink and Dottle work doggedly to remedy the situation, Bemish "clasped Aunt Sophronia in his bosom, covering her head with his hands and arms and he kept murmuring comforting words" (50). Though his protection of Sophronia appears chivalrous and even heroic, the black men deem this act yet another instance of white male appropriation of black women. Instead of lauding Bemish's selflessness, Chink and Dottle perceive it as a rather ironic and bizarre variation of the Muriel cigar story: a white man's total access to women—an access routinely denied black men.

Though he is physically no threat to them or to Sophronia, both Chink and Dottle perceive B(l)emish as a blight to their community in general and to their relationships with black women specifically. Bemish upsets their tenuous and flawed sense of patriarchal privilege, which grants them an unencumbered dominance of black women. This mutual loathing of Bemish spawns the "marriage" of Dottle and Chink, a union forged to eradicate the white male menace in the name of black manhood. Sophronia's welfare now becomes ancillary. Petry thus inverts the dynamics of power and privilege inhered in Dottle's Muriel cigar story, which now becomes an intratext that parallels Dottle and Chink's actions in the "official" story. The conclusion of "Miss Muriel," in which the black men literally run Bemish out of town—he laments to the narrator that he must flee to Massachusetts because Dottle and Chink have threatened to "sew me up" (55)—is the quintessence of black male power run amok. In their hierarchy of social ills, male perfidy eclipses homosexuality, thereby making Dottle's sexuality moot in the preservation of black male hegemony.

Black men's constricting notions of manhood, as seen in numerous works of fiction by black male writers, routinely short-circuit the lives of black women with whom they come in contact. Bigger Thomas's remorseless murder of his black girlfriend, Bessie Mears, is perhaps the sine qua non in discussions of this particular narrative dynamic. Petry interrupts this discursive pattern by exposing the dire consequences of black men behaving as faux white men. In doing so, she employs her unique brand of irony, revision, and inversion to dramatize what might be deemed the "price of black masculinity." Perhaps informed by her reading of Douglass and Johnson, she reinscribes an ever-present circumstance in black literature in which black men are forced to flee in the face of transgression against white women. Conversely, black men preside over the expulsion of a white man for his supposed violation of sexual taboos. Bemish's northern destination, Massachusetts, further links him geographically if not racially with the incarnation of "strong" black manhood, Frederick Douglass. Re-wri(gh)ting the leitmotifs of several black men's texts, Petry raises profound questions about gender, authority, race, and distorted notions of phallocentric gender praxes. Perhaps the most cogent question the narrative raises is this: How valuable is black male subjectivity if it simply replicates white male hegemonic behavior, evidenced by the threats against and potential brutalizing of Bemish, a man who is in some ways is a parody of the very "masculinity" that black men have internalized? Concomitantly, is the black man's vaunted new role that of master/ oppressor, whose behavior black men now emulate?[8] Dottle and Chink achieve a Pyrrhic victory, one that has the unintended effect of reinforcing stereotypes about the bestial black menace, which American society has demonized as the apogee of Otherness and violence.

Forcefully and perspicuously, Ann Petry asks us to consider the meaning of black men accepting and reenacting the very oppressive behaviors that have enervated them throughout history. "Miss Muriel" functions as a cultural intercession, questioning the value of a particular gender-social politics that held sway during the Black Nationalist period of the 1960s. During this volatile cultural moment, many black men felt justified in promulgating sexism, homophobia, and, occasionally, violence in their zeal to repair and "reclaim" a tattered masculinity.[9] The verbal grenades launched by figures such as Amiri Baraka and Eldridge Cleaver have their fictive analog in "Miss Muriel," an underread but artistically and culturally resonant cautionary tale where gender, sexuality, and culture intersect and often collide.

NOTES

1. I take this critical position in a 1992 article on *The Street*, "A Distaff Dream Deferred? Ann Petry and the Art of Subversion."

2. See, for instance, Lindon Barrett's incisive *Blackness and Value: Seeing Double*, which includes extensive interpretations of *The Street* and *The Narrows* from a poststructuralist critical framework

3. Early interpretations of Petry's novels include Robert Bone's seminal *The Negro Novel in America* and Carl Milton Hughes's *The Negro Novelist: A Discussion of the Writings of American Negro Novelists, 1940–1950*. Most recent commentary on Petry's position in the context of 1940s literary discourse can be found in Bernard Bell's *The Afro-American Novel and Its Tradition* and Lawrence Hogue's *Discourse and the Other: The Production of the Afro-American Text*.

4. I invoke here the definition of *Otherness* posited by the pioneering critic George E. Kent, who used it in *Blackness and the Adventure of Western Culture* (see the essay "Faulkner and the Heritage of White Racial Consciousness: Notes on White Nationalism in Literature," especially page 179) to identify Faulkner's erasure of Dilsey Compson's place within her family and native black community—the author's failure to enter the spaces of the immortal character's life that fell outside the purview of her relationship with the disintegrating Compson family.

5. Petry's 1988 interview with Mark Wilson in Old Saybrook, Connecticut, reveals how her father's life informs Samuel's portrayal: "The drugstore was the public part of our lives. My parents never let it intrude on their private lives. . . . My father sang in the church choir. He helped raise the money to build this town hall. He and three other men used to sing stuff from Gilbert and Sullivan all over the country. In other words, *he was part of the community, and yet not part of it*. He had a big family, warm and close-knit, and my mother did too" (Wilson 77, emphasis added). Certainly, these comments shed light on Samuel's own liminality—the connectedness and disconnectedness he experiences as a black male entrepreneur in the North trying to negotiate personal, racial, and public spaces.

6. For a discussion of the musical underpinnings of Petry's short fiction, see novelist Gayl Jones's "Jazz/Blues Structure in Ann Petry's 'Solo on the Drums'" in her book *Liberating Voices,* (article reprinted in the present volume).

7. Petry's comments on New England convey her ambivalence about the North. In fact, her unequivocally *southern* roots help explain her representation of Wheeling, New York, as an imperfect haven and the story's portrayal of the South as the cradle of black life and culture: "But my grandfather James (that was on my mother's side) was a runaway slave from a plantation in Virginia; and so when he sang to his children, dangling them on his knee, it was: 'Run little baby, run; paterollers goin' to come!'. . . . All right, so that's part of my background; that does not a New Englander make. In other words, this is another breed entirely. And though we take on all of the—what shall I say?—the speech patterns, we accept the kind of food, the cooking, the houses, and so forth, nevertheless truly we're not Englanders—and never will be, as far as I can see" (Wilson 81). William H. Robinson provides one of the few contextual studies of black New England authors in an informative book *Black New England Letters: The Use of Writings in Black New England* (1977).

8. Contemporary novels questioning the efficacy of black vigilantism to avenge racial offenses include John Edgar Wideman's *The Lynchers* (1973) and Toni Morrison's *Song of Solomon* (1977).

9. In his recent biography of civil-rights activist Bayard Rustin, historian Jervis Anderson quotes a letter from activist and author Pauli Murray in which she

upbraids the predominantly male power brokers of the movement who excluded black women from positions of leadership: "The time has come to say to you quite candidly, Mr. [A. Philip] Randolph, that 'tokenism' is as offensive when applied to women as when applied to Negroes, and that I have not devoted the greater part of my adult life to the implementation of human rights to [now] condone any policy which is not inclusive" (259). Unabashedly, Murray's letter "calls out" the problem of male hegemonic power and its attendant scourge, sexism, in the quest for black liberation in the 1960s.

WORKS CITED

Anderson, Jervis. *Bayard Rustin: Troubles I've Seen*. New York: HarperCollins, 1997.

Barrett, Lindon. *Blackness and Value: Seeing Double*. Cambridge: Cambridge University Press, 1999.

Bell, Bernard W. *The Afro-American Novel and Its Traditions*. Amherst, MA: University of Massachusetts Press, 1987.

Bigsby, C.W.E., ed. "The Negro in American Culture." *The Black American Writer, Volume I: Fiction*. Baltimore: Penguin, 1969. 79–108.

Bone, Robert A. *The Negro Novel in America*. Rev. ed. New Haven, CT: Yale University Press, 1965.

Clark, Keith. "A Distaff Dream Deferred? Ann Petry and the Art of Subversion." *African American Review* 26 (1992): 495–505.

Edley, Nigel, and Margaret Wetherell. "Masculinity, Power and Identity." *Understanding Masculinities: Social Relations and Cultural Arena*. Ed. Maíatin Mac an Ghaill. Buckingham: Open University Press, 1996. 97–113.

Ervin, Hazel Arnett. *Ann Petry: A Bio-Bibliography*. New York: G. K. Hall, 1993.

Gibson, Donald. "Politics of Literary Expression." The Politics of Literary Expression: A Study of Major Black Writers. Westport, CT: Greenwood, 1981.

Greene, J. Lee. *Blacks in Eden: The African American Novel's First Century*. Charlottesville, VA: University Press of Virginia, 1996.

Hall, Leland K. "Support Systems and Coping Patterns." *Black Men*. Ed. Lawrence E. Gary. London: Sage Publications, 1981. 159–68.

Hogue, W. Lawrence. *Discourse and the Other: The Production of the Afro-American Text*. Durham, NC: Duke University Press, 1986.

Holladay, Hilary. *Ann Petry*. New York: Twayne, 1996.

hooks, bell. *Yearning: Race, Gender, and Cultural Politics*. Boston: South End Press, 1990.

Hughes, Carl Milton. *The Negro Novelist: A Discussion of the Writings of American Negro Novelists, 1940–1950*. New York: Citadel Press, 1953.

Jones, Gayl. "Jazz/Blues Structure in Ann Petry's 'Solo on the Drums.'" *Liberating Voices: Oral Tradition in African American Literature*. Cambridge, MA: Harvard University Press, 1991. 90–98.

Kent, George E. *Blackness and the Adventure of Western Culture*. Chicago: Third World Press, 1972.

Lorde, Audre. *Sister Outsider: Essays and Speeches*. Freedom, CA: Crossing Press, 1984.

Mobley, Marilyn Sanders. "Ann Petry." *African American Writers*. Ed. Valerie Smith. New York: Scribner's, 1991. 347–59.

Nero, Charles. "Gay Men." *The Oxford Companion to African American Literature*. Ed. William L. Andrews, Frances Smith Foster, and Trudier Harris. New York: Oxford University Press, 1997, 312.

O'Brien, John, ed. "Ann Petry." *Interviews with Black Writers*. New York: Liveright, 1973. 153–63; Reprint. Hazel Arnett Ervin. *Ann Petry: A Bio-Bibliography*. New York: G. K. Hall, 1993. 72–77.

Petry, Ann. "Miss Muriel." *Miss Muriel and Other Stories*. 1971. Boston: Beacon Press, 1989. 1–57.

Polanyi, Livia. *Telling the American Story: A Structural and Cultural Analysis of Conversational Storytelling*. Cambridge, MA: MIT Press, 1989.

Robinson, William H. *Black New England Letters: The Uses of Writings in Black New England*. Boston: Trustees of the Public Library of the City of Boston, 1977.

Scarry, Elaine. *The Body in Pain: The Making and Unmaking of the World*. New York: Oxford University Press, 1985.

Silverman, Kaja. *Male Subjectivity at the Margins*. New York: Routledge, 1992.

Washington, Gladys. "A World Made Cunningly: A Closer Look at Ann Petry's Short Fiction." *College Language Association Journal* 30 (1986): 14–29.

Wilson, Mark A. "A MELUS Interview: Ann Petry—The New England Connection." *MELUS* 15 (1988): 71–84.

Riot as Ritual: Ann Petry's "In Darkness and Confusion"

George R. Adams

One of the most noteworthy examples of sociology transformed into art is Ann Petry's story, "In Darkness and Confusion" (1947),[1] which recreates the Harlem riot in 1943[2] and foreshadows studies like those of the Kerner Commission.[3] What is most striking about the story, however, is that within the narrative itself a similar transformation occurs. What begins as a riot ends as a traumatic experience which transmutes the inarticulate and patient protagonist into an enraged and aggressive one. The transformation thus moves beyond the levels of sociological awareness and psychological response to the level of archetypal participation, in which, through rites of passage, an innocent is initiated into the communal experience of the culture.

In accord with the implicit theme of riot as ritual initiation into the mysteries of the community, the transformation in the Black protagonist, William Jones, is presented in terms of darkness and confusion. Before the riot, "darkness" refers to the sociological fact of William's skin color and the ghetto dwelling which his blackness had forced him to rent; psychologically, "darkness" describes the condition of ignorance and restricted awareness which is the result of William's sociological circumstances. The range of William's ignorance is wide. For example, he is not aware, on the eventful Saturday morning before the riot, that the summer heat is raising the level of irritability of the whole ghetto, although he perceives the heat himself (162).[4] He does not know, until later in the day, that his son, Sam, has been shot and arrested (172–173). He does not understand why his adopted daughter, Annie May, once a "nice little girl," is so rebellious (163), and he does not know what she does with herself when she is not

working (164). He cannot think what to write to Sam, away in the army
(166). He is not sure whether or not Sam at 16 "had already explored the
possibilities" offered by the "bold-eyed women" of the ghetto (167). In
short, William's life had not allowed him either the education or the leisure to become reflective, to philosophize on his condition, which means
that he has not allowed himself to develop what Grier and Cobbs calls
the "black rage"[5] which comes from the Black man's consciousness of his
condition.

That consciousness is in large part sociological, an awareness of milieu.
William does in fact respond to certain characteristics of his surroundings:
the "startlingly black" skin of his wife, Pink,[6] the "dark thin hands" of
Annie May, the "hallways so dark that he knew if he wasn't careful he'd
walk over a step" (165) in contrast to the "brilliant sunlight outside," the
dangerous streets where "at night shadowy," vague shapes emerged from
the street's darkness, "lurking near the trees" (167). But William cannot
put these perceptions into an analytical framework or draw a systematic
conclusion from them. At most he can come to a desperate decision: "We
gotta move this time for sure" (167). And he certainly cannot be aware of
the defense mechanisms he uses to protect himself against the hostile
white society, mechanisms based upon the values of that society. For example, he never thinks of himself as "boy" or "Willie" or "Bill," but always
"William,"[7] he is always on time to work, he works hard, and he never
misses a day. He is conscientious father and husband, and wants Annie
May to be "good" and responsible (169). He wants to move to a better
neighborhood. And he is determined that Sam is going to earn a living
"wearing a starched white collar, and a shine on his shoes and a crease in
his pants" (165); a likely career, William thinks, is "a druggist instead of
a doctor or a lawyer" (169), so long as Sam "could make enough to have
good clothes and a nice home" (168).[8]

If William is unable to make sociological analyses, he is even more incapable of noticing symbolic patterns in his life, such as the recurrence of
darkness at periods of stress. Such moments occur when William worries
about Annie May's "staying out practically all night long" (163) and about
his wife's bad heart (during his walk through the dark hallways (165)),
when he remembers Sam's graduation on "a warm June night" (165) or
Pink's fears about Sam in Georgia (expressed "one night" (166)) when he
attempts "one night" to write Sam a letter (166), when he is alarmed by
the "shadowy, vague shaped" which emerge from the ghetto darkness
(167), when he is depressed after work at "eight o'clock that night" (170),
and when he discovers later in the barbershop that Sam is in jail (172).
All of William's life, in short, is bounded and circumscribed by the darkness of his skin, his milieu, his mood, and his fate.

Closely linked to the thematic function of darkness is the thematic use
of confusion. William's confusion is of two kinds, psychological and so-

ciological. On the personal level, he cannot cope with Annie May's change from "good little girl" to "Jezebel," and he alternates among worry about it (163), frustrated threats of punishment (164), false analysis (164), and physical action (the ejection of Annie May from the house (175)). His confusion is manifested in his inability to articulate what he dimly perceives or deeply feels but cannot analyze. For example, all he can say to Pink the Saturday before the riot is "Hot, ain't it?" He is nonplussed by Annie May's silent rebelliousness, and finally can only say, "You know you ain't too big to get your butt whipped" (164). Earlier, with great effort, he had penned a brief letter to Sam: "Is you all right? Your Pa" (166). The maximum of confusion came with a direct confrontation with the oppressive white society, when William encountered Annie May's teacher and was "buried under a flow of words" which left him "confused and embarrassed" (170). When he does articulate his analysis, the conclusions he draws are clichés dictated by his society. He can talk freely in the Black barbershop but his comments are obvious ones based upon limited and generalized opinions ("Them Japs ain't got a chance"). His conclusion about Annie May is equally trite and predictable; like the girls who come into the drugstore with "Too much lipstick" and "Their dresses . . . too short and too tight" (169), she has gone bad, become a "Jezebel," given up her sense of morality and her sound familial and social values.

William's conception of sound values represent his greatest confusion. As I suggested earlier in describing William's defense mechanisms, all his values are white, handed to him ready-made. We can see his value-system at work in his self-image ("William"), his characterization of Annie May as worthless because she will not work regularly (169), his failure to react when his employer calls him "Boy" (166), his dislike at living in a neighborhood of brothels and bars, and his rejection of Pink's continued churchgoing. More importantly, we can see William's introjection of white middle-class values in his plans for Sam. In William's fantasies "Sam wasn't going to earn his living with a mop and broom" but with a "starched white collar" as befitted a young man who had "made the basketball team in high school" and whose picture "had been in one of the white papers" (173). Ann Petry subtly points out the unreality of William's vision by counterpointing to Williams's "white" illusions the Black reality that William is subconsciously aware of. He is afraid that Sam had already begun to find his place in the world defined to him by whites. At sixteen he apparently had already "explored the possibilities" of the brothels (167), he worked as a redcap at Grand Central (165), he is going to a Black college, Lincoln (165), he can become a "druggist instead of a doctor or a lawyer" (119), and he is in a Georgia army camp. Reinforcing the reality which Sam, and to a certain extent William, has accepted is the reality which William unconsciously perceives but hopes, vainly, to reject, e.g., the ghetto apartment, the eight-to-eight menial job, the "limp work coat" in contrast to Mr. Yudkin's "crisp white laboratory coat" (169), and the natural community in the Black barbershop. In short, William's whole world is defined by his plans for Sam, but that this is a fantasy world is made clear by what happens to Sam and the riot it triggers, a concrete realization of the confusion of values in William's mind. But because he is ignorant and confused, we are not to take William as obtuse or to reject him as too imperceptive to carry the value-statement of the author. On the contrary, Ann Petry is very careful to define William's problem as perceptions without a means to analyze or define them and frustrations without a means to articulate them or act them out. This repressed locked-in psychological and sociological condition, this darkness and confusion, is a necessary cause and justification for William's activities as a rioter. It is only by an event which goes deeper than riotous reaction, that is, an event which brings William in touch with the deepest desires of his community, that William can begin to articulate and act upon his accumulated if unconscious knowledge of his condition. To emphasize William's metamorphosis, Ann Petry created a tripartite narrative structure that juxtaposes William as puzzled novice, William as initiate, and William as active member of the new life.

His false value-system is represented by the events of Saturday, which occur in three major segments. As usual, William rises early to cook his breakfast; but this morning is different: it is extremely hot, he ruins his breakfast, and he has an argument with Annie May. This opening segment ends with the empty mailbox and William's walk down depressing Harlem streets (161–168). The second segment begins with William at his menial chores from eight in the morning to eight at night. It ends with the scene in the barbershop, where Sam's friend Scummy reports that Sam, refusing to move to "the nigger end of a bus," had been shot by a white MP and then imprisoned for twenty years for shooting back (169–174). In the third and last segment (174–177), William goes home to the heat and smell of the ghetto and, after a quarrel with Annie May, goes to sleep so that he will not have to tell Pink about Sam.

Throughout the Saturday section of the narrative, Ann Petry carefully lays the psychological and sociological groundwork for William's transformation into rioter. Within the stifling atmosphere of the hot, stinking, violent ghetto, William stores up a dangerous complex of past and present experiences: Annie May's smart-aleck rebelliousness, Pink's failing health, the dark tenement apartment, Pink's crying at Sam's departure for Georgia, which "tore him in little pieces," Mr. Yudkin's snarl, "Boy, what the hell's the matter with you," the futile search for better housing, his mother's comment on Georgia ("They hate niggers down there"), the episode with Annie May's white teacher, the news about Sam, the urge to stand up in church and yell. Thus, William comes to the night of the riot in a state of acute tension and resentment. He is ready for riot.

The events of Sunday are balanced against those of Saturday. In the morning segment (177–179), William stays home while Pink goes to church; he meditates on Sam, suffers from the heat, and watches the random violence of the ghetto. The first segment ends with his decision, "I gotta get me some beer." The second segment begins in the bar, where William is caught up in the undirected, restless energy of the crowd, the loud jukebox, the loveless sexuality, the false joviality of drunkenness. But under this influence, he begins talking aloud to himself, musing on Sam's probable future ("whoring" on Sunday afternoon). Like segment one, the second segment ends with violence, the shooting of a Black soldier by a white policeman. Aroused by the beer and the symbolic connection between the shooting of Sam and the shooting of the soldier, William spontaneously says, "Come on, what are you waiting for?" and leads the crowd outside (179–181). The third segment (181–186) deals with the increasing anger of the crowd and William's increasing identification with it: "He got the feeling that he had lost his identity as a person with a free will of his own" (182). At first he is frightened, but then "he began to feel powerful"; an important indication of his growing sense of communal power is his speaking to himself and his Black brothers. A meaningful component of this articulation of power is his social commentary: "They got us coming and going, he thought" (182). And he suddenly remembers a poignant and proleptic scene of loss and pain, when Pink had lost a child: the white nurse commented that Blacks have too many children anyway, and William stared at her white face and uniform and muttered, "It's too bad your eyes ain't white, too" (184). The violence (and growing perception by William) culminates in the concluding action of the third section, when Pink, finally told of Sam's fate, throws a bottle through a plate-glass window and initiates the riot.

Pink's act concludes the first stage of William's initiation; the remaining "mysteries" are the subject of the last section of narrative (186–191). The first section (Saturday) presents William as silently impotent, closed in by his life and milieu; the second (Sunday) shows his increasing identification with his Black brothers and his progressive ability to articulate his feelings and perceptions. To this dialectic pattern of thesis-antithesis the closing pages of the narrative (Sunday night) add the synthesis of William's experiences, in which the suppressed anger and shock of Saturday is released in the communal experience of Sunday, culminating in the final blood-rites of the riot on Sunday night. And the riot is clearly a ritual requiring the shedding of blood. As Ann Petry makes clear early in the story (171), William "didn't like violence," and when he notices that many of the looters (including Pink) have cut their hands during the looting (188, 190) he begins to lose his rebellious energy and wants only to return to the familiar and protective home and values which the darkness and confusion of the riot had temporarily displaced (188, 191). But William, once a participant in the ritual transformation, has to see it through.

As Sam's fate and the bloody hands of the rioters suggest, the ritual is based upon the sacrificial shedding of blood: at the same time, on the sociological and psychological levels it is the ritualized shedding of the past, that is, of false evaluations of self and society. The link between the ritual and sociological levels is the symmetrical arrangement of the protagonists. The first sacrificial victim, the young male member of the family, is Sam; his is a literal shedding of blood, both his and that of the dominant white society. Like Sam, the young female member of the family, Annie May, is symbolically killed by being arrested in the riot, to be categorized as no longer "delinquent" but "criminal." The two members on the other side of the generation gap, Pink and William, have fates similar to that of the children. Pink, like Sam, does literally shed blood (both in the riot and in the flashback in which she loses her baby in a white hospital), and she is killed by the riot. William, in accord with his role as ritual initiate, sacrifices the most: his son is shot and jailed, he abandons his middle-class value system, he takes part in violence, and he loses his daughter and wife. In short, he undergoes a ritual transformation, completing the symmetry of the rebellious family and closing the generation gap by identifying with Sam and Annie May. When William cries aloud over the dead body of Pink, "The sons of bitches" (191), the articulated expression of shock, loss, and hatred is the culmination of the ritual transformation of William into aggressive and rebellious Black.

What begins in sociology, then, ends in archetypal experience. The thematic reason for this progression is clear: Ann Petry is concerned to justify Black riots. On the sociological and psychological levels we are made to see the result of just one repressive act too many on a hot summer day in Harlem, 1943. On the archetypal level we come to understand the universal meaning of William's "riotous" act. It is not simply that he is lashing out at a repressive and dominant society, it is that he is breaking out of a mode of existence. But the physical experience, realistically, is only temporary, that is, will be nullified by further repression (including arrest) and loss (e.g., William's family), so that William's milieu is unchanged. But the Black psyche is changed; more importantly, it is oriented to communal experiences; to the brotherhood of the oppressed against the oppressor. William does not feel this rationality but intuitively; it will take much longer for him to rationalize this experience, to develop an ideology for action. Therefore, his transformation is truly a ritual one; on the outside, in his body and milieu, little is changed for William. But in the realm of ritual transformation, in the universal religious experience of being born again through sacrifice into a new life, of breaking through the darkness and confusion of this life into a clearly-perceived new life, William is much changed. For Ann Petry, as for William Jones, riot becomes ritual.

NOTES

1. I am using the text printed in Abraham Chapman, ed. *Black Voices: An Anthology of Afro-American Literature* (New York: Mentor Book, 1968) 161–191.

2. For another Black writer's use of the Harlem Riot, see James Baldwin's *Notes of a Native Son* (Boston, 1955).

3. Report on the National Advisory Commission on Civil Disorders (New York, 1968). A brief comment on the Harlem riot is on p. 224 of the Bantam edition.

4. For a similar use of summer heat as one cause of violence, see Katherine Anne Porter's "Noon Wine."

5. William H. Grier and Price M. Cobbs, *Black Rage* (New York, 1968); See also Baldwin in *Notes*.)

6. He is also aware of the futility of her constant church-going (178–179).

7. This is an assumption based upon the author's use of "William," but nowhere in the story is the protagonist's referred to in any other way.

8. Note also the value-judgment implied in his wife's name, "Pink."

"Ain't No Room for Us Anywhere": Reading Ann Petry's "In Darkness and Confusion" as a Migration Narrative

Deirdre Raynor

In her explanation for writing *The Street*, Ann Petry has stated she was interested in showing "how simply and easily the environment can change the course of a person's life" (Ivey 48). Robert Bone in *The Negro Novel in America* and James Ivey in "Mrs. Petry's Harlem" have criticized Petry's sociological approach to "what life is like for the [working-class] African American" in urban America. According to Bone and Ivy, the implications in the story are that "bigotry" (Ivey 154) and "racial discrimination [are] responsible for [the urban] slums" (Bone 180) and for protagonist Lutie Johnson's failures (Ivey 155).

Petry's short story, or more accurately her novella, "In Darkness and Confusion" (1947) has a thesis similar to the thesis found in *The Street*, and the short narrative easily lends itself to a sociological reading. But when the short story is read against Farrah Jasmine Griffin's *"Who Set You Flowin'?" The African-American Migration Narrative*, it yields less of an interpretative sociological background and more of a background that is cultural and historical.

Farrah Griffin defines the African American migration narrative as "one of the twentieth century's dominant forms of African American cultural production" (3). In such a narrative, the recurring motif is the migration of characters to the North (i.e., to freedom or to the figurative Promised Land). Recurring also in such narratives are what Griffin calls "pivotal moments" that allow cultural and historical readings of characters and their backgrounds. As Griffin writes, the migration narrative possesses

(1) an event that propels the action northward;

(2) a detailed representation of the [character's] initial confrontation with the urban landscape;

(3) an illustration of the migrant's attempt to negotiate the urban landscape and his or her resistance to the negative effects of urbanization; and

(4) a vision of the possibilities or limitations of the North and . . . South. (3)

"In Darkness and Confusion" might be read as a migration narrative. It encourages a critique of William Johnson and his family as migrants (or minorities) confronting their urban landscapes, as migrants (or minorities) negotiating their spaces in their southern and northern communities, and as migrants (or minorities) who develop a new level of social consciousness about American society.

As the first pivotal moment in the African American migration narrative, there is in "In Darkness and Confusion" an event that moves the action northward. The event occurs midway in the story, however. Protagonist William Jones learns about the jailing of his son, Sam, in Georgia. Each time William thinks of Sam being in Georgia, he remembers what his mother told him about the plight of blacks in Georgia and her admonition, "They [whites] hate niggers down there. Don't you never let none of your children go down there" (262). In describing the impact of violence and inequity experienced by African Americans at the hands of whites in the South, Petry writes, "The very sound of the word Georgia did something to [William Jones] inside" (262). In fact, William believes being in Georgia is worse than being in the army. The jailing of Sam coupled with the stories about Georgia that William hears from his own mother emphasize for him, as well as readers, why many African Americans made the sojourn to urban and more cosmopolitan environments (i.e., to the North or to the figurative Promised Land). And, again, as Griffin reveals, sometimes the migration narrative is less than a "straightforward linear progression from the south to a vision" (3).

Before discussing further how Petry's short story develops as a migration narrative, I would like to provide an overview of the "stories about Georgia"—about the South—that propel the Great Migration following World War I. Many African Americans left the South in search of better opportunities in the urban/northern industrialized environment (e.g., jobs in auto factories, meat-packing plants, and other types of factory work) (Franklin 339–40). Other motivating factors to leave the South were gender related. For instance, during Reconstruction or economic slumps, there was a rise in lynching, especially against African American men. Fed up and desiring a better and more wholesome life, a number of African American men made the exodus to the North in hopes of escaping racial violence and inequality directed against them and their families.

Similar to African American men, African American women attempted to escape race-based violence such as lynching, but the women also migrated North to avoid rape and other forms of sexual exploitation. According to Darlene Clark Hine, for African American women in the early twentieth century, there was a definite desire for "sexual autonomy and sexual preservation" (215), and many of the women migrating North believed they could realize this desire in the urban environment. Other reasons for African American women to migrate from the South to the North, similar to men, included the search for better jobs. In contrast, African American women, particularly working-class women, did not necessarily find jobs in the factory industry. The most-available job for them was domestic work.

Petry alludes to the control of African Americans via violence and discriminatory practices in employment and housing in the South through her depiction of what happens to Sam, but she also shows how African Americans living in the North encounter some forms of control as well. Griffin terms the encounter in the North as "initial confrontation with the urban landscape" or the encounter with controlling whites in the urban North. The "initial confrontation" becomes the second pivotal moment in migration narratives. According to Griffin, during confrontations, the migrant experiences "a change in time, space and technology," and the change can be positive or negative (5).

In the story "In Darkness and Confusion," Petry reveals how the city has the potential to negatively transform Sam and Annie May as they navigate the streets. With the character Annie May, Petry expands her analysis of the sexual exploitation of black women living in the urban environment—an analysis that she began in *The Street* (1946). Moreover, by emphasizing the predatory nature of "the street" and its inhabitants, Petry shows how "the city silently and invisibly operates on its inhabitants" (Griffin 17). The theme of sexual exploitation in "In Darkness and Confusion" parallels a similar theme in Calvin Hernton's "The Significance of Ann Petry." According to Hernton, Petry's *The Street*, and I would argue "In Darkness and Confusion," shows that "the black ghetto is not only a social, political, educational, and economic colony, but the black ghetto is also . . . a sexual colony" (83). Hernton goes on to describe African American women as "sport and game" for both white and black men in the ghetto. In "In Darkness and Confusion," Petry shows how both African American women (e.g., Annie May and her friends) and men (the youthful Sam and his friends) become "sport and game" for inhabitants of the ghetto and possibly outsiders. In so doing, Petry further demonstrates that William (who cautions Annie May and Sam) understands the nuances and dangers of life in an urban community.

During "initial confrontation" or the second moment in the migration narrative, the migrant is also confronted by the "sophisticated [and not so sophisticated] uses of power and control" that whites exert over blacks (e.g., health care, specifically the high mortality rate for African Americans in Harlem and when Pink loses her baby; education, specifically when Annie May's teachers conveniently label her as "slow" and start her on a path of remedial education; and police brutality, specifically the murder of the African American soldier). The suggestions here are that inhabitants of the ghetto are abandoned by the larger American society and/or relegated to the periphery of American society, particularly as regards political and social institutions, as a result of racist notions about the place of African Americans in the larger American society.

Through her depiction of Annie May, Pink, and William as characters who attempt to negotiate the urban landscape, Petry shows evidence of the third pivotal moment in migration narratives. Interestingly, Pink and Williams identify "safe spaces" that allow them refuge and the confidence to resist the negative effects of urbanization. Patricia Hill Collins identifies safe spaces as a place where African Americans are free to speak and "where domination does not exist as a 'hegemonic ideology'" (in Ervin 429). Griffin expands on Collins's definition. She points out that these spaces "are more often the locus of sustenance and preservation" as opposed to being sites of resistance exclusively (in Ervin 429). For Pink and William respectively, the church and the barbershop are "safe spaces." In these places, the characters are said to "freely express themselves and learn strategies for resolving personal and communal problems." Furthermore, whites do not control these sites.

The depiction of the church as a "safe space" reiterates the central role of the black church in the experience of the migrant. As Griffin writes,

Black churches [provide] another arena where migrants were able to convene community; in some instances, church was a place where migrants could invoke the south as a means for sustaining them in the city. (62)

Here, Griffin makes direct reference to African Americans bringing southern traditions and values to their black churches in the North. In "In Darkness and Confusion," traditions are found in the author's references to the African American spirituals and to call and response. Another tradition is found in William Jones's references to spirituality. As William contends, "[H]e could find relief from the confusion of his thoughts by taking part in the singing and shouting that would go on in the church" (274).

Like the church, the barbershop reiterates a specific function. It is a "safe space"; it is a site where African American men, as do the men in the story, voice their opinions, rage, and fears about the war, economic realities facing both the individual and the community, and politics—all without facing reprisal from whites. The exchange between the men in the barbershop further illustrates the migrants' understanding of the "manifestation of power in the white controlled north" (Griffin 5). The barbershop also offers escape, for William believes that listening to the debates between the men in the shop will, for instance, push "the nagging worry about Sam . . . so far in the back of his mind, he wouldn't be aware of it" (266).

Unlike Pink and Sam, Annie May seeks refuge and/or escape not in traditions but from "a stranger." According to Griffin, "within the context of the African American community, the stranger is that figure who possesses no connections to the community." She continues,

On the pages of the written migration narrative . . . , the migrant often meets a literal stranger who offers (mis)guidance, advice, and a new worldview. The stranger exists in a dialectical relationship with the ancestor (found in the church, the barbershop, etc.). While the ancestor originates in the South and lives in the North, for the most part the stranger is a Northern phenomenon. (in Ervin 427)

Informed by sociologist Robert Park, Griffin concludes that "the stranger" evolves into "marginal man"; his or her "energies that were formerly controlled by custom and tradition are released. . . . He or she . . . looks upon the world . . . with something of the detachment of a stranger" (427). Throughout the story, Annie May is referred to as a "Jezebel" or as being "lost" or detached. In short, Annie May is detached from the community in ways that her mother and father are attached.

William Jones is the character that comes to understand the various manifestations of power in both the South and the North, and, as the story progresses, the limitations of the North for African Americans. William's new level of social consciousness marks the fourth pivotal moment in migration narratives. In scenes in the hospital, school, barbershop, and even during the riot in the story, William provides both subtle and overt commentary on white privilege and racism, and on the failure of the Great Migration. He comes to understand that in 1943 it is race that determines one's fate and that "White folks got us comin' and goin' backwards" (292). Following the murder of a soldier in his community, William concludes further, "We don't belong anywhere [South or North]. There ain't no room for us anywhere" (291).

The background in "In Darkness and Confusion" might easily be categorized as sociological, but a more enlightening approach to the story is a review of the construction of an African American racial identity and the intersections of race, class, and gender in a migration narrative.

WORKS CITED

Bone, Robert. *The Negro Novel in America*. New Haven, CT: Yale University Press, 1965.

Ervin, Hazel Arnett, ed. *African American Literary Criticism, 1773 to 2000*. New York: Twayne, 1999.

Franklin, John Hope. *From Slavery to Freedom: A History of African Americans*. New York: Alfred Knopf, 2000.

Griffin, Farrah Jasmine. *"Who Set You Flowin'?" The African-American Migration Narrative*. New York: Oxford University Press, 1995.

Hernton, Calvin. "The Significance of Ann Petry." *The Sexual Mountain and Black Women Writers, Adventures in Sex, Literature, and Real Life*. New York: Anchor/Doubleday, 1987.

Hine, Darlene Clark. *A Shining Thread of Hope*. New York: Broadway Books, 1999.

Ivey, James W. "Ann Petry Talks about First Novel." *Crisis* 53.2 (February 1946): 48–49.

———. "Mrs. Petry's Harlem." *Crisis* 53.5 (May 1946): 154–55.

Petry, Ann. *The Street*. 1946. Boston: Houghton Mifflin, 1974.

———. "In Darkness and Confusion." *Miss Muriel and Other Stories*. Boston: Houghton Mifflin, 1971. 252–95.

Apartheid among the Dead; Or, on Christian Laughter in Ann Petry's "The Bones of Louella Brown"

Gene Fendt

Metuunt cupiuntque, dolent gaudentque, et quia rectus est amor eorum, istas omnes affectiones rectas habent.

(They fear and desire, grieve and rejoice, and because their love is right they have all those other passions rightly.)

—De Civitate Dei 14.9

If we support, with Kant, that "laughter is an affection arising from a strained expectation being suddenly reduced to nothing,"[1] and that our expectations and what reduces them are, to some extent, culturally constructed, we must come to the conclusion that the evocation of laughter by a joke or absurdity or some other "reduction to nothing" has a range of communities in which it will work better or worse, or may fail to work. In Ann Petry's comic masterpiece, "The Bones of Louella Brown,"[2] a reader begins to hear the joyful and loving laughter of the community of saints. Old Peabody, the undertaker, hears it, and Governor Bedford, the WASP builder of the glorious new family mausoleum, fears to hear it; and every reader joins in it—to a greater or lesser extent—and precisely that ability to join in it—or not—is a confession of the extent to which our own spirits are being constructed in accord with that happy community—or not. If we do not hear this laughter, or can't participate in it, we are on the wrong side of a deeper and more lasting division than any racial, cultural, or economic apartheid present in, or suffered by, the bones of Louella Brown. This final division between audience members is, in fact, the only real division, the one that performs the erasure of all the other forms of apartheid a culture or a history might practice or put its faith in.

In "The Bones of Louella Brown," (1947) such erasures have a lightness of touch that exhibit Petry as a masterful writer rather than a heavy-handed apologist or embittered racialist. I will point out some of those horsetail-fine erasures in retelling the bones of the story.

The bones of the poor, black laundress, Louella Brown, had passed through the underground workroom of Whiffle and Peabody, Incorporated, in 1902 on their way to Yew Tree Cemetery—"the final home of Boston's wealthiest and most aristocratic families" (166). Without speaking at all symbolically, as one might by pointing out that the yew is traditionally a symbol of eternal life, we know at the time this statement is made that it is already under erasure, since all of the aristocratic Bedfords, as well as Louella, have been recently removed: the cemetery has proved not to be their final home. The supposed dead are on the move; there is a kind of life in them yet. And they are more than corpses. Soon after the exhumation, Old Peabody is "a little disconcerted, for he suddenly saw Louella Brown with an amazing sharpness. It was just as though she had entered the room" (166). Not just the bones, but the very ghost had been raised. Her final home seems not to be among the dead.

Half a century previous to the time of the story, Old Peabody's father had bent to the will of his wife, who was very fond of the old, black laundress, and had made what, at the time, had been a small crack in "the careful discriminatory practices of generations" to place Louella in the cemetery, albeit at the very edge, "in a very undesirable place" (166). Through "enlargement"—a wonderful word—she now lay in one of the choicest spots—in the exact center. So the old washerwoman, who perhaps had been born a slave, and in any case inhabited a very undesirable place in her cultural hierarchy, had, through death, come to occupy the very center. We see that the former slave, the cultural captive, is enlarged through dying. We see, too, that those very small acts of love on the part of Old Peabody Sr. for his wife and the wife's for the washerwoman have been enlarged, as well, through death. Dying into the Yew Tree—who could think it would be so powerful? Is it perhaps true that the smallest act of love is an erasure of discrimination? But it takes so much dying for us to recognize that fact, for it to become visible that the discrimination is already erased though it continues to be practiced, indeed even more rigorously enforced. Despite all of this, we see that what happens in the Yew Tree is that through lots of dying these two small acts of love are enlarged and come to occupy the very center.

Old Peabody intends to rectify his father's "truly terrible error in judgment" by moving Louella to "one of the lesser well-known burying places on the outskirts of the city. That's where she should have been put in the first place" (165). But the course of the story shows us that the enlargement brought about by this dying into eternal life is not reversible, however much embarrassment it might cause to those who have not yet been so enlarged. It is against this background of enlargement that smallness becomes quite humorous:

"Colored?" said Young Whiffle [who is 75] sharply. "Did you say 'colored'? You mean a black woman? And buried in Yew Tree Cemetery?" His voice rose in pitch. (166)

"We're ruined—ruined—ruined—" he muttered. "A black washerwoman!" he said, wringing his hands. "If only she had been white—"
    "She might have been Irish," said Old Peabody coldly. . . . "And a Catholic. That would have been equally as bad. No, it would have been worse. Because the Catholics would have insisted on a Mass, in Bedford Abbey, of all places! Or she might have been a foreigner—a—a—Russian. Or, God forbid, a Jew!"
    "Nonsense," said Young Whiffle pettishly. "A black washerwoman is infinitely worse than anything you've mentioned." (171–72)

Young Whiffle stood up and pounded on the dusty windowsill. "Because black people, bodies, I mean the black dead—"
    He took a deep breath. Old Peabody said, "Now relax, Mr. Whiffle, relax. Remember your blood pressure."
    "There's such a thing as a color line," shrieked Young Whiffle. (173)

So many expectations; so much nothing. Young Whiffle, an undertaker all his life, cannot quite figure out how the line should be drawn: "black people"—well, they were people, or—, but now—"bodies"—but that can't be the source of pollution for an undertaker—"the black dead," and perhaps at this point Whiffle remembers that all the dead turn black in decay. The incapacity of Whiffle to finish any line he begins to draw is merely presented to us; we must see and feel his whiffing. We see and feel it, if we see and feel it, against a background much larger than any of the race, class, or religious lines he attempts to stabilize. Further, by siding, in her narrative voice, with the living, division-making characters, Petry shapes us to a laughter that does not encourage a malicious sense of superiority, but rather encourages our own playfulness with all these deeply unimportant, death-dealing divisions from within:

Old Peabody shouted: "Will you stop that caterwauling? . . . Louella Brown was a neatly built little woman, a fine woman, full of laughter. I remember her well. She was a gentlewoman. Her bones will do no injury to the Governor's damned funeral chapel."
    It was a week before Young Whiffle actually heard what Old Peabody was saying, though Peabody made the same outrageous statement, over and over again.
    When Young Whiffle finally heard it, there was a quarrel. . . .
    By the end of the day, the partnership was dissolved, and the ancient and exclusive firm of Whiffle and Peabody, Incorporated, went out of business. (178)

Old Peabody's statement is outrageous because it dissolves all the distinctions "the ancient and exclusive firm[s]" have to depend on; it dissolves them in the gentleness and laughter of Louella Brown. We might say that it is as a result of her resurrection that the firm embodying the exclusive and discriminating is dis-incorporated. For, in fact, Old Peabody himself, having suffered under the gentle laughter of Louella, is clearly cured of his original (and problem-causing) judgment that Louella had been misplaced by his father. He clearly no longer considers such discrimination to carry any weight—it has been reduced to nothing for him. May all of our sorry distinctions be granted such dissolution. Just as Louella's laughter dissolved Old Peabody's demanding apartheid, the laughter charmed forth from us by this story begins the process of dissolving ours.

But notice what beliefs underlie this comic catharsis, what movements of the spirit we must be imitating in this purification through laughter. This catharsis requires we share in and submit to the dissolution of the distinctions we incorporate in the so-called real world, the world of apartheid history and exclusive culture (economic, racial, sectarian). We could not laugh at the sputtering smallness of Whiffle (e.g., in the passage quoted above) unless we ourselves were already enlarged. We do not, on the other hand, accomplish this dissolution of distinctions into a realm of abstract personhood—legal or fictional. The laughter we share in, the laughter that reduces these distinctions to nothing does not require the dissolution of difference into sameness or vacuity, the loss of distinction and personality.[3] In Petry's mimetic art we do not become disembodied ghosts in our enlargement; Louella Brown appears as she was in life—a neat, small-boned, laughing black woman, unbent by servitude to anything less than perfectly erect posture. If anything, she is more clearly herself—more perfectly, soulfully distinct while enlarged beyond all exclusion (whether walls or color lines). Not only does this enlargement appear in the fact that hers is the brightest and presiding spirit of the story, but also in the fact that mere bodies are discovered, in the story, to be incapable of exact-enough distinction: spirits are larger. Stuart Reynolds, sometime assistant and researcher for the firm, discovers this when he opens the caskets of Louella and of Elizabeth Bedford, Countess of Castro: the same bone structure, each their own teeth—no repairs, each about 70, both with even the same type of hair (168).

Reynolds considers this a revelation:

"Why, it's sensational!" he said aloud. And as he talked to himself he grew more and more excited. "It's a front page story. . . . It's more than front page news, why, it's the biggest story of the year—" (168)

And the sentence is left unfinished—as if it might be even bigger news than that. Reynolds has discovered the Gospel, that in Christ there is no slave or free, but he clearly thinks his science has discovered (and proves) this thought that no one could think—and the first thing he thinks to do is to go and tell the news. To go forth and tell is, of course, the right response to a true and groundbreaking discovery, but that the discovery is his is the comedy. His news, in a world where the Gospel is such old news that it is nearly forgotten, appears as the light dawning on a child who suddenly sees that two plus two are and always will be four. The child would be right that the discovery is momentous, and of a piece with an unimaginable and infinite journey, and the child would be right that it is true, but that it is his discovery, not something older than the hills, is high humor.

The world in which we are laughing (if we are laughing) is a world in which the dead are not dead, in which they can visit "every night and frequently during the day" (179) at their own sweet will. It is a world in which the quick-moving, merry little woman is easily identifiable, but not by the distinctions of our science; she can be bodily present without bodily limitation; and Petry presents all of these miracles as the plainest everyday thing. Let those who have eyes to see with see.

Reynolds's discovery leads to the last erasure of distinction. Like the other distinctions we have been examining, in all probability there were people who, when this story was first published, found it (or would have found it, had they read it) disgusting. Perhaps most would have disliked it because it is structured on the lines of race, class, and sect in which they believed, and everywhere the clean line crumbles into dust like a mummy's winding cloth at the slightest touch. But some might have been disturbed, as well, by the disturbance of another kind of apartheid—that marking the division between the living and the dead. When, after the exhumation of all the dead Bedfords and Louella, Stuart Reynolds calls in the night city editor of the *Boston Record* to take note of the similarity in bone structure of the laundress and the countess, the editor orchestrates a "merry-go-round" (169) of encorpsed undertaker's tables. The countess and the laundress go wheeling, within the larger roomful of the dead, on the arms of the night-shift journalist's assistants, until Reynolds loses track of who is who. The editor and his crew

Invaded the sacred premises. . . . He had no sooner asked Reynolds to pose in one position than he had him moved, in front of the tables, behind them, at the foot, at the head. Then he wanted the tables moved. The photographers cursed audibly as they dragged the tables back and forth, turned them around, sideways, lengthways. And still the night city editor wasn't satisfied. (169)

Again, it is written as if the narrative voice agrees with the sacred-line drawers: there is invasion and cursing in the holy premises. It is all (one might say) disgustingly disrespectful; but if one can see spirits among these wheeling dead (as Old Peabody has already begun to find himself doing), one might see them enjoying the merry-go-round—the twinned countess and laundress laughing at their ride together among the more staid and proper Bedfords, and the Harvard medical student getting his picture taken again and again between the laundress and the countess, gazing at both of them with "surprise, amazement, pleasure" (169). And if you can hear that laughter, has not that final line, between the living and the dead, collapsed to dust? This community of saints is the end of all apartheid; it is realized in our laughter.

Even Governor Bedford, if he does not join this laughter in the story, fears it, and so he humbles himself before that judgment by agreeing with Old Peabody on the appropriate epitaph. If the laughter of Louella Brown is the laughter of the saints in the life of Christ (in whom there is no slave or free—nor any death), the Governor's final act is a confession. As he agrees to the epitaph out of fear, we must say that just as he is on the outside of crypt and looking in (to a place Peabody recognizes he does fear [179]), he is on the outside of the community of saints and looking in. But as he agrees on the epitaph, we must also see that he recognizes the truth of that community's judgment, and though he cannot laugh at the divisions in which his present life is so completely invested, he knows that he should, for the epitaph he agrees to confesses to the inconcinnity of those divisions and the singular power that overcomes them:

HERE LIES
ELIZABETH, COUNTESS OF CASTRO
OR
LOUELLA BROWN, GENTLEWOMAN
1830–1902
REBURIED IN BEDFORD ABBY JUNE 21, 1947
"They both wore the breastplate of faith and love;
And for a helmet, the hope of salvation" (180)

This last sentence is the only one that openly quotes the New Testament,[4] but as it is the epitaph both to the good women in the story and for the story itself, we must take it as the author's own gospel confession. While there has been much fussing about who is to get into the Bedford Abby crypt, it is clear that something entirely different is needed to get through the door of the other kingdom—the one whose coat of arms is the yew tree—which one might enter as quickly through the pauper's cemetery as through the abbey. In fact, someone might get into the abbey door, but not get into the kingdom. The final epitaph is an admission that there is a better place than Bedford Abbey, that both women knew it, that the careful discrimination which set the hurly-burly of the story in motion mattered not to them. Their breastplate was faith and love; their helmet, the hope of salvation. These are not the coat of arms of Bedford. What mattered, and what is now carved in marble, is what the countess shared with the laundress, what the rich can share with the poor, what inseparably must unite the white and the black, wherever their bodies are: that they wear the breastplate of faith and love, and for a helmet, the hope of salvation. It is that armor in which Louella stood "very erect" (166) during all those years of good service and devotion (174) and that called forth from Old Peabody's mother the debt of gratitude and the unremitting fondness that the story exhibits as enlarged through death. Insofar as they stand erect in that armor, all their other passions and affections—as Augustine says—including laughter, are also correct. And the same will be true of the audience—or not.

NOTES

1. Immanuel Kant, *The Critique of Judgement*, trans. James Creed Meredith (Oxford: Oxford University Press, 1952), 332. Pagination according to the Akademie Ausgabe of Kant's works.

2. This story may be found in Ann Petry, *Miss Muriel and Other Stories* (Boston: Mariner Books, 1999), 163–80, which is the edition I have used. Further references to the story will be in the text.

3. Such political or ethical (perhaps even Kantian!) egalitarianism, while it may be democratic, is not Christian. C. S. Lewis points this out in his essay, "Membership," in *The Weight of Glory* (New York: HarperCollins, 2001). The "egalitarian fiction [of politics] . . . is our only defence against one another's cruelty. . . . It is medicine, not food. . . . Equality is a quantitative term and therefore love often knows nothing of it" (169–70).

4. The epitaph is taken from Ephesians 6:14–17. This chapter also urges "Bondservants, be obedient to those who are your masters in the flesh , . . . not with eye service, as men pleasers, but as bondservants of Christ, doing the will of God from the heart, with good will doing service, as to the Lord and not to men, knowing that whatever good anyone does, he will receive the same from the Lord, whether he is a slave or free. And you, masters, do the same things to them . . . knowing that your own Master also is in heaven, and there is no partiality with Him" (5–9).

The Narrator as Feminist Ally in Ann Petry's "The Bones of Louella Brown"

Amy Lee

When Petry's "The Bones of Louella Brown" was published in 1947, post-war American society represented a fading ideal for many women. After the war, the government tried to urge women back to their domestic duties. This return to domesticity had implications for women of all classes and races. Most of Ann Petry's novels are devoted to the experiences of African Americans, especially working-class women that leave their own kitchens in order to serve in those of white families (Taylor 249). Yet in Petry's "The Bones of Louella Brown," one finds women characters (Louella Brown, the black laundress, and Mrs. Peabody, the white aristocrat) that do not entirely reinforce the practices of the patriarchy. To detect the women's resistance and challenge to and visions within a patriarchal society, one has to look for the fissures and silences that permeate the narrative.

Analysis of textual silences and gaps becomes a fascinating adventure into the unmasking of composite oppression by various forces upon women, as well as the unveiling of "forbidden sexual feelings or equally forbidden anger and protest" (Showalter 88). Virginia Woolf's ideas in *A Room of One's Own* of "a witch being dunked and of a woman possessed by devils" (48) and Alice Walker's "Crazy Saints of black culture" (232) emerge from the reinterpretation of women silenced by the mainstream patriarchal discourse. In short, feminist critics like Woolf, Walker, and others see their mission as rescuing the hidden voices from a patriarchal literary history and reinstating the memory of the silenced women and their stories. Ann Petry's short story "The Bones of Louella Brown" provides a fertile text for exploration of this kind because Louella Brown, the dead and buried black laundress, simply refuses to be forgotten. Death, which is the ultimate silencer, cannot stop her presence from continuing to be felt, her voice from being heard, and her name from being repeatedly uttered.

Naming is a fundamental act of presence. To have a name, and thus to be able to name things from a subject position, is the key gesture against oppression and silencing. In *The Pedagogy of the Oppressed* (1970), Paulo Freire describes how he engages illiterate Brazilian peasants in dialogical educational praxis to help them emerge from their "culture of silence." Having won back "the right to say his or her own word, to name the world" (15), these individuals learned to think critically, and to gain political consciousness. Freire states that "[b]y making it possible for people to enter the historical process as responsible subjects, *conscientizacao* enrolls them in the search for self-affirmation and thus avoids fanaticism" (18)" This process of *conscientizacao* (conscientization) is analogous to the feminist idea of consciousness-raising.

An important part of the process of coming to consciousness is the development of a sense of group identity and solidarity. Feminist theologians Pauli Murray and Letty Russell have made specific comments on individual and group identity within the process of "conscientization." According to Murray, both the individual and the group "deal with the question of identity, the retrieval of lost history, the destruction of self-deprecation, and liberating self-affirmation" (406). According to Russell, "the search for a usable past" is an essential part of the liberation process, for "an unexamined history [that] operates as fate" (85). The way unexamined history silences and wipes out female talents, or even identity, is stressed again and again in the works of feminists writers such as Woolf and Walker. According to Russell, a major objective of feminist criticism is to "enable women—as readers and as writers—to break their culture of silence, to locate within a political spectrum, and to envisage and work toward alternatives" (85). Although women from different groups may suffer various kinds of oppression, Russell maintains that an awareness of gender inequalities generates a basic solidarity among members of the same sex and helps in the devising of transgressive strategies.

How does "The Bones of Louella Brown," a story of mistaken identity published in the 1940s, figure in the context of feminist criticism? And how do we view the creative venture undertaken by Petry to raise a new level of feminine consciousness among individuals and groups of women? In an interview with *Artspectrum* (Windham Regional Arts Council) in the early 1950s, by way of response to whether she considered herself a feminist, Petry answered:

I don't like labels like that. I'm just an individual who has a special way of looking at the world. But I'm an ally of feminists, there's absolutely no question about that. (in Ervin 100)

Petry's unquestionable sympathy for feminists that work to create alternatives to the patriarchal repression of women—even if this occurs through silences and gaps in female writing—is present in "The Bones of Louella Brown." Petry's unquestionable sympathy for feminists spills over into the fiction, as she, like feminists, to borrow from Josephine Donovan, "take[s] a stand . . . on the 'poetics of domestic values'—on ethics, human ties, and in the end human change" (ix).

In content, "The Bones of Louella Brown" is about a black laundress, long-since dead and buried, who steals the limelight in a major event in Boston. The opening of "that marble masterpiece, Bedford Abbey" (170), and the removal of all the Bedford graves from the Yew Tree Cemetery to the abbey itself were to make the headlines because of the wealth and status this family enjoyed. Louella's bones, which had been buried in the respectable, white cemetery, were shown to be identical to those of the most noble among the Bedfords, the Countess of Castro. The prestigious undertakers Whiffle and Peabody attempt in vain to uphold traditional patriarchal and racist values by erasing the black woman's name—that is, the supposedly less-than-ideal woman—as well as silencing any talk about the bones of the black and white woman being indistinguishable. At the end of the story, Louella Brown gains her place alongside the Countess in Bedford Abbey, sharing the same tomb, under the same marble slab that bears the name of both women. Silenced by her race, class, social status, and finally by death itself, Louella nonetheless emerges at the end of the story triumphantly. The gaps in her story allow readers to fill them in with questions about the double standards for the ideal woman via the servitude, miscegenation, and domesticity surrounding the working-class black woman. In ideology, Louella is supposedly less than the ideal image, yet her bones are identified to be identical to the ideal white woman. The very silence on such revelation stirs discussion.

In *Marxism and Form* (1971), Frederic Jameson cites Paul Ricoeur's distinction between

Negative and positive hermeneutics, between the hermeneutics of suspicion and the hermeneutics of a *restoration of some original, forgotten meaning*, between hermeneutic as demystification, as the *destruction of illusions*, and a hermeneutic which offers renewed access to some essential source of life. (119, emphasis mine)

In other words, "a work is established against an ideology as much as it is from an ideology" (Macherey 113). In "The Bones of Louella Brown," reflected in various narrative arrangements, there are strategies that challenge patriarchal, racist, and class values on the one hand and that rediscover an alternative feminine language on the other. When the reporter from *Boston Record* features a picture of the magnificent Bedford Abbey on its front page, the caption shakes the governing power structure to its foundations: "the white countess or the black laundress?" (170). In response to reporter Clarence Ludastone's authoritative comments on the identity of the bones, the newspaper "reproduces" the birth certificate of the head embalmer in order to satirize the myth of his seniority:

This reporter has questioned many of Boston's oldest residents but he has, as yet, been unable to locate anyone who remembers a time when Whiffle and Peabody employed a two-year-old child as embalmer. . . . (175)

The birth certificate, a token of patriarchal authority on identity, is used here to deconstruct and demystify the very authority men in the past have relied on for authentication.

In Boston society in the 1940s, which is strictly patriarchal, the newspaper the *Boston Record*, which is dominated by a cigar-smoking male, is turned into a deconstructive tool and against its very power of authority. At times, the voice of the establishment at the *Boston Recorder* takes the narrator's position and unfolds the triumph of Louella at every step. Together, the voices function to expose the emptiness of the ideological practices.

The Governor's statement ["Nobody could tell which be the black laundress and which the white countess from looking at their bones"] went around the world. . . . Sermons were preached about the Governor's statement, editorials were written about it, and Congressmen made long-winded speeches over the radio. The Mississippi legislative threatened to declare war on the sovereign State of Massachusetts because Governor's Bedford's remarks were an unforgivable insult to believers in white supremacy. (176–77)

When filling in the gaps—that is, what does not get said—the Governor, preachers, newspaper editors, and congressmen, who are all males in the 1940s, are having difficulty with the fact that "Nobody" could distinguish the bones of the black and white woman. Their ambiguity raises other questions, for instance: Could anybody distinguish the bones of black and white men? If not bones, then what else in cultural or patriarchal ideology and practices might not hold true?

In addition to undermining the patriarchy, "The Bones of Louella Brown" opens up a space for the liberation of feminine desires. At the source of the whole problem concerning Louella, there is old Mrs. Peabody, mother of the undertaker Peabody. Very fond of Louella, Mrs. Peabody had insisted that Louella be buried in the Yew Tree Cemetery, "the final home of Boston's wealthiest and most aristocratic families" (166). Mrs. Peabody's motives are not stated. But when read against the 1940s and the strong cultural push for the ideal woman (which was considered white) to remain in the home, one is forced to fill in the gaps. Is there a feminine desire to break down the Peabodys's or white male's "careful discriminatory practices" (166) and to give voice to women on the question of ideal image, liberty, and the pursuit of happiness? Mrs. Peabody's request suggests a new level of feminine consciousness during her time among some individuals, for her decision to treat her laundress as her equal challenges the issues of value and propriety in the public and political realms.

"The Bones of Louella Brown" contains not a single word spoken by a living or dead female character. Nevertheless, feminine desires find expression through the deconstruction of patriarchal language. The alternative textual space of the feminine language can be read as a manifestation of the positive mode of hermeneutics or as stated by Jameson in *The Political Unconscious* as a "political 'allegory of desire'" (79). The power of feminine desire is expressed not only actively in the wishes of the female characters, but also passively in the communications of desire—that is, by extension of things in reality. For instance, although death has silenced the Countess of Castro and despite the superficial differences of race and class, articulated through her remains is solidarity with other women:

[The] countess and Louella Brown had resembled each other in many ways. They both had thick glossy black hair. Neither woman had any children. They had both died in 1902, when in their early seventies, and been buried in Yew Tree Cemetery within two weeks of each other. (167)

This silent intrusion presents itself as "an ironic subtext or a formal design that contradicts the content" of patriarchal ideology (Donovan xvii).

After months of psychological torture, haunted by Louella's laughter, Peabody announces

Louella Brown was a neatly built little *woman*, a fine *woman*, full of laughter. I remember her well. She was a *gentlewoman*. Her bones will do no injury to the Governor's damned funeral chapel. (178, emphasis mine)

It is interesting to note that the triumph of Louella Brown, Mrs. Peabody, and Elizabeth Peabody does not come from recognition of Louella's race, but as a fine specimen of the female gender. It seems that what the story proposes is the creation of a common front for all women for solidarity, despite their class and race. Ann Petry claimed herself to be an ally to feminists. Her stance can be seen in her more-inclusive approach toward the appropriation of voice and method to name things according to female needs.

WORKS CITED

Donovan, Josephine, ed. *Feminist Literary Criticism: Explorations in Theory.* Lexington, KY: University Press of Kentucky, 1989.

Ervin, Hazel Arnett. *Ann Petry: A Bio-Bibliography.* New York: G. K. Hall, 1993.

Freire, Paulo. *The Pedagogy of the Oppressed.* Trans. Myra Bergman Ramos. London: Penguin, 1970.

Jameson, Fredric. *Marxism and Form: Twentieth-Century Dialectical Theories of Literature.* Princeton, NJ: Princeton University Press, 1971.

———. *The Political Unconscious: Narrative as a Socially Symbolic Act.* Ithaca, NY: Cornell University Press, 1981.

Macherey, Pierre. *A Theory of Literary Production.* Trans. Geoffrey Wall. London: Routledge and Kegan Paul, 1978.

Murray, Pauli. "Black Theology and Feminist Theology: A Comparative View." *Black Theology: A Documentary History, 1966–1979.* Ed. Gayraud S. Wilmore and James H. Cone. Mary Knoll, NY: Orbis, 1979.

Petry, Ann. "The Bones of Louella Brown." *Miss Muriel and Other Stories.* 1971. Boston: Beacon Press, 1989. 163–80.

Russell, Letty M. *Human Liberation in a Feminist Perspective: A Theology.* Philadelphia: Westminster, 1974.

Showalter, Elaine. *Hystories: Hysterical Epidemics and Modern Culture.* London: Picador, 1997.

Taylor, Ula. "The Historical Evolution of Black Feminist Theory and Praxis." *Journal of Black Studies* 29.2 (November 1998): 234–53.

Walker, Alice. *In Search of Our Mothers' Gardens: Womanist Prose.* San Diego: Harcourt Brace Jovanovich, 1979.

Woolf, Virginia. *A Room of One's Own.* 1929. London: Granada, 1977.

Taking the Cake: Ann Petry's "Has Anybody Seen Miss Dora Dean?"

Barbara Lewis

The name of Dora Dean, an African American beauty known for her skill as a cakewalk performer, is recurrent in an Ann Petry tale from the Wheeling, New York, cycle. When Dora Dean emerged as a star in the 1890s, Petry's family had owned, for several generations, a pharmacy in a small Connecticut town straight out of Rockwell country that is similar to the fictional setting of Wheeling. More than likely, that pharmacy is the basis for the drugstore that provides the setting for the vivid yet haunting childhood memory that interrupted the pattern of daily composure in "Has Anybody Seen Miss Dora Dean?" (1958). The narrator grew up in "the building that housed my father's drugstore. . . . Whether I sat inside the store or outside it, I had a long sweeping view of the church, the church green, and the street. The street was as carefully composed as a painting: tall elm trees, white fences, Federal houses" (91–92). Petry's background as the daughter and heir of propertied African Americans provided an unusual niche from which to observe and comment upon the ramifications and interruptions of race in a New England setting.

Depending on the weather, when the narrator was a girl, she would perch either on a bench or on a wooden outdoor step, and from there, she would watch and listen to the goings-on in the family and in the store as though she were attending the theater. As an adult, Petry became involved with the American Negro Theatre (popularly known by the acronym ANT). While living in Harlem early in the 1940s, Petry acted in the ANT's inaugural production, *On Striver's Row*, which incidentally addresses the subject of class striving. Drama can, and sometimes does, bring voice and visibility to an emergent alternative vision. In the case of the ANT, the burgeoning crossroads of Harlem spawned a new phalanx of cultural talents who went on to imprint their faces and perspectives on the American landscape. The ANT, the era's most important Harlem theater, nurtured the careers of Harry Belafonte, Alice Childress, Ossie Davis, Ruby Dee, and Sidney Poitier. Petry was in the best of company, and her theatrical perspectives and acuity are apparent in her focus on the cakewalk, a vital but overlooked aspect of African American performance history. As a further testament to her dramatic leanings, in the story Petry describes, with great awareness of costuming and set, a scene in which the narrator imagines, in the form of a drama, the final minutes in the life of John Forbes, who belonged to her parents' social circle:

The play takes place on the wrong side of the railroad tracks, where the land is all cinders, in a section where voluptuous, big-hipped foreign women go barefooted, wrap their heads and shoulders in brilliant red and green shawls, and carry bundles on their heads—that is, those who work. Those who do not work wear hats with so many feathers on them they look as if they had whole turkeys on their heads. The houses in this area are built entirely of packing cases and orange crates. There is the sound of a train in the distance, and a thin, carefully dressed black man, in a neat black suit and polished shoes, walks swiftly onstage and up the slight incline toward the railroad tracks—no path there, no road. It is a winter's night and cold. This is Forbes and he is not wearing an overcoat. The train whistles, and Forbes walks up the embankment and lies down across the tracks. The train comes roaring into sight and it slices him in two—quickly, neatly. And the curtain comes down as a telephone rings in a drugstore miles away. (102)

The narrator had never met John Forbes, husband of Sarah Forbes, a childhood friend of her mother's. Before she was born, he had stopped coming to Wheeling in the summers and had remained instead in Bridgeport, Connecticut, year-round. His widow, Sarah, however, the narrator knew well and continued to know her as an adult, taking pleasure in her yearly visits when Sarah could be engaging and delightful company. Over time, however, and through protracted disappointment, Sarah's voice had become, on occasion, disagreeable, and her body had fattened fore and aft, taking on the pouter-pigeon stance associated with the exaggerated s-shaped body position of the cakewalk that accentuated the reproductive portions of the body. George Walker, the dandy half of the cakewalking blackface-comedy team of Williams and Walker, was famous for "throwing his chest and buttocks out in opposite directions, until he resembled a pouter pigeon more than human being" (Emery 212). It was as though Sarah's posture, in later years, had settled into the alignment of her finest hour.

The narrator was nine years old when, one dreary, wet afternoon, Sarah called with a hush of news about Forbes. In later years, the narrator heard so many conflicting stories about him from both parents that he became mysterious as well as legendary. The narrator's father faulted Forbes for his utter passivity, his rather feminine docility. The narrator's mother considered his behavior exemplary, describing him as "a perfect gentleman" (101). Somewhere in between lay the truth. Even after Forbes was no longer living, the truth of his existence remained elusive. Why did he deliberately surrender his life to those railroad tracks? Why was this man, who was always so careful and even pristine in his habits, visiting the seedy side of town, the haunt of immigrant prostitutes?

On the day of his passing, as soon as the narrator's mother heard the peal of the telephone, she knew this was no ordinary call. She was right. It was a call of death—violent, public, and self-inflicted. The hand of the past can reach quite far into the future. Thirty-three years later, there was another insistent ring from a telephone. Like her mother, the narrator intuited this was a call that could not be refused. It had to be answered promptly. Dora Dean, who was featured with her husband Charles Johnson in a pioneering 1890s musical called *The Creole Show,* showcasing a chorus line of African American female pulchritude, figures indirectly in both calls. Dean had been an object of fascination for John Forbes, whose passing was the subject of the first call. In the second call, with great urgency, John's son Peter was summoning the narrator to his mother's sickbed. As a young mother, Sarah Forbes had resembled Dora Dean. In their prime, John and Sarah Forbes had been the Johnson and Dean of their particular small-town milieu.

The narrator informs us that Peter's name has been changed, and so have the names of all the others in the short story. To the reader, this disclosure implies the existence of a significant strand of truth in this fiction. Our curiosity is piqued. We begin to feel that we are nosing inside family closets and leafing through faded photograph albums. Indeed, the narrator describes for us a photograph of an unmarried Sarah Trumbull in the flush of youth. With a sensitivity to characterization associated with an understanding of the dramatic, her description seems to invest Sarah with a living quality and ends with an emphasis on the role of costume and what it can accomplish or signify:

I have a full-length photograph of her taken before she was married. She might well have been one of those beautiful girls in "The Creole Show." In the photograph, she has a young, innocent face—lovely eyes, and a pointed chin, and a very pretty mouth with a quirk at the corner that suggests a sense of humor. Her hair is slightly frizzy, and it is worn in a high, puffed-out pompadour, which serves as a frame for the small, exquisite face. She is wearing a shirtwaist with big, stiff sleeves, and a tight choker of lace around her throat. This costume makes her waist look tiny and her neck long and graceful. (98)

Johnson and Dean, the celebrities whose careers and aspirations impacted so forcefully John and Sarah Forbes, were noted for the cakewalk, a contest dance so named because those judged to be its most accomplished practitioners were awarded a cake. The Petry story bears the same name as a ragtime song that the comic actor Bert Williams wrote and sang with his partner, the aforementioned dandy, George Walker. "Has Anybody Seen Miss Dora Dean?" was popular at the turn of the last century when Dean, a legendary African American beauty who was also a cultural icon, was enjoying national and international renown as a cakewalk performer, half of the Kentucky-born team of Johnson and Dean. When Williams and Walker, champion cakewalkers themselves, arrived in New York in 1896, they were singing that song. It was their calling card, and it served notice that a new aesthetic was afoot. Dora Dean represented a departure: the image of the black woman as darling, no longer the drudge.

The precolon title of this paper, "Taking the Cake," has triple resonance. Certainly, it refers to the winning couple in a cakewalk competition getting a tasty treat for their efforts. Dessert symbolizes a new stage of achievement for African Americans. Prior to Emancipation, savoring delicacies, whether gustatory or material, was a luxury afforded very few, and regulated, more often than not, by white hands. Having access to cake on their own terms and because of their own efforts was an emblem of liberation, a life that could be filled with confection. The title also refers to the promise of a better tomorrow for African Americans, yanked back by the federal sanctioning of segregation, the public and private separation of black and white on the nation's railroads and elsewhere as a result of the ruling of *Plessy v. Ferguson* (1896). In addition, the title signifies the African American resilience and predisposition to create cultural batter from the social and economic ingredients they encounter.

In the face of the affront to their citizenship that public banishment represented, they stirred up resistance in public display, with their bodies and their influence culturally very visible in a multiplicity of venues: in social gatherings of the highest order, in advertising, in film, and in international expositions. In the 1890s, and into the beginning of the twentieth century, everyone was wild about the cakewalk. The moneyed set led the pack. William K. Vanderbilt, a scion of one of America's wealthiest families, signed up for cakewalk lessons and even displayed "his newly acquired talents at an exhibition" (Baldwin 210). An 1893 coffee advertisement depicted a cakewalking couple with "the woman smiling coyly as her partner struts proudly by" (Baldwin 205). This was one of countless commercial images of the cakewalk, many of them outrageously exaggerated or minstrelized, that appeared on postcards, sheet music, product trade cards (a precursor of today's baseball cards), board games, and in Currier and Ives prints for home decoration. Several short 1-minute films featuring the cakewalk came out in 1903, and the first filming of *Uncle Tom's Cabin*, a 10-minute version that Edwin Porter directed for Thomas Edison, was released the same year with a long segment focused on slaves dancing the cakewalk. John Philip Sousa, the legendary bandleader, also invested in the cakewalk phenomenon. He "featured cakewalk syncopation in his 1900 performance at the Paris Exposition and the 1904 St. Louis World's Fair" (Baldwin 216).

Clearly, the nation was enthralled with the cakewalk. Indeed "[b]y the mid-1890s Madison Square Garden was holding national cakewalk championships for competing hometown couples from around the country" (Sundquist 288). Though it seemingly unleashed new rhythms, the cakewalk was actually an old dance performed during plantation days that had renewed itself at different stages of its long history. Its roots reached back to Africa, where it celebrated harvests, the yield of the season. In the New World, it served as a repository of the past that also accommodated the present. On the minstrel stage, the cakewalk served a finale or culmination. Once slavery ended, the newly emancipated African Americans seized upon the cakewalk as dance of celebration and continuance, as something that was theirs and had been theirs during the different phases of their existence in this country, something they could control and shape to their purposes. The cakewalk became a mating dance performed by couples, a dance of community and belonging, a dance of reward. The deeper meaning of the cakewalk, its posturing toward new attitudes and authenticity, its carnivalesque nose thumbing at oppressive hierarchies, was ignored or suppressed by the dominant or intervening society that interpreted the dance as mere entertainment, a fad to be caricatured and consumed. Even if African Americans were ultimately prevented from fully empowering themselves in the performative, status-changing transaction of the cakewalk, they still held fast to some prizes, some of the gains they earned through their collective cultural exertion.

Johnson and Dean, who were managed by the exclusive William Morris agency, exuded status in their performances. They were also associated with the avant-garde. In the early days, their act included fancy strobe lighting that gave the impression their gestures and movements were being captured on film, a brand-new medium at the time. As further evidence of their position out front of the throng, from 1915 to 1930, Johnson and Dean appeared in six films, two of which were named *Bouncing Babes* and *Georgia Rose*. Their clothes were expensive, and they danced with dignity and command. Their savoir faire, increased by their European tours, was undoubtedly a crucial part of their appeal to the African American community that lionized them as role models. Because of the possibilities for identification they provided as performers, the gap between the races was perceived as being a little less wide, not quite so impassable. If Johnson and Dean could make inroads into privilege, the thinking went, so could some of the other members of the group they represented. Johnson and Dean were ambassadors of civility: "They were so universally admired that the *Dramatic Mirror* lowered its ban against printing Negro photographs that were not paid advertisements and ran their picture over the heading 'Popular Colored Artists'" (Charters 35).

It didn't hurt that the cakewalk was a favorite social pastime in aristocratic circles, with some of the more prominent members of the upper classes inviting well-known minstrel performers to give them authentic cakewalk lessons. Johnson and Dean, along with Williams and Walker, were trendsetters who moved in and out of the most luxurious suites and living rooms in America and Europe, not to mention a palace or two, Buckingham being high on the list. Their talent was of such dimension that they received unprecedented opportunities. Johnson and Dean personified dignity and brought distinction to their performance of the cakewalk. They were considered royalty, the king and queen of cakewalk:

Their act was marked by the elegance of their costuming and of their bearing. Dora Dean was the first black entertainer to wear thousand-dollar costumes. As a dancing duo, they were the first successful blacks in ballroom dancing, and certainly the most elegant and sophisticated. . . . They toured Europe and in fact spent more time there than in the United States in the early 1900s. (Haskins 30)

In the Petry short story, the mysterious and ultimately tragic John Forbes is so enamored of the lovely Miss Dean that he whistles the ragtime tune that pays tribute to her beauty and her suitability as a wife. He repeats the tune in his leisure moments as he bicycles along quiet roads in the fictional summer resort of Wheeling, New York. Late in life, when he is 40, he marries a Dora Dean look-alike named Sarah Trumbull, who is 20 years his junior. John, a disciplined and fastidious man, had met Sarah in 1900 when both attended a dance at a social in New Haven. Sarah, a minister's daughter, was wearing a white muslin dress. She was also playing ragtime on the piano, a pastime that the members of her father's church never approved. Ragtime was associated with bawdy houses. But Sarah found immediate favor in John's eyes.

They danced the cakewalk together that evening—and outlasted everyone else to claim the cake as their prize. The cakewalk was the first dance craze of the twentieth century, and it registered the temperature of the times. There was a great desire, especially on the part of African Americans, for democratic inclusion. The world had changed. A major war that had divided and scarred as well as liberated the nation had been fought, leaving behind winners as well as losers. People wanted to forget the past. They wanted to lose themselves in the moment. The old century had expired. A new one was being born, and the dancers, as acolytes of possibility, were renewing themselves in celebration. Petry describes the dance that was unleashing pandemonium everywhere in 1900:

About fourteen couples took part, and they walked in time to music—not in a circle but in a square, with the men on the inside. The participants were always beautifully dressed, and they walked with grace and style. It was a strutting kind of walk. The test of their skill lay in the way they pivoted when they turned the corners. The judges stopped the music at intervals and eliminated possibly three couples at a time. The most graceful couple was awarded a beautifully decorated cake, so that they had literally walked to win a cake. (99)

The cakewalk was a dance of community in which multiple partners participated. Those who performed the dance did so in public gatherings and were always careful to present themselves with great panache. While performing the dance, they also affected a posture of pride. The winners were singled out for their ability to dance with astonishing skill.

More than a dance, the cakewalk symbolized license and possibility. It also symbolized the tradition of courtship and marriage for many within the African American community. During slavery, African Americans had not been accorded the privilege of inviolable unions. Their marriages were not considered binding or sacred. They could be broken at any moment by any outside authority. After Emancipation, many African Americans wanted to live the solid promise of freedom and believed it essential to generate authority and establish unbreakable lineage within their own institutions. They saw marriage as the institution that would allow them to create a line of continuance and establish themselves as owners of property rather than property to be owned.

The cakewalk replicated the marriage ceremony in at least four ways: the presence of witnesses, an emphasis on dress, a performative utterance that altered the status of one couple relative to the group, and the symbolic nature of the cake. Like a marriage, the cakewalk attracted observers and well-wishers and perhaps some naysayers, many of them arriving as couples. Marriage connoted an orderly society focused on the future and committed to safeguarding and acquiring property and transmitting it from one generation to the next. Like the cakewalk, the marriage ceremony required a certain self-presentation that emphasized proper attire and behavior.

John Forbes was an elegant man, and he had manners to match. He was also skilled and performed a number of duties for the Wingates, the family that employed him: "[A]fter Mr. Wingate's death, he ran the house for Mrs. Wingate. He could cook, he could sew, he could act as coachman if necessary; he did all the buying and all the hiring" (95). Mrs. Wingate, who owned a summer home in Wheeling near the Long Island Sound as well as a winter home in Bridgeport, belonged to the set of whites drawn to the cakewalk. The refined and aristocratic classes were among the first to popularize the dance and the music with which it was associated, ragtime. Many of the songs that were sung to the syncopated ragtime beat were called coon songs and were full of demeaning lyrics that harkened back to slavery. The cakewalk reminded the previous master class of plantation days.

Ragtime, the music to which people danced the cakewalk, had an irregular or syncopated beat, "traceable to African styles" (Baldwin 209). In ragtime, a polyrhythmic form, the intervals between notes became portals for the insertion of additional sound. In this sense, ragtime, which for a time was only acceptable in bordellos, was disruptive, a departure from the status quo. It made space for a new expressiveness within the musical structures of the past, and also "provided the necessary bridge to the popular performance style that came to be called 'jazz' . . . America's only truly endemic musical form" (Dormon 467). Ragtime and cakewalk, "the first African American dance to gain popularity both as a stage form and a ballroom dance" (Dixon-Gottschild 114), exerted an influence in Europe as well, where it was again championed first by the highest ranks in society.

In the first decade of the twentieth century, just when it seemed that the appetite for the cakewalk was about to reach its peak, the rage for it grew even stronger in America and abroad when the King of England, Edward VII, requested lessons for the royal family in 1903. The occasion was the ninth birthday of the king's favorite grandson, later the Duke of Windsor (Smith 71). In short order, the cakewalk was also the rage in Germany, where images of African Americans dancing the cakewalk were featured on sheet music. In France, *Le Rire*, a Parisian periodical, dedicated "the cover of its 1903 special edition to the phenomenon" (Archer-Straw 44). "The old plantation walk-around reached the immortality of literature in 1905 when a play by Jose Jockson Veyan, *El Cake Walk*, was published in Madrid" (Blesh 100). In 1908, Claude Debussy, the French composer, wrote "Golliwog's Cake Walk," which remained popular as a piano exercise for much of the first half of the century; the golliwog was a "black doll-like creature popular in Europe" (Baldwin 210) up through the last quarter of the twentieth century, when it lost favor because of political correctness. Interest in and familiarity with the cakewalk spread wide and persisted much longer than the dance craze.

The cakewalk held onto its heyday until World War I, and was revisited from time to time in popular culture. During the Harlem Renaissance, it was transformed into the Charleston, a dance that obliterated social barriers and had whites traveling uptown to Harlem:

Downtown specialists who have wearied of the tricks of Broadway come northward to this new center of pleasure. In some of the fifteen cabarets black and white eat together, dance together in the rich abandon of the race which evolved that first jazz classic, the Memphis Blues; which refined the cakewalk into the fantastic fling of the "Charleston." (Mary Green in Lemke 84)

The cakewalk also influenced later national and international dances such as the turkey trot and the tango (Sundquist 290). In 1943, the cakewalk was featured in the film *Stormy Weather*. In the 1940s and 1950s, the cakewalk influenced Alvin Ailey's classic *Revelations* and was featured in Katherine Dunham's *Tropical Revue*. At the end of the twentieth century, Peter Feibleman's play *Cakewalk* (1996), about the tense and libelous interactions between Mary McCarthy and Lillian Hellman, was produced. In the twenty-first century, the Cakewalk Web site is available for those musicians and songwriters who want to mix and record their own materials. The history of the cakewalk may no longer be well-known, but its name has been retained as a synonym for diversion or an easy feat, whether or not the use is ironic.

In its more evolved forms on stage and off, the cakewalk came to signify, in the passage from the nineteenth into the twentieth century, a performance of collectivity and continuance within the African American community. Its history of being understood and portrayed one way by the observing community and quite differently by the originating community was conducive to the dance being associated, for some, with its history in the plantation era. It was also interpreted as the occasion for lascivious fraternizing, as manifested by this 1899 editorial in the *Musical Courier*: "Society has decreed that ragtime and cakewalking are the thing, and one reads with amazement and disgust of historical and aristocratic names joining in this sex dance, for the Cakewalk is nothing but an African *danse du ventre*, a milder edition of African orgies" (in Baldwin 210). Still others saw the cakewalk as an ambassador of change and also as a demonstration of worth. At the juncture between the centuries, when the African American community was emerging out of bondage, the cakewalk evolved into a public wedding ceremony, a ritual of legitimation and elevation.

In studies of the performative, the marriage ceremony is classic. The linguist J. L. Austin argues that the pronouncement is key in the change of status fundamental to performativity. In the cakewalk, the bodies give consent, and represent the authority. All the elements are present: the couple, the costume, and the cake. The couple that took the cake was made into one flesh, and the community of witnesses was merged into solidarity. The plurality of couples participating in the communal dance represented a quorum of the society. A people denied the legitimacy of marriage during slavery and burdened by the taboo against love between blacks on the traditional stage cleared a way through no way and forged a link between the popular and the sacred in dance. They reached back into their history as slaves and extracted the value of that collective experience to move forward into an uncharted future. Their desire, like their labor, was finally theirs to direct, and they celebrated this new reality by performing a ritual of mass elevation. The cakewalk was clearly an expression of class ascendance: "Its copper-hued belles in velvet ballet skirts or long gowns and great ostrich-plumed hats, and its silk hatted dusky gentlemen in tails, were leaders of the Darktown four hundred, materialized in the flesh from the pages of the songs" (Blesh 96).

For most whites, however, the cakewalk had no such connotations, or if it did, those aspirations were anathema. It was perceived simply as a dance that allowed the upper classes to give rein to their libido. They became so enamored of it that they felt they owned it. "[B]y 1898 white popular culture had . . . so infiltrated itself into the production of ragtime music, that white society was convinced that the dance was now its rightful province" (Baldwin 210). As a performance genre, the cakewalk had been tempered in the fires of minstrelsy, also fully under white control. The cakewalk was subsumed under the umbrella of minstrelsy, symbolized by Jim Crow, universally adopted as the mascot of segregation. The cakewalk was often much maligned and lampooned in print and in other forms of public reproduction that called attention to the ridiculous airs of African Americans who dared to dress up in finery and push their bodies into such exaggerated positions. The cakewalk was the locus on which a cultural struggle was waged:

Plans to seize control of the cakewalk from blacks hit some snags. Black performers remained and dancers *really* in demand, and still had to be imported into white shows. And while racist lyrics abounded, it was black composed *tunes* that were whistled and danced all over America. . . . Blacks continued to make America aware of the power and attractiveness of their cultural forms, despite white attempts to make it seem that they were not really black art forms at all . . . the burden of proving black racial inferiority was returned to white caricaturists, who had to make it seem as if black culture had never existed at all. They attacked the very strengths of the race which threatened to disprove their stereotypes. Cakewalkers were made to appear ludicrous. Their dance, which satirized white manners, was presented as a ridiculous and unsuccessful attempt to emulate white culture. Their dress was depicted as tastelessly gaudy; their postures distorted. Instead of projecting grace, caricatured cakewalkers projected awkwardness. This image was then repeated and repeated and repeated until it was reinforced in the minds of all those people who bought postcards, sheet music, stereo cards and toys. Finally, this image supplanted the true one in American popular culture. (Baldwin 216)

The cakewalk spanned the divide between the plantation and the city. It represented the point of articulation from the end of bondage to the beginning of an integral community engendered by the legitimized family brought into being by these mass nuptials. Dora Dean and Charles Johnson, as symbolic black bride and groom, signified this progression. In a highly public way, the cakewalk made visible the values and attitudes of an African American generation of marriageable age at the beginning of a new century. They were starting fresh, they were legitimizing themselves, they were honoring their history. It must be repeated here that the cakewalk had its origins in Africa, was continued and mutated during slavery, and was featured in the antebellum and postbellum eras on the minstrel stage, where is was sometimes referred to by the alliterative term "peregrinating for the pastry" (Charters 35). When minstrelsy lost favor to the new genres, giving way to vaudeville and film, the cakewalk survived to serve a new purpose. That new purpose was to dance into being another world, a different world, out of the movement of their flesh clothed in finery.

For the generation that was young and potent when the twentieth century was in its infancy, Dora Dean was seen as the ultimate glamour symbol. She was the ideal, the perfect wife. Petry's story is about a courtship and a marriage that went bad, about hopes that were dashed, about the dreams and expectations of a time that were not fully realized. John and Sarah, who wed in 1901, did not have a successful union, in the traditional sense. Only a few weeks after their marriage, Mrs. Wingate, his employer, demanded that John return to her service full-time, including the stipulation that he live in her house, not with his wife. John Forbes and Mrs. Wingate entered into a contract that competed with and altered the marriage contract that John had made with Sarah.

Forbes was dutiful in the discharge of his duties toward the white family for whom he had worked his whole life. Through long and patient service to the Wingates, he was ultimately able to improve his station and that of his family. His first responsibility was to Mr. Wingate, and after that gentleman died, he devoted all his energy to Mrs. Wingate. Despite being a vain woman, she had begun to put on girth, becoming so corpulent that she had to be lifted in and out of carriages and then cars. Petry describes Mrs. Wingate as becoming more and more of a burden: "Mrs. Wingate grew fatter and fatter, until, finally, getting her in and out of carriages, and then, during a later period, in and out of cars—even cars that were specially built—was impossible unless Forbes was on hand" (97). Mrs. Wingate interposed her pink flesh into the union between John and Sarah Forbes, and became a colossal weight to carry.

Mrs. Wingate symbolizes the subservient past from which John Forbes attempted to escape, without total success. She is opposed to, yet paired with, Sarah. They are connected to the same man, who frustrates each of them in his way, probably because he doesn't fully belong to either one. In compensation, perhaps, each of the women grows fat, eating too much metaphoric cake, trying to feed their hungers, some of which, in the case of Mrs. Wingate, may have been sexual. In the Petry tale, it is never made clear whether or not Forbes is sexually involved with Mrs. Wingate, but her utter dependence on him, her comment that he is everything to her suggests that her need of him is too strong to ever be appeased. The narrator's mother recalls that Mrs. Wingate referred to Forbes as "her mind, her heart, her hands" (96). He was everything to her, and she prevents the marriage between Sarah and John from following its traditional course of cohabitation. The blonde Mrs. Wingate increases Forbes's pay and promises him an inheritance so that he will agree to live with her rather than with his wife, thus interrupting their cakewalk and taking away the prize of conjugal companionship. Her dependence on Forbes asserts precedence over Sarah's claim to her husband. As the narrator's mother exclaims, "Sarah used to call Forbes by his first name, John, when he was courting her and when they were first married. After he went back to live at Mrs. Wingate's, she called him Forbes. All the rest of his life, she called him by his last name, just as though she was talking to Mrs. Wingate's butler" (103).

From Sarah Forbes, the narrator receives a legacy that by rights should have gone to Peter Forbes and his heirs. But Peter has inherited the dissolute ways of his father, and Sarah chooses to express her disapproval of the males in her immediate family, including her grandsons, by leaving an honored possession to the daughter of a childhood friend. The gift manifests a bond forged on the anvil of memory. Sarah wants to be remembered, and she fears that her male progeny will be too distracted by female flesh to fulfill that responsibility. The narrator, who is now more than 40 years old, has not forgotten John Forbes. She may never have met him, but his suicide scarred her childhood, left an imprint on it that, over the years, has proved indelible. That scar or wound, the deep gash in her mind, scarred the narrator's memory. Because of it, she came to a greater understanding of the depth of racial suffering that contrasted, starkly, with the halcyon setting of her small-town world. The enigma of his voluntary death—in which he is literally broken apart—urged her toward contemplation and creative wondering, expressed in the dramatic vignette that she summoned up in her mind in order to witness and make sense of his dismemberment.

Forbes was prevented from sustaining his marriage in conventional terms. He was deprived of his better half, and symbolically as well as actually, he was cut in two by a train—"easily one of the most charged symbols of racial politics in American culture" (Sundquist 439). He was rendered a transient, someone who did not have a true home, someone caught betwixt and between, someone lost and left wandering. He was separated from his wife and from his community by the demands that Mrs. Wingate imposed. In return for his coerced and extra service, Mrs. Wingate had left him $35,000, which he used to buy six tenement buildings in Bridgeport during the Harlem Renaissance. His body was severed down the middle, but his inheritance, the lifelong value of his labor, was intact. Sarah was able to hold on to those houses through the Depression, after which time she sold them at a profit. Being able to make those properties pay through hard times was a testament of her tenacity and dogged management style. Sarah "said that the bank that held the mortgages and notes had congratulated her; they told her that no real estate operator in Bridgeport had been able to do what she had done—bring all his property

through the depression intact" (109). The switch to the masculine pronoun
is curious. It is as though Sarah was regendered by the economic responsibilities she assumed, just as John Forbes was by being forced to become
the petted servant for Mrs. Wingate.

When the story begins, the life of Sarah Forbes is almost over. If we
follow the chronological clues imbedded in the story, we can reconstruct
a trajectory that takes us from 1860, when John Forbes was born; to 1901,
when he married Sarah; and to 1925, when he died. At the time, the narrator was nine years old. Thirty-three years later, which would have been
1958, the narrator was informed of Sarah Forbes's fragility. It was winter.
It was also snowing. The phone rang, and the narrator was summoned to
Sarah's sickbed. Peter, Sarah's son, told the narrator: "She's got some
dishes she wants you to have" (90). Peter made it clear that there was no
time to tarry. After a slow, halting trip on a winding road "all hills and
sharp curves" (90), the narrator arrived at Sarah's sickbed. The change in
this once vibrant and vivacious woman surprised her.

The moment I saw Sarah, I knew that she was dying. She was sitting slumped
over in a wheelchair. In the two years since I had seen her, she had become a gaunt
old woman with terrible bruised shadows under her eyes and she was so thin that
she looked like a skeleton. Her skin, which had been that rich reddish brown, was
now overlaid with gray. (104)

It wasn't long before two sets of china, one white and the other choco-
late, were brought out. The white set of six flawless cups and matching
saucers had come to Sarah from her grandmother. It is perhaps ironic that
the set inherited through her African American forebears is white, the
conventional sign of the unsullied. This inheritance also sets up a matri-
lineal line of heritage and testifies to the class status of Sarah's grandmother, born probably in the 1830s or 1840s, who was still able, despite
living during slavery, to make her mark materially on and be remembered
by another time, thus transcending her own. Sarah Trumbull did not come
from impoverished people, either economically or emotionally. They had
goods and personal connections of their own that they cherished, and they
knew something of the refined life. They understood and answered the
claims of posterity, the obligation of one generation to give the next not
only a keepsake but also a lineage.

The other set of china, which Sarah told the narrator had once belonged
to a French king, had been a wedding present from Mrs. Wingate. It also
signified class, with royalty as the height of class aspiration. Being an
aristocrat, whether born to the manor or invited there, was the ultimate
badge of belonging, and many of those who had performed the cakewalk
wanted very much to belong to family and to nation. Through these cups
and saucers, receptacles and their matching base of transformed clay, rep-

resenting harmony, transcendence, and connectedness across time and across social barriers, the narrator is being entrusted with the unwritten, precious, and painful history of the Forbes family. It is thus her inherited duty, which she fulfills, to carry the story of the cups and their meaning to the future, to fill them with nourishment for another era.

Through her husband's employer, Sarah had benefited—at great cost. John Forbes, born in 1860—before slavery ended officially—leased his body to Mrs. Wingate, becoming a virtual prostitute whose body was for hire. Hence, his final hours on the wrong side of the train tracks translate into metaphor. In return for loaning out his limbs, his back, and his presence, he made sure that he would have an inheritance, something tangible to pass on to his family, the duty of a husband. He was not able to have a traditional marriage, but he adhered, in his fashion, to the contractual obligations the cakewalk as wedding ceremony implied. He was a partner with flair, who improvised his steps in accordance with the beat, however irregular, of the times. The dual line of heritage, one from kin and the other from a lifetime of labor, plus the combination of Sarah's financial stewardship and his nest egg, solidified and enriched the family's prospects.

Both sets of china are all of a piece with the winning cake of the cakewalk. After the dance was done and while the cake was being consumed, the dancers and their friends would have enjoyed tea or coffee from similar cups and saucers. The delicate crockery would have added a finishing flourish to an evening spent performing the cakewalk. The porcelain table service in perfect condition connoted the ultimate in manners and etiquette, the absolute right way to do things, the cream of the good life. It signified a leisured life and the investment on which Sarah and John Forbes had made good. Transition into the ranks of the propertied classes—that was the cake they took.

WORKS CITED

Archer-Straw, Petrine. *Negrophilia: Avant-Garde Paris and Black Culture in the 1920s.* New York: Thames and Hudson, 2002.

Austin, J. L. *How to Do Things with Words.* Cambridge, MA: Harvard University Press, 1962.

Baldwin, Brooke. "The Cakewalk: A Study in Stereotype and Reality." *Journal of Social History* 15.2 (1981): 205–18.

Blesh, Rudi, and Harriet Janis. *They All Played Ragtime.* New York: Oak Publications, 1971.

Charters, Ann. *Nobody: The Story of Bert Williams.* New York: Macmillan, 1970.

Dixon-Gottschild, Brenda. *Digging the Africanist Presence in American Performance: Dance and Other Contexts.* Westport, CT: Praeger, 1996.

Dorman, James H. "Shaping the Popular Image of Post-Reconstruction American Blacks; The 'Coon Song' Phenomenon of the Gilded Age." *American Quarterly* 40.4 (1988): 450–71.

Emery, Lynne Fauley. *Black Dance in the United States from 1619 to 1970.* Palo Alto, CA: National Press Books, 1980.

Ervin, Hazel Arnett. *Ann Petry: A Bio-Bibliography.* New York: G. K. Hall, 1993.

Haskins, James. *Black Dance in America: A History through Its People.* New York: HarperCollins, 1990.

Lemke, Sieglinde. *Primitivist Modernism: Black Culture and the Origins of Transatlantic Modernism.* Oxford: Oxford University Press, 1998.

Petry, Ann. "Ann Petry." *Contemporary Authors: Autobiography Series,* Vol. 6. Detroit: Gale Research, 1988. 253–69.

———. "Has Anybody Seen Miss Dora Dean?" *Miss Muriel and Other Stories.* Boston: Houghton Mifflin, 1971. 89–111.

Smith, Eric Ledell. *Bert Williams: A Biography of a Pioneer Black Comedian.* Jefferson, NC: McFarland, 1992.

Sundquist, Eric. *To Wake the Nations: Race in the Making of American Literature.* Boston: Harvard University Press, 1994.

"The Man Who Cried I Am": Reading Race, Class, and Gender in Ann Petry's "The Witness"

Carol E. Henderson

... black men suffer the double jeopardy of a social and representational sort simultaneously.
—Maurice Wallace, *Constructing the Black Masculine*

He looked now for the first time sharply about him, and wondered [why] he had seen so little before. He grew slowly to feel almost for the first time the Veil that lay between him and the white world. . . .
—W.E.B. Du Bois, "Of the Coming of John"

In "Can you be BLACK and look at this?" Elizabeth Alexander poses a central question relative to the current discussion concerning the African American racial memory and the paradoxical nature of "witnessing" as it pertains to the process of *recognizing* one's self in that which one sees. She asks: "What do the scenes of communally witnessed violence . . . tell us about the way that 'text' is carried in the African-American flesh?" (95). Embedded in Alexander's striking question is a series of cultural touchstones—mnemonic wounds—that, when examined, return the reader to a litany of cultural scenes filled with black bodies in pain. For more than 400 years, people of African descent have been subjected to vindictive and vicious acts of physical, spiritual, and cultural erasure—what Cornel West terms *institutionalized terrorism* (123)—in an effort to control not only their progress as a people, but their bodies as well. "One of the best ways to instill fear in people is to terrorize them," writes West. And "this fear is best sustained by convincing them that their bodies are ugly, their intellect is inherently underdeveloped, their culture is less civilized, and their future warrants less concern than that of other people" (122).

West's observations make clear the objectives of a racial subtext rooted in white-supremacist ideology. It is this subtext that underwrites, in many respects, the social policies concerning the rightful "heir ship" to America's citizenry—a citizenry that has, more often than not, left African Americans disenfranchised. One needs only to return to the founding documents of this country for evidence of this cultural misstep. As Alexander aptly argues, "African-Americans have always existed in a counter-citizen relationship to the law; how else to contend with knowing oneself as a whole human when the Constitution defines you as 'three-fifths'?" (94). This fact alone reaggravates the cultural wounds evident in the African American racial memory. Such mis-affirmations relegate African Americans to the margins of society, imprisoning them in their own flesh—dooming them to be participants and witnesses to those devices that seek to undermine their integrity as human beings while simultaneously making them strangers in their own land—a land bought and paid for by the blood, sweat, and tears of their ancestors.

What is less clear, however, is the extent of the damage done to those individuals subjected to these daily assaults visited upon their persons. "African-American viewers have been taught a sorry lesson of their continual, physical vulnerability in the United States," writes Alexander, "a lesson that helps shape how it is we understand ourselves" (95). Such awareness has led many African American writers, including Ann Petry, to chart with painstaking acuity the depth of this cultural angst in their narratives in an attempt to understand how these degrading acts have left their tinge in the psychic wounds and scars written on the souls of black folk. Petry herself is quoted elsewhere as saying her characters are the walking wounded—figuratively marked, I would argue, by those dehumanizing conditions of life that take various forms: decay and/or disease or mutilation and/or fragmentation of the mind, body, and spirit. As a journalist and a teacher, her daily encounters with the broken spirits of New York's Harlem district allowed her to witness the stifling effects of poverty on its residents; she saw the pain and anguish in the eyes of mothers, fathers, and children weaving their way through life's urban maze.

But Petry has not limited herself to the urban center. She has written about quaint New England towns as well as rural country cities. In each instance, Petry explores the dynamic interpersonal relationships of *people*. Much of her writing can be said to deal with the human experience, an experience not limited by geography or class. Critic Heather J. Hicks maintains that Petry's representations of life are tantamount to "taking down the fourth wall," so to speak. Petry admits that her objective in writing about Harlem and other cultural spaces was to expose her primarily white reading audience to the intimate details and challenges of living in places many of them could only imagine (Hicks 89). In many respects, Petry builds upon the traditions of her literary antecedents, adopting a mode of writing that calls forth the political and historical fervor of her fore-mothers and forefathers as she redefines the ways in which we come to understand the social significance of institutionalized oppression in the twentieth century. Just as Harriet Jacobs and Harriet E. Wilson wrote about the goings-on behind the fourth wall of southern plantations and the rural North respectively, redirecting attention, I would argue, to the cause for freedom and economic equality, Petry examines the vast pano-rama of African American experience in the 1950s and 1960s, drawing parallels between the past and the present humiliations suffered by Af-rican American people. Petry's figurations of the migratory experiences of the grandchildren and great-grandchildren of ex-slaves who left the rural areas with dreams of a better life in the city build upon many of the same social and political concerns of yesteryear, yet one can safely argue that her portrait is complicated, particularly in "The Witness," with vi-sions of the *illusory* promise of American prosperity—a promise guaran-teed after the abolishment of slavery and its attendant evils.

While it is true that African Americans have been some of the most ardent supporters of the American Dream, despite the monumental dis-appointments they have suffered in achieving the maxims promised to those fortunate enough to "pull themselves up by their bootstraps," most African Americans feel, as Richard Yarborough aptly points out, that "race" has been the determining factor that has prevented many from entering America's sanctum sanctorum, "that imaginary arena of freedom and fair play where an individual may prove his or her worth and, upon doing so, earn the security, peace, material comforts, and happiness iden-tified with success in the United States" (33). Thus, in speaking on those issues, Yarborough argues that African American writers "have had to perform a peculiar kind of thematic gymnastics in order to reflect in their works both the realistic awareness that racist oppression has persisted after slavery and the idealistic faith in America as the land of opportunity for all" (34). I argue here that Petry performs such a task in writing "The Witness" (1971) as she explores the nexus of race, class, and gender from a perspective that shows that even an assimilated middle-class black pro-fessional can never forget his blackness.

THE SOULS OF A BLACK MAN

> How does it feel to be a problem?
> —W.E.B. Du Bois, *The Souls of Black Folk*

According to Kelly Oliver, "the paradoxes inherent in bearing witness to one's own oppression teaches us something about the dialogic nature of subjectivity," a subjectivity that requires witness. This witness is key to the process of understanding the *trauma* of oppression, as such witness is a necessary part of personal and political transformation (85). However, Charles Woodruff's experiences in "The Witness" point to a more troubling paradox associated with human nature and the effects "witnessing" has on the inner man of the seer. As Ralph Ellison so poignantly illustrates in *Invisible Man*, the "sleepwalkers" are those with the most power—to see or not to see. They can choose to acknowledge the character of a man or subsume his character under myths of distorting glass so insidiously created by American society. Woodruff's flight at the end of the narrative alerts the reader that "[a]nother poor scared black bastard who was a witness" (234) to the potency of these myths has experienced the unyielding power these traditions have over those individuals who create them and use them freely.

But Petry's character suffers from a number of issues. He is, after all, a man struggling with his multiple identities. As a widowed, black, 65-year-old man, Woodruff's professional status places him in the borderlands—betwixt and between—the major (r)evolutionary developmental periods of African American consciousness and thought. To borrow an apt phrase from critic Houston Baker, "the journey back," and I would argue the journey in between, is, after all, a critical prospective of the future, the sound of your own voice returning to you—amplified—in the discourse of your immediate and distant communities. If, as writer Gloria Anzaldua determines, the borderlands are any physical space or territory where two or more racial, cultural, or economic groups edge each other (ix), Woodruff's lived experience has allowed him to catch a glimpse of some of the most monumental changes in American society: He has witnessed the ravaging effects of racism on the psyches of southern blacks. He has experienced some form of the economic, cultural, and spiritual depression of the 1930s. Likewise, Woodruff has seen, I would surmise, the promise of the future in the eyes of those students he taught at Virginia's College for Negroes. He has also heard or knew of The Tuskegee Airmen, the troops of Company G, 24th Infantry, and thousands of other black men who went to war to fight for a country that did not acknowledge their humanity. This lack of respect was evidenced in the many men who found themselves lynched in their military uniforms upon their return to the states. The reality of their existence is intertwined with his; Woodruff knows that his blackness confines him to certain segments of society and prevents him from entering others. Therefore, until the politics of the country had changed, his life revolved around the limitations of his blackness, and in some respects, his gender.

Oddly enough, it is his African American heritage that provides a way for him to change his immediate circumstance, making plain the paradox of race matters and underscoring in hypervisible terms the political and ethical dimensions of blackness. As the narrative discloses, Woodruff's new job came as a result of affirmative action:

Everybody was integrating and so this little frozen Northern town was integrating, too. Someone probably asked why there were no black teachers in the school system and the school board and the Superintendent of Schools said they were searching for "one"—and the search yielded that brand-new black widower, Charles Woodruff (nigger in the woodpile, he thought, and then, why did it pop up like that . . .). (213–14)

Although Woodruff's previous occupation as a college professor placed him in a position of privilege—a status relegated to the "talented tenth" that Du Bois spoke of in *The Souls of Black Folk*—in his new position as a high-school teacher, Woodruff was just "another nigger," categorized, at this point, by a generic term used to degrade and humiliate. The doubleness evident in the psychological interplay illustrated in this instance mirrors the uneasiness Woodruff feels at being an "alien presence" in an all-white town. Petry's constant references to the "whiteness" of the snow that blanketed the walkways where Woodruff traveled daily to get to the school and to the congregational church he visited and her detailed description of the whiteness of the inhabitants of Wheeling, New York, make plain the rhetorical strategies she employs to point up the competing forces that figuratively veil Woodruff's being. If the history of the "American Negro is the history of . . . strife—this longing to attain self-conscious manhood, to merge his double self into a better and truer self" so that neither of the older selves are lost (Du Bois 3), Woodruff's apt description of his Du Boisan experience emphasizes not only the complexities of his existence as a black man but also the way he feels trapped in his body.

He envisioned himself as a black beetle in a fur-collared coat silhouetted against the snow trying to scuttle out of danger. Danger: Why should he think he was in danger? Perhaps some sixth sense was trying to warn him and his beetle's antenna (did beetles have antennae, did they have five senses and some of them an additional sense, extrasensory—) picked it up—by the pricking of my thumbs, something wicked this way comes. (217)

If double consciousness is the "peculiar sensation" of "always looking at one's self through the eyes of others," then Woodruff's ability to recognize the tenuousness of his predicament raises a number of questions about the benefits of "progress" and its detrimental effects on his moral character. Specifically, in this example, Woodruff's alien status animalizes him—makes him a freak reminiscent of Kalka's beetle-man in his haunting tale *The Metamorphosis*. Like Gregor, Woodruff searches for wholeness in an environment that has mongrelized him, encrusted him in flesh that is spiritually and culturally contaminated due to the way others view him.

Those daily encounters Woodruff must have surely experienced being the only black man in his town, those halfhearted approaches by other town citizens who eyed him in curious wonder or who simply let their distain for progress be known through their indignant and callous behavior towards him must have added another layer of contention to an already-volatile situation. Woodruff's entomological change can then be viewed as a crisis of witnessing, a poetic posturing of a self-reflexive nature that seeks to join those discarded selves fractured under the gaze of a dominant culture. This dizzying recapitulation of those "incidents" that help to mark him, to submerge him in the irrational reality of race matters, doom him to be a witness and a participant in his own transmutation, his own metamorphosis. And as was evident in that tale as well, "the dream" can become a nightmare at a moment's notice.

According to critic Michael Barry, Petry's writings have, more often than not, been preoccupied with one central question: Is the world getting better? And if it is, better for whom? Such questions not only lie at the heart of her social critiques of universal human foibles, but these concerns also frame her struggles with questions surrounding the moral progress of American society and civilization in general. As Barry contends, "We can best appreciate Petry's view of history by sifting through the ironies of her texts; her view is ultimately progressive, but qualified by hints of determination and even of a liberating ahistoricism—an affirmation of cyclicalness that offers an escape from linear narrative that is not, after all, experienced universally as progress" (143). In placing Barry's comments within the context of "The Witness," it becomes clear that Woodruff is a product of the "cyclicalness" of history. His fear that "something wicked this way comes" functions as a mantra for African American men who feel they have somehow stepped outside of "safe space." Because the high profile of race makes the black male body a walking magnet for all the fears and fascination possessing our cultural imagination, Woodruff, as medium for those fears, absorbs and deciphers them accordingly through his behavior. Woodruff readily admits that he was a prime candidate to be picked out of the pool of applicants because he posed the least threat: he was a newly widowed black man who was 65 years of age—trained, from experience, in the ways of "white folk." The fact that he lived in Virginia ensures that he possesses the "qualities" and likewise the social posture of an assimilated black man who could easily blend in with his environment.

But as Petry makes abundantly clear, *physical* integration (i.e., environmental change) does not necessitate cultural acceptance and physic healing. Woodruff carries the ghosts of history with him always. The fact that he believes his good fortune, his dream, will dissipate is evidenced very early on in the narrative when he fears that someone would call the state police because there was a "black man, repeat, a black man . . . standing in front of the Congregational church in Wheeling, New York" (213). The generic police description that follows—"thinnish, tallish black man, clipped moustache . . ."—is offset by Petry's attention to the material possessions that Woodruff embraces to counter the insecurities he feels in his new environment: "(extravagantly expensive, outrageously expensive, unjustifiably expensive) overcoat, felt hat like a Homburg, eyeglasses glittering in the moonlight . . . " (213). As the narrative relates, Woodruff had not planned to buy the coat initially because his deceased wife, Addie, had she been alive, would have opposed vehemently such an indulgence. But during a Christmas trip to New York, Woodruff succumbed to the tantalizing appeals of the salesman who told him, "Try it on sir—it's toast-warm, cloud-light, [and] guaranteed to make you feel like a prince" (212). The expensive overcoat, a dark-gray cashmere color adorned with a black Persian-lamb collar and his felt Homburg hat serve as obvious reminders of his class status—a status challenged only by his race. The irony of this pairing, however, is how hypervisible Woodruff's blackness becomes in his coat. The narrative suggests that it is Woodruff's elitism that makes him conscience of his status in this small town. What he also comes to realize is that no matter how comfortable one becomes, one is never *really* comfortable enough to fit in. Like the one drop of black paint that gets lost in large barrel of white paint in the Liberty Paints episode in *Invisible Man*, Woodruff finds himself lost in his class status, in his blackness, in the very alienation that marks his troubled existence in Wheeling, New York.

ON THE MEANING OF PROGRESS

> One of the ways that has been used to simplify the answer [of who and what America is] has been to seize upon the presence of black Americans and use them as a marker, a symbol of limits, a metaphor for the "outsider."
> —Ralph Ellison, "What America Would Be Like without Blacks"

Petry's commentary on the challenges that face many African Americans who seek to resist the delimiting social order that tries to keep them away from the prosperity promised to those who are born and/or "naturalized" as American citizens is telling. In particular, Petry's focus on material "enslavement" serves to underscore the bondage awaiting those who foolishly embrace the seductive lure of wealth at the expense of the integrity of their mortal souls in an effort to embrace America's promise of prosperity. And here again, Petry's rhetorical interplay—her literary ingenuity—becomes clear in this way. The overcoat—the very material possession that marks Woodruff's prosperity—becomes the very thing that restricts him when he is kidnapped by the group of delinquent youth he is encouraged to counsel:

[Woodruff] shouted, "My car. Damn you, you're stealing my car." . . . They took his coat off and put it around him backward without putting his arms in the sleeves and then buttoned it up. The expensive coat was just like a strait jacket— it pinioned his arms to his sides. He tried to work his way out of it by flexing his muscles, hoping that the buttons would pop off—and thought, enraged, They must have stitched the goddamn coat to last for a thousand years and put the goddamn buttons on the same way. The fur collar pressed against his throat, chok-ing him. (223)

Key in this encounter is Petry's use of the term "strait jacket." There are several associations one can make with this term but one glaring connec-tion is its relevant correlation to the psychological conundrum the pro-tagonist finds himself. Woodruff's inability to "work his way out" of his situation, to "flex his muscles"—may that be economic or social—ampli-fies, in glaring fashion, the self-alienating disjunction of race and man-hood in American culture. Woodruff senses that his past, present, and future are "stitched together" by an array of representational logics and material practices tied to the doctrines of racism and sexism. Half-blind without his glasses and uncertain of what he sees through his optical prisms, Woodruff thrashes around in his coat, immobilized by the fur collar that threatens to suffocate him. Like Woodruff's black skin, the over-coat becomes his sign of bondage and likewise his psychical impairment as he attempts to decipher "the shadows on the wall" (225).

Interestingly enough, Petry inverts the color palette in this short story and challenges the reader's expectations about certain stereotypes by ex-posing the "darker" side of this quaint New York town. The youths that assault Woodruff and hold him hostage in the preceding illustration are described elsewhere in the narrative (218) as being very intelligent but possessing a character so evil, so cold, so dark that their blackness calls forth the archetypal image of the hole from which D. H. Lawrence's snake emerges. The ringleader, Rambler, is said the have an IQ in the genius bracket. These intellectual qualities, combined with the privilege that comes with being white, afford Rambler and his crew the opportunity to be "reformed" by the church's minister and other members of the com-munity. Woodruff's middle-class status allows him access to the inner workings of this world—a world he would have been barred from except for his *alleged* special skills at reaching the unreachable:

'Dr. Shipley, do you think we are accomplishing anything?' He had said 'we' though he was well aware that these new young outlaws spawned by the white middle class were, praise God, Shipley's problem—the white man's problem. This cripplingly tight shoe was usually on the black man's foot. He found it rather pleasant to have the position reversed. (216)

Petry's rhetorical layering of Woodruff's dark skin with that of the char-acter of these youths allows her to rend the veil on the upper middle class's smug exterior as she complicates the nexus of race, class, and gender. The focus on the delinquent juveniles in this instance is only one prong in a larger narratological structure that seeks to turn the narrative on itself as Petry dismantles the power structures encoded in the ideological precepts of race, class, and gender, and subverts the practices of surveillance and spectatorship through an examination of the modes of discourse that resist neat classifications. Petry's self-conscious negotiation of those issues relevant to the black experience produces a commentary on racial politics that effectively exposes and disassembles our systems of knowing. Moreover, Petry exposes the falsehoods of -isms associated with certain groups of individuals, as these become the posts of the structure that supports our discourse on race. Thus "blackness," in this instance, becomes a signifier for not only social ignorance but also a metaphoric indicator of the darkness of the spirit—a spirit bound to the precarious quest for self-esteem and the immature, cathartic gestures that bespeak an obsession with difference.

It becomes very evident in the narrative that Rambler and his crew function as a figurative manifestation of the resentments many members of the select elite feel at having their space "infringed upon." That Rambler and his gang understand the dynamics of race and class early in their young lives points up the propensity of white America to formalize a two-dimensional vision of black men. Even more haunting is how closely associated these images are to the notion of power—a power these boys readily assume when they kidnap Woodruff.

'Here you go,' the boy said. He pulled a black wool cap down on Woodruff's head, over his eyes, over his nose.

He couldn't see anything. He couldn't breathe through his nose. He had to breathe through his mouth or suffocate. The freezing cold air actually hurt the inside of his mouth. The overcoat immobilized him and the steady pressure of the ... collar against his windpipe was beginning to interfere with his normal rate of breathing. He knew that his whole circulatory system would gradually begin to slow down. He frowned, thinking what a simple and easily executed method of rendering a person helpless—just an overcoat and a knit cap. Then he thought, alarmed, If they should leave me out in the woods like this, I would be dead by morning. (224)

Besides playing on the trope of lynching and a long line of historical memories (formulated in slavery) that find the black man victimized by his circumstance, these boys' behavior conjures up repetitious formulations of national discourse centered on "maleness"—formulations that continue to serve as a chief mechanism for defining relations of power in America. History has demonstrated that whenever this power is threatened, reconfigured, or socially realigned, violence—be it literal or figurative—becomes the method of defense. In Woodruff's case, this violence is confirmed not only in the defilement of his personal possessions (the car, the coat, his glasses), but also in the defilement of his person. Only the alleged rape of the young white woman Woodruff tries to rescue matches the symbolic gestures of figurative castration and emasculation evidenced in this encounter.

RETURN OF THE REPRESSED

> For the 'monster' always constitutes the return of the socially or po-
> litically repressed fears of a society, those energies, memories, and
> issues that a society refuses to deal openly with.
> —Ed Guerrero, *Framing Blackness*

Woodruff's encounter with the delinquent youths of Wheeling recalls all those ancestral aspects of memory that undermine black masculinity. If, as Ed Guerrero argues above, the "monster" returns embodied in those energies of a society that refuses neither to accept its past nor to embrace its future, Woodruff's internalized metaphorization of his own body—he envisions himself as a black beetle at one point and as a chicken and a spider at other moments—speaks to the corporeal images of terror recorded in his mind's memory bank as knowledge. Woodruff's "sixth sense" derives from this series of cultural visions whose history moves from slavery to lynching, from public beatings to sexual violation. Each of these scenes dance across the collective memory of African Americans with unabated agility, returning its subject time and time again to the socially repressed racial subtext that misrecognizes—does not acknowledge—black communal pain. In the memory code of African American history, this misrecognition is reinvoked each time the narrative space between individually experienced bodily trauma and collective cultural trauma is crossed. For Woodruff, this memory trace is activated by his attempt to prevent the kidnapping and rape of Nellie, a young high-school townie. Woodruff's conflicted duties as man and protector (participant) and bystander (witness) collides head-on with his subconscious being, that being that tells him "he ought to go home where it was quiet and safe, mind his own business—black man's business; leave this white man's problem for a white man" (221). Woodruff's need to seek shelter in a bungalow he rents, a bungalow with an open porch and a "ridiculous type of architecture" for the cold climate, speaks to the inadequacy he feels at being unable (and some would argue unwilling) to prevent this tragedy or offer himself as a sacrifice for the life of another. As Woodruff tells himself, "Wait, slow down, cool it, you're a black man speaking with a white man's voice" (221), a voice of authority that earns Woodruff the "stare down" and the unwanted attention from the boys when he asks them what they are doing to Nellie.

But sacrifice is what Woodruff feels he did. There were seven of them—young, strong, and virile. HE was a black man in his sixties, conditioned all his life to avoid AT ALL COSTS associations with white women. The moment Woodruff decided to intervene in front of the church, he knew he had become a spectator to his own demise. "You're our witness, ho-daddy. You're our big fat witness," (227) the boys explained. Woodruff himself acquiesces:

They knew he wasn't going to the police about any matter which involved sex and a white girl, especially where there was the certainty that all seven of them would accuse him of having relations with the girl. They had used his presence in that tool shed to give an extra exquisite fillip to their dreadful game. (233)

This exchange is important because it demonstrates at once the relationship between the *politics* of identity and the *poetics* of identity. Such a relationship finds the black man spectacle-ly "framed" as he labors against the dam of overwhelming representations poised to keep him in his place. According to Maurice Wallace, "We are made to see black masculinity from new angles, new looks that powerfully revivify what would seem fossilized by the camera/gaze" (13). Put another way, black masculinity, as seen through the delimiting lenses of history and social culture, objectifies and reifies the performative disfigurement of the black male body in ways that reconcile the nation's anxieties about black men as it also replicates within black men privately as the angst of entrapment and racial domination. As in Woodruff's case, his mind, body, and spirit become calcified in the cultural remnants of a frozen Northern town intent on reappropriating its one black male subject. Woodruff's efforts to shelter his psyche from the deteriorating effects of his immediate environment reveal the complex interplay of race as the patterns for relating across human differences lay bare the intrinsic values of "blackness" in determining white subjectivity. Woodruff understood the rules of *this* game all too well—his immediate resignation and subsequent flight from Wheeling, New York, demonstrates that. But more haunting is the image we are left with of Woodruff and his coat:

He put on his elegant overcoat. When he got back to Virginia, he would give the coat away, his pleasure in it destroyed now for he would always remember the horrid feel of the collar tight across his throat, even the feel of the fabric under his finger tips would evoke an image of the cemetery, the tool shed, and the girl. (232)

Death appears to be the only resolution to Woodruff's quandary—the death of his dream, his person, his soul.

What happens to a dream deferred? Woodruff's plight suggests that it festers like a sore and hangs like a heavy load. But Petry may also be arguing something simpler: Know who you are and do not be caught up in the hype. After all, we do not design the rules of engagement, so study the blueprint well—in this way you will not become a witness to your own demise.

WORKS CITED

Alexander, Elizabeth. "'Can you be BLACK and look at this?': Reading the Rodney King Video(s)." *Black Male: Representations of Masculinity in Contemporary American Art.* Ed. Thelma Golden. New York: Whitney Museum of American Art, 1994. 95–110.

Anzaldua, Gloria. *Borderlands/La Frontera: The New Mestiza.* San Francisco: Aunt Lute Books, 1987.

Baker, Houston. *The Journey Back: Issues in Black Literature and Criticism.* Chicago: University of Chicago Press, 1980.

Barry, Michael. "'Same Train Be Back Tomorrer': Ann Petry's *The Narrows* and the Repetition of History." MELUS 24.1 (Spring 1999): 141–61.

Du Bois, W.E.B. "Of the Coming of John." *The Souls of Black Folk.* 1903. New York: Bantam Books, 1989. 161–76.

———. *The Souls of Black Folk.* 1903. New York: Bantam Books, 1989.

Ellison, Ralph. *Invisible Man.* 1952. New York: Vintage Books, 1995.

———. "What America Would Be Like without Blacks" *Going to the Territory.* New York: Vintage Books, 1986. 104–12.

Guerrero, Ed. *Framing Blackness: The African American Image in Film.* Philadelphia: Temple University Press, 1993.

Hicks, Heather J. "Rethinking Realism in Ann Petry's *The Street.*" MELUS 27.4 (Winter 2002): 89–107.

Jacobs, Harriet. *Incidents in the Life of a Slave Girl.* 1861. Cambridge, MA: Harvard University Press, 1987.

Kafka, Franz. "The Metamorphosis." *The Complete Stories.* Ed. Nahum N. Glatzer. New York: Schocken Paperback, 1971.

Oliver, Kelly. *Witnessing: Beyond Recognition.* Minneapolis: University of Minnesota Press, 2001.

Petry, Ann. "Ann Petry." *Contemporary Autobiography Series,* Vol. 6. Detroit: Gale Research, 1988. 253–69.

———. "The Witness." *Miss Muriel and Other Stories.* 1971. Boston: Houghton Mifflin, 1999. 211–34.

Wallace, Maurice O. *Constructing the Black Masculine: Identity and Ideality in African American Men's Literature and Culture, 1775–1995.* Durham, NC: Duke University Press, 2002.

West, Cornel. *Race Matters.* New York: Vintage Books, 1993.

Wilson, Harriet E. *Our Nig; Or Sketches from the Life of a Free Black.* 1859. New York: Vintage Books, 1983.

Yarborough, Richard. "The Quest for the American Dream in Three Afro-American Novels: *If He Hollers Let Him Go, The Street,* and *Invisible Man.*" MELUS 8.4 (Winter 1981): 33–59.

Traumatic Reenactment and the Impossibility of African American Testimony in Ann Petry's "Like a Winding Sheet" and "The Witness"

Eva Tettenborn

Ann Petry's "Like a Winding Sheet" (1945) and "The Witness" (1971)[1] are sure to shock their readers with graphic depictions of violence unparalleled in Petry's other short stories.[2] "Like a Winding Sheet" details a day in the life of the African American factory worker Johnson in an environment that exploits, oppresses, and ridicules him based on his race and class. The story culminates in a scene in which Johnson responds to his frustrations about racism and to his impotence in a white world by acting out his fierce anger in a violently sexist way: he attacks his wife May with uncontrollable brutality. By contrast, "The Witness" sketches a horrific incident in the life of the widowed African American middle-class teacher Charles Woodruff. Woodruff, unlike Johnson, does not act out violently when he is abducted by his criminal and brutal white middle-class students to be present at a gang rape he attempted to prevent. Woodruff's response to this experience is flight from the white community where the horror occurred. The reactions of these men to their experiences seem morally wrong as they victimize women: Johnson becomes the cruel wife beater he never wanted to be, and an apparently cowardly Woodruff abandons his commitments to middle-class justice and avoids reporting a white girl's rape to the police. While I do not want to devalue the traumatic effects on the women affected by Johnson's and Woodruff's respective actions, I want to suggest that it is necessary to think beyond these facts by investigating the reasons behind the behavior of the protagonists. If we are to comprehend their motivations, and if we want to understand the statement Petry makes about witnessing African American life, we need to turn to trauma theory.

Trauma theory has recently emerged as a compelling critical view on the works of many African American writers, and it will be crucial in defining the motives behind the actions of Petry's characters.[3] A reading informed by trauma theory seeks to expose the psychosocial pressures powering the protagonists' actions. At the same time, trauma theory offers insights into the challenges women encounter in the face of a patriarchy structured by racism. Such a reading sheds light on Petry's political intentions as an African American author passing on some of the traumatic shock of the events portrayed in these two stories. In *Ann Petry*, Hilary Holladay has pointed out that "Petry calls her characters 'the walking wounded'" (4), and I want to explore Petry's focus on traumatic wounds in "Like a Winding Sheet" and "The Witness."

Trauma is a response to an event—or a series of events—that cannot be represented by an acceptable narrative of what happened. An involuntary reenactment of the traumatic event is often what takes place instead of verbal testimony and witnessing. In the "Introduction" to her collection *Trauma: Explorations in Memory*, Cathy Caruth explains the psychic mechanisms of trauma. She points out that if an individual lives through a traumatic experience, "the event is not assimilated or experienced fully at the time, but only belatedly, in its repeated possession of the one who experiences it." To be traumatized is precisely to be possessed by an image or event. The traumatized, we might say, carry an impossible history within them, or they become themselves the symptom of a history that they cannot entirely possess (4–5). Adding to her explanation of the impossibility of possessing or narrating the traumatic event, Caruth points out that the traumatic flashback is marked by "literality" and that it remains "nonsymbolic," simply preserving the original event as it happened without ascribing narrative meaning to it (5). Trauma is therefore tied to the conservation of an officially unacknowledged history, and Petry's short stories portray just such traumatic preservations of officially unrecognized events. Naomi Morgenstern has argued in "Mother's Milk and Sister's Blood: Trauma and the Neoslave Narrative" that "if trauma endangers the subject, it would seem to keep 'history' safe" (104). What Morgenstern suggests is that the involuntary traumatic flashback of a horrific event serves to document history almost perfectly as it replays the event. It does so, however, at the high cost of endangering the traumatized person's psychological well-being. This is another marker of trauma Petry utilizes in both of the short stories discussed here. The traumatized subject, based on his or her horrific experience, is no longer able to safeguard or control a record of his or her experiences. Rather, the experiences seem to control the traumatized subject. Dori Laub explains this phenomenon in "Bearing Witness or the Vicissitudes of Listening": "Trauma survivors live not with memories of the past, but with an event that . . . attained no closure, and therefore, as far as its survivors are concerned, continues into the present and is current in every respect" (69). The immediacy of the past thus resides at the center of the traumatic manifestation of an event. What cannot or must not be remembered returns to play itself out over and over again. "Like a Winding Sheet" and "The Witness" engage questions of how unspeakably hurtful experiences return to those who suffered through them and how primary racial trauma can lead to the production of traumatic situations that hurt and endanger others. In the case of these short stories, the endangered are women.

While the assessments of trauma mentioned previously mainly focus on large-scale horrific events like the holocaust or slavery, it does not always take an event of that magnitude to traumatize a human being. Petry's short stories explore the torturous and traumatic quality of ordinary and extraordinary occurrences is everyday African American life. The traumatic quality of "normal" life has been explored recently by some critics. In *Quiet as It's Kept: Shame, Trauma, and Race in the Novels of Toni Morrison*, J. Brooks Bouson locates the possible sources of traumatization in everyday social and political realities.

[R]ecent investigations of the impact of trauma and shame on the individual as well as sociological inquiries into the ubiquity of shame and pride in daily social interactions can help bring into bold relief the effect of racist practices on African American identity. A race-cognizant application of shame and trauma theory . . . shows that African-Americans have been forced to deal not only with individual and/or family shame or trauma but also with cultural shame and racial trauma as they are designated as the racially inferior and stigmatized Other and thus become the targets of white discrimination and violence. (6)

In other words, the source of trauma can, for marginalized people, reside in everyday racist practices as well as in singular horrific events they come to experience.[4] Ann Petry's "Like a Winding Sheet" and "The Witness" recognize the many sources of African American trauma and take into account both historical collective and contemporary individual experiences as causes for the disturbing reactions of the African American male protagonists.

I argue that in both stories, Petry portrays the impossibility of traumatic *witnessing* and proper *testimony* to the dehumanizing incidents the protagonists live through. This impossibility is grounded in the respective life experiences of Johnson and Woodruff in a racist world. In this sense, the short story title "The Witness" is actually ironic, as Hilary Holladay has also observed (110). Instead, given the absence and the impossibility of a proper representation of their traumatic experiences, both men can only live through a traumatic reenactment of the original event in their own ways by becoming cruel and cowardly, respectively. The factory worker Johnson takes out on his wife his original (but impossible) reaction to a racial insult when she jokingly uses the same slur in an attempt to brighten his mood. The teacher Woodruff, who feels implicated in a girl's rape by his mere presence, suddenly recalls scenarios that use black men as scapegoats for actual or alleged sexual assaults on white women. As a result, he flees his town. His reaction alludes to the flight of many endangered black men who tried to escape the anger of a white lynch mob. As I will show, although both actions seem like acts of avoiding the original cause of their frustration, fear, and fury, they actually serve to gesture towards and preserve the original injury both men received in the only way possible: as repetition and reenactment. In both stories, whiteness is associated with social or racial death, as Petry makes clear what constitutes the threat to the self of both men and what generates their trauma. In both cases, women pay the price for the reenactment of the black men's traumata. Petry thus depicts a world in which racial trauma causes reactions that play out in violently sexist ways, always making it clear that the original problem resides with the white racist patriarchal power structure that routinely ignores the impact of African American experiences with racism.

In "Like a Winding Sheet," the factory worker Johnson's self is wounded because of his exposure to daily racism and economic exploitation. His traumatization is continuous rather than singular, and the threats to his self that traumatize him are contained in the daily acts of racism that seek to obliterate his humanity and subjectivity. The fact that his experiences are not unique is signaled by his common last name, a last name he shares with the female protagonist of Petry's *The Street.* The traumatic assault on his self is composed by two powers that are juxtaposed to each other: race and gender relationships. Johnson feels like he needs to uphold a proper position as a man in the patriarchal system. However, his goal is undercut by his position as a black person in a white racist world that continuously violates his humanity. The impossible pressure to negotiate both societal demands, that is, to be an assertive male and a submissive black person at the same time, constitutes a continuous threat to the integrity of his "self."

Whiteness is seen as death-bringing in "Like a Winding Sheet," and Petry points out that the white world is the traumatizing factor in the life of men like Johnson. The short story opens with the depiction of a seemingly loving black couple who communicates patiently and respectfully. However, Petry is quick to direct her short story away from any romantic undertones. Mae Johnson announces to her husband, who just woke up to get ready for his evening shift: "You look like a huckleberry—in a winding sheet—" (199). Mae's description of her husband as a very dark berry framed by sheer whiteness denotes his social and racial position: "He looked at his arms silhouetted against the white of the sheets. They were inky black *by contrast* and he had to smile in spite of himself" (199, emphasis mine). Johnson can only be defined by contrast to the white world surrounding him. White society does not ascribe any worth to him. Moreover, this scene gestures to the dangers looming over the integrity of his self as the white winding sheet is associated with death.

Mae's joke also functions as a subtle foreshadowing of what is to happen to Johnson that day. The short story achieves this foreshadowing through literary allusion. Many readers will no doubt associate Mae's unusual comparison with Mark Twain's *The Adventures of Huckleberry Finn*. Johnson's association with Twain's novel denotes two things: First, the pun plays on Huckleberry Finn's lower-class existence and his exclusion from mainstream American society and culture. Adrift in the world, Huck Finn does not belong. Neither does Johnson, despite his routine African American working-class life. Second, Petry's allusion to Twain's novel foreshadows the racial slur that Johnson will have to face that day, as it is the same word that Twain's characters use when referring to the slave Jim. Through the symbol of the winding sheet, and through her literary allusion to *The Adventures of Huckleberry Finn*, Petry makes it clear that Johnson is always already at risk of being socially and racially traumatized in the white world surrounding and framing him.

Petry signifies Johnson's fragile position in a racist white world by portraying him as a person whose legs ache constantly. Having woken up, Johnson complains to Mae about his condition as a shift worker: "He pushed his legs out from under the covers experimentally. Some of the ache had gone out of them but they weren't really rested yet. 'It's too light for good sleeping. And all that standing beats the hell out of my legs'" (199). Johnson thus literally cannot rely on having a strong foundation in the world he faces. Holding himself upright seems a painful task, as symbolized by the condition of his legs.

Mae's prophetic huckleberry joke comes true once Johnson reaches his work environment. Exposed to the demands of working-class African American life, he experiences an assault on his racial and masculine self. Significantly, the disabling pain in his legs increases before he experiences the traumatic moment around which the story revolves: "And this job he had—this job that forced him to walk ten hours a night, pushing this little cart, well, he'd turn it into a sitting down job" (201). The conditions under which Johnson works underscore this social and racial displacement: forced to wander around, his work reinscribes his social position that makes it painful for him to uphold the integrity of his body and his self. Johnson's black male self is threatened when his white female superior reprimands him for being late: "'Excuses. You guys always got excuses,' her anger grew and spread. 'Every guy come in here late always has an excuse. . . . And the niggers is the worse. I don't care what's wrong with your legs. You get in here on time. I'm sick of you niggers—'" (202). What the tirade of Johnson's female supervisor makes clear to the reader is that

Johnson cannot ever allow himself to be a free person like Huckleberry Finn. Rather, this society likens him more to the slave Jim and addresses him with the accompanying racial slur. This key scene of the short story constitutes Johnson's racial trauma—for this particular day, that is. Like a carelessly crushed berry, his self is damaged on the basis of his race, as the white woman feels free to degrade him. In terms of his gendered self, his manhood is also assaulted by the woman. Johnson prides himself on not committing violent acts against women. He has never hit Mae: "he couldn't bring himself to talk to her roughly or threaten to strike her like a lot of men might have done. He wasn't made that way" (200). Johnson's understanding of his position in patriarchy is one of protecting Mae in particular and women in general. This is his definition of masculinity, and his female supervisor attacks his male values by exploiting and mocking his outlook with a blatant verbal assault.

While Johnson experiences this scene actively, it becomes traumatic for him as it is designed to obliterate his self-respect. Even more traumatic is the fact that he cannot react to it. He is not allowed to beat his supervisor, and he cannot bring himself to hit a woman. Furthermore, in the world of his time, he is not allowed to seek justice against racist whites. The latter is the most crucial of all taboos, and at the end of the day, he will channel his anger in gendered terms rather than allow its racial dimension to make him act. While Johnson cautiously talks back to his boss, he has to keep his pent-up anger inside. Before she can finish her tirade, Johnson warns her: "You got the right to cuss me four ways to Sunday but I ain't letting nobody call me a nigger" (203). What Johnson is not allowed to do is to act on his tentative warning. Out of this taboo emerges a significant inequity: the white boss insults Johnson primarily as a black person, that is, on the grounds of *race*. Johnson, however, thinks he cannot retaliate the way he would like to because above all, he sees the boss as female. Johnson thus thinks he is holding back his rage because of *gender*.

Faced with the social and political circumstances of his time, Johnson is forced to see his lack of response in terms of gender rather than race because this allows him to mask the actual trauma: he would never be allowed to seek justice against a white person. While it is his choice not to hit women, he does not have a choice when it comes to hitting white people. In order to get some kind of hold on his anger and outrage about the racist remark, Johnson thus immediately directs his anger in the direction of gender: "He stood motionless for a moment and then turned away from the sight of the red lipstick on her mouth that made him remember that the foreman was a woman. And he couldn't bring himself to hit a woman. He felt a curious tingling in his fingers and he looked down at his hands. They were clenched tight, hard, ready to smash some of those small purple veins in her face" (203). The story signifies Johnson's gendered anger by his fixation on women's lips and lipstick. This fixation is the result of his inability to act on the racial component of the insult.

Johnson convinces himself that he has survived the situation unharmed and that he was in control of it at all times, rather than the other way around, as is usual for trauma. However, his body reenacts what happened—or rather, what he could not make happen: "An hour went by but the tension stayed in his hands" (204). His hands tell the untold story in the absence of a proper verbal narrative:

And he thought he should have hit her anyway, smacked her hard in the face, felt the soft flesh of her face give under the hardness of his hands. He tried to make his hands relax by offering them a description of what it would have been like to strike her because he had the queer feeling that his hands were not exactly part of him anymore—they had developed a separate life of their own over which he had no control. (204)

The language Petry uses to describe Johnson's rage is phallic in its description of hard anger meeting softly receptive flesh. Thus, this passage serves to underline Johnson's shift of his anger from hatred against the insult of a white person to resentment for being emasculated by a woman. Significantly, Johnson remembers how he was unable, almost impotent, to hit his boss (204). Moreover, by developing the feeling that his hands are no longer a part of him, Johnson displays symptoms of traumatic disintegration. This is a feeling of being acted upon by the traumatic event rather than having mastery over it.

The traumatic cancellation of his self comes back to haunt him in unexpected situations. When his shift is finally over, Johnson goes to an all-night restaurant to have some coffee. However, his joyful anticipation is cut short by the server: "The white girl looked past him, put her hands up to her head and gently lifted her hair away from the back of her neck, tossing her head back a little. 'No more coffee for a while,' she said" (206). What Johnson perceives as yet another act of racism is in reality the result of an empty coffee urn that needs to be refilled. However, the incident demonstrates that Johnson finds it entirely imaginable to be refused service because of his race, as he has come to expect such actions. Johnson's mind and body seem to go through a traumatic flashback and replay the scene at the plant. His traumatic flashback makes the two white women seem interchangeable, as the action Johnson wants to—but must not—take is exactly the same: "What he wanted to do was hit her so hard that the scarlet lipstick on her mouth would smear and spread over her nose, her chin, out toward her cheeks, so hard that she would never toss her head again and refuse a man a cup of coffee because he was black" (207). Once again, Johnson is painfully aware of the fact that he is not allowed to react to racist insults, including this perceived one. Hence, he reevaluates his anger in gendered terms and, once again, convinces himself that the reason he does not react is because he "couldn't even now bring himself to hit a woman" (207). This redirection of his rage allows him to make it seem as if he has in fact saved part of his self by insisting on his chivalry and his masculinity, if not his race.

When the traumatized Johnson reaches his home, he experiences a third and final traumatic flashback. This time, he does not hold himself back, as the taboo of black-on-white violence no longer prevents him from reacting. Upon Johnson's arrival, the story immediately directs our attention to Mae's mouth. She is "chewing gum vigorously" (208), which aggravates Johnson (209). To make matters worse, Mae unwittingly repeats the gesture of the coffee server: "[she] lifted her hair away from the back of her neck, ducking her head forward and then back. He winced away from the gesture" (209). When Johnson finally sits down and wrinkles Mae's work clothes, she assumes a confrontational tone and tells him to sit elsewhere, thus reminding him of his supervisor (209). Ironically, Johnson and Mae seem to resolve all these tense moments that replay earlier insults, since Mae starts to laugh and tease him. However, after the seeming aversion of a domestic catastrophe, Mae jokes, "You're nothing but an old hungry nigger trying to act tough and—" (210). What Mae cannot know is that her joke, just like her huckleberry simile, sums up Johnson's experience and points to the original event of that day's traumatic assault on his manhood. Since the race barrier is removed at home, this time Johnson's body and mind truly reenact the original event without holding back. Johnson's racial anger and fury become fully gendered, and he replays his inner reaction to his supervisor's insult, abusing Mae's body:

[T]that funny tingling started in his finger tips, went fast up his arms and sent his fists shooting straight for her face. There was the smacking sound of soft flesh being struck by a hard object and it wasn't until she screamed that he realized he had hit her mouth—so hard that the dark red lipstick had blurred and spread over her full lips, reaching up toward the tip of her nose, down toward her chin, out toward her cheeks. (210)

Johnson's phallic violence bears all the signs of traumatic reenactment in which the event plays itself out even if the survivor of trauma is not conscious of it. Johnson's detached manner suggests that he has very little control over what he is doing. The language Petry chooses makes Johnson seem like an inanimate puppet in the reenactment of his original wish: his arm is like a "hard object," and it is the odd tingling that makes his arm aim for Mae's face, not he himself. This impression is also reinforced by the fact that he does not seem fully conscious of his brutality: "The knowledge that he had struck her seeped through him slowly and he was appalled but be couldn't drag his hands away from her face. He kept striking her and he thought with horror that something inside him was holding him, binding him to this act, wrapping and twisting about him so that he had to continue it. He had lost all control over his hands" (210).

Johnson makes an attempt to find words for what is happening to him. He tries to replace his traumatic display of power (that actually barely masks his lack thereof) with a narrative of the events that deeply scarred him: "And he groped for a phrase, a word, something to describe what this thing was like that was happening to him and he thought it was like being enmeshed in a winding sheet—that was it—like a winding sheet" (210). Unfortunately, his attempt to give words to what happened and thus stop his violence must fail, as the comparison to a winding sheet only ends in a repetitive link to violence. His thought of Mae's joke about the winding sheet is circular in two ways: First, situating himself in the narrative of the winding sheet is in and of itself traumatizing, as Johnson recognizes that there can never be an escape from a winding sheet. A body in a winding sheet is always already dead and acted upon, the body's situation final and unchangeable. Second, Johnson's remembrance of the winding-sheet metaphor brings his thoughts back to Mae, who is the only immediately available potential recipient of his violence. Thus, his attempt to replace the traumatic flashback with a narrative is so hopelessly frustrating that "his hands reached for her face again and again" (210). Hilary Holladay has called the incident a result of a "long history of thwarted communication" (114) and has written about Johnson's rage: "Though violence appears to be the only avenue of communication available to him, the assault on his wife will only exacerbate his troubles: It will ensure his alienation from the one person who provides him comfort and affection" (27). Beating Mae appears to be Johnson's hopeless attempt to take action against the passive position he must occupy in a white world, yet this action is destined to cause new trauma.

Ultimately, Ann Petry's "Like a Winding Sheet" thus turns into a story about an African American woman who is draped in a winding sheet that consists of the fists of her formerly loving husband. Petry thus sheds light on the social and racial trauma of African Americans, culminating in a traumatic reenactment that seemingly only relates to scenes of domestic violence and marital problems. One could say that Petry attempts to bear witness to the trauma experienced by many black men and women and to break the cycle of violent traumatic reenactment by offering a narrative in place of the physical flashback.[5] One could even argue that the act of writing "Like a Winding Sheet" gestures towards its connection to traumatic, unmediated, and spontaneous witnessing. In an interview with John O'Brien, Petry has said, "there were no changes in a story entitled 'Like a Winding Sheet' "—that is, the process of her writing to a degree mirrors the sudden expression of Johnson's flashback. By exploring the psychological motivations behind the actions of "ordinary" men like Johnson, Petry thus politicizes the African American domestic sphere and assigns responsibility to the social forces at work around the individual human being.

Ann Petry's "The Witness" explores the effects of racial trauma in a way that differs from "Like a Winding Sheet" in several ways. Instead of focusing on the replay of the original hurtful episode in a traumatized African American man's life, "The Witness" points to the limits of official African American testimony and witnessing in a white world. "The Witness" demonstrates how, under traumatic circumstances, it is impossible to replace unspeakable trauma with narrative rediscovery. Furthermore, the short story suggests that the flashback Charles Woodruff suffers, the fear that makes him flee from his environment, is rooted in communal as well as personal African American memory. Once again, it is a woman who is victimized by the destruction of black male testimony.

"The Witness" opens with a foreshadowing of the assault on the black protagonist's self by covering the body in threatening whiteness, thus echoing the opening scene of "Like a Winding Sheet." Charles Woodruff stands in front of a white church. We learn that "it had been snowing for twenty-four hours" (212). The whiteness surrounding Woodruff is clearly tied to his endangerment, and the protagonist is aware of this situation: "If he kept it up long enough, someone would call the state police and a bulletin about him would go clattering out over the teletype: 'Attention all cruisers, attention all cruisers, a black man, repeat, a black man is standing in front of the Congregational church in Wheeling, New York" (213). Here Petry's use of snow to signal the dangers the white world holds for a black man is in line with Ralph Ellison's use of snow in *Invisible Man* and Richard Wright's use of snow in *Native Son*. No doubt, Petry relies on this association striking her readers.[6] Woodruff knows that as a middle-class black man who visibly displays his wealth in the form or an expensive overcoat and a new car, he is perceived as a threat to white society. He feels that merely standing in this environment is incriminating. He even refers to his "alien presence" and imagines that "the entire population of the town had died and lay buried under the snow and that he was the sole survivor" (213). Thus, compared to the tightly organized white community, Woodruff sees himself as alive and as a survivor in a hostile world. However, this is about to change as the white community around him functions as another type of winding sheet.

The assault on his African American male self begins soon after his exposure to the freezing white world. He is assisting minister Dr. Shipley in the hopeless attempt to educate and socialize juvenile delinquents who are the spoiled sons of established Wheeling families. During one of the lessons he and Shipley give to the merciless and unresponsive boys, Woodruff receives a "collective stare" that is extremely "hostile" (215). Woodruff feels about the boys that "there was around them an aura of something so evil, so dark, so suggestive of the far reaches of the night, of the black horror of nightmares, that he shivered deep inside himself whenever he saw them" (218). The story makes it very clear that these boys will emerge as nothing but a constant source of trauma for others. While Woodruff thinks about the boys in terms of blackness, he differentiates their blackness from the color of his skin and likens the blackness associated with their immorality to "the hole from which D. H. Lawrence's snake emerged" (218). What Woodruff does not realize is that the metaphorical blackness of these criminals is actually a form of white male privilege taken to the utmost extreme in a display of cruel irony.

Woodruff is traumatized by these criminally racist and sexist offspring of the white middle-class when he tries to save a white girl from being raped by all seven boys. The mere presence of the boys already endangers his black self, and at first he considers not interfering. What he wants to do is "leave this white man's problem for a white man" (221). Yet, his recognition of the girl's position in relationship to the boys, which is not unlike his own, makes him interfere. By the power of his status as a teacher, Woodruff attempts to forbid the students what they have planned. In the instant that he claims his position of having witnessed something sinister, that is, the beginning of their assault on Nellie, the boys immediately make it clear that as an African American man in a white world, he cannot occupy the position of a witness to the trauma they are inducing. The text demonstrates this by their physical assault on him: "One of them suddenly reached out and knocked his hat off his head, another one snatched his glasses off then threw them in the road and there was the tinkling sound of glass shattering. . . . He was half-blind without his glasses, peering about, uncertain of the shape of objects" (222). The way these boys disable his capacities to bear witness and to deliver a testimonial narrative of what has happened and of what is about to commence is indicative of the status of African American experience under white racism.

The boys recognize their full capacities to assault not only Nellie, but also the subjectivity of their black teacher. They deliver their calculated strike in two ways. First, the witnessing of a rape is in itself traumatic. Second, the boys traumatize Woodruff by rendering him incapable of narrating Nellie's and his own horrific experiences. In a way, however, these boys need only take advantage of the long-standing traumatization of a man like Woodruff who grew up with immanent threats to his African American subjectivity. The elimination and breaking of the respective selves of Nellie and Woodruff is underlined by the background of death the criminals select for their crimes: after both victims are abducted, the gang rapes the girl in the dead of night in a cemetery covered in snow, whose deadly qualities have been established earlier in the short story.

What Woodruff witnesses is nothing but the very impossibility of being a witness to the crime of this gang. It is as if the boys derive their cruel phallic potential from the knowledge that they can obliterate an African American's authority by their power to annihilate and negate their teacher's testimony. They use the black man as a prop or as part of the scenery in their personal landscape of violence:

They stood him against the back wall, facing the wall.
    "He's here and yet he ain't here."
    "Ho-daddy's here—and yet—he ain't here."
    "He's our witness." (225)

Woodruff's presence at the crime thus only figures in terms of his social death and absence that the boys have established. Forced to turn towards the wall, deprived of his glasses, and robbed of his subjectivity and authority, Woodruff's witnessing is always already impossible as he can neither fully perceive what happens to Nellie, nor turn her trauma into a testimonial narrative.

The boys are not satisfied with the extent to which they have already destroyed the selves of two human beings whom they render socially worthless. They seem to encourage Woodruff to rape the white girl as well, thus reducing him to the stereotype of the black rapist. As Hilary Holladay has argued, "[b]ecause Woodruff would know and fear the racist stereotype of a black rapist terrorizing white women, they seize on him as a means of covering up their gang rape" (110). Even though he did not rape the girl, the unconscious victim cannot know this, and the boys go to extremes to implicate him in their crime. In addition to offering him the opportunity to become an offensive stereotype and to rape the lifeless girl, they force him into a wicked parody of this role once they see his refusal: "someone grabbed one of his hands and placed it on the girl's thigh, on her breast, and then they laughed again" (226). It appears that the boys want to pin the rape on the black man, the person most likely to be pronounced a suitable suspect in a white town, and by forcing him to touch their victim they also obliterate any chance that he might become an actual witness to their crime. The short story is ironic in as far as it calls the perpetrators "the boys," while their sexuality marks them as rapacious men. By contrast, the boys do not accept Woodruff's black masculinity and his authority as an adult. As Woodruff realizes later, the boys "were bright enough to know that he would quickly realize how nearly they had boxed him in and thus would keep quiet" (230). By touching the lifeless body, Woodruff also becomes aware of the fact that there are parts of the crime that only he witnessed and that not even the girl, who fainted, can confirm. At the same time, since he had to face the wall when the girl was raped, there are parts of the horror that only the girl will ever remember. His touching her only serves to demonstrate that even though he came so close to the girl and to the violence that was visited upon her body, he cannot, and is not allowed to, fully grasp, understand, and testify to what happened. A merging of the black male and the white female perspectives into a more complete testimony against the white boys is not possible.

Once Woodruff returns home from his ordeal, he faces the social implications of his witnessing. While he is at first determined to call the police, he neglects to do it. I want to suggest that Woodruff suddenly recalls, as it were, the communal trauma of African American men falsely accused of raping white women. Significantly, he has this kind of realization, a traumatic flashback to collective African American memory, in one of his rooms that "had a southern exposure" (229). This southern perspective seems to allude to the fate of many black men from the South accused of rape and brought to "justice" with a lynching.[7] The thought of leaving enters his mind in this southern room (229), and he imagines the town's accusations of him: "Would the police believe him? The school board? The PTA? 'Where there's smoke there must be fire.' 'I'm not going to let my daughter stay in his class'" (229). Woodruff's trauma is thus far more than just an individual experience. As a black man connected to the rape of a white girl, he is also always already faced with the communal trauma experienced by black masculinity and forced to relive its consequences.[8]

When Woodruff feigns a heart attack to resign from his position, his chosen symptom points to the obliteration of his subjectivity he has suffered. While the doctor suggests that he could return to his duties within a few months, Woodruff only thinks, "Come back here and look at that violated little girl? Come back here? Ever?" (231). This means that he would rather be socially dead and abandon his career than be forced to face constant flashbacks to the traumatic night in the form of the students he has to teach.

As Johnson does in "Like a Winding Sheet," Woodruff also suffers an actual personal traumatic flashback in addition to being plagued by the communal trauma suffered by black masculinity. On his way out of town, Woodruff once again observes something to which he cannot become an official witness, and he is reminded of the absence and illegitimacy of his own testimony. When he sees the boys in the car again, his memory makes him ill: "he heard close at hand the loud explosive sound of an engine—a familiar sound. He was so alarmed that he momentarily experienced all the symptoms of a heart attack, the sudden terrible inability to breathe and the feeling that something was squeezing his chest, kneading it so that pain ran through him as though it were following the course of his circulatory system" (232). Even more painful and terrible is the fact that "[t]he thin blond girl was in the front seat—a terrible bruise under one eye" (232). The sighting of the young criminals and the victimized girl triggers a traumatic flashback and an involuntary reaction. However, unlike Johnson, Woodruff turns his aggression not against another person but against himself. The symptoms of death he experiences can be seen as a reminder of the communal memory of those black men who did die at the hands of violent whites who assumed a black man had disobeyed—"the knowledge that 'White women taboo for you'" (233). As Woodruff reminisces, the boys "used his presence in that tool shed [where the rape took place] to give an extra exquisite fillip to their dreadful game" (233).

The symbolism Petry employs is once again very subtle: while she gives the white girl a so-called black eye, the same girl is actually painfully deprived of the eyes of a black witness, the eyes of Woodruff. His inability to turn both of their traumata into a narrative leads to a metaphorical and actual traumatic reenactment: Nellie is once again abducted in the boys' car, presumably to be violated again. Woodruff must once again relive the previous night when he, like Johnson, hears a phrase that was hurled at him as an insult by whites: the car radio plays a song with the lyrics "ho-daddy, ho-daddy" (234), and this returns him to his state of helplessness at the time of the crime. Hilary Holladay has described this helplessness: "Perhaps, worst of all, Woodruff is a witness who will never tell his tale. As readers, we witness his fear and shame and imagine the terrible aftermath of his silence" (110). This silence screams the absence of Woodruff's testimony.

Nellie's deprivation of Woodruff's testimony and his perspective on what happened to her is based on the fact that the white world is likely to construct this black man as someone who raped her out of *violent desire* for her white body. However, the white world is less likely to imagine him to be capable of an act of *humanist love* for a female white fellow human being. The black man is by definition barred from lending his testimony to the girl who has none, as he is always already defined in terms of extremes: seen as hypersexualized and hypervisible by virtue of his black masculinity, he seems like a threat to the icy white community. Consequently, he is restricted to seeing himself as only "[a]nother poor scared black bastard who was a witness" (234). Petry thus ends her short story with a literary allusion similar to the one incorporated in the snowy-white opening paragraphs. The portrayal of the fleeing Woodruff recalls Bigger Thomas's panic in Richard Wright's *Native Son*, and "The Witness" thus claims not only literary kinship to other African American works of fiction, but also a strong relevance to the communal memory of African American men faced with stereotypes in a racist world.

In "Like a Winding Sheet" and "The Witness," Ann Petry explores the impossibility of proper black testimony at the times she wrote these stories. Both stories point to the horrors of the racist hegemony's presence in everyday African American life. Petry seems to focus on black men as their position was particularly tentative in the decades when these stories were composed. Johnson is forced to negotiate his position as a working-class black man in a white patriarchy, suffering an assault on his self by a white woman. Woodruff has to face the fact that even though he is above his students in terms of class, education, and age, they insult his subjectivity and devalue his humanity on the basis of his race in a matter of hours. In both cases, Petry thus foregrounds race as the component of American identity formation that signifies most prominently and inevitably in the traumatization of her protagonists. "Like a Winding Sheet" and "The Witness" thus insist on the political dimensions of identity in relation to the social realities and possibilities of African American testimony and witnessing in the face of racism. Where testimony is impossible, Petry seems to argue, painful traumatic reenactment will follow that gestures to the story that cannot be told.

NOTES

1. As Hazel Arnett Ervin has pointed out in *Ann Petry: A Bio-Bibliography*, Petry first published "Like a Winding Sheet" in *The Crisis* in 1945 (2), and "The Witness" first appeared in *Redbook* in 1971 (6). I will refer here to the versions of both stories as reprinted in *Miss Muriel and Other Stories*, a collection that includes a slightly altered version of "The Witness" (Ervin 6).

2. Hilary Holladay has termed "The Witness" "the bleakest of the Wheeling stories" (109).

3. Deborah Horvitz has examined the connection between historical trauma and so-called Freudian hysteria in female African American literary characters in her essay "Hysteria and Trauma in Pauline Hopkins's *Of One Blood; Or, the Hidden Self.*" Lisa Garbus has offered a comparative study of the respective cultural and individual traumata generated by the holocaust and slavery in "The Unspeakable Stories of *Shoah* and *Beloved.*" Lisa Woolfork's dissertation, "Trauma and Racial Difference in Twentieth-Century American Literature," includes explorations of the traumatized self in African American literature.

4. This problem has also been identified by Saidiya V. Hartman. In *Scenes of Subjection: Terror, Slavery, and Self-Making in Nineteenth-Century America*, she explores at length the subjection of African Americans under and beyond slavery through everyday activities, that is, "the terror of the mundane and quotidian" (4). The fact that trauma gestures beyond the experience of the individual has also been highlighted by Deborah M. Horvitz in *Literary Trauma: Sadism, Memory, and Sexual Violence in American Women's Fiction*. She emphasizes the political dimensions of trauma when writing, "having distinguished here between 'psychological' and 'political' processes, I want to emphasize once again that, in the experience of trauma, such distinctions fall apart, and . . . the categories merge" (11). That is, personal trauma can very well carry political meaning. In *Worlds of Hurt: Reading the Literatures of Trauma*, Kali Tal has also recognized the political dimensions of traumatic witnessing. As Tal writes: "The battle over the meaning of a traumatic experience is fought in the arena of political discourse, popular culture, and scholarly debate" (7).

5. David Madden has termed Petry a witness to black experiences in New York City in "Ann Petry: 'The Witness'" (24).

6. In her interview with Mark K. Wilson, Petry explains: "I read [Richard Wright's] novels and short stories as they were published. And I also read the work of Langston Hughes, James Baldwin, and Ralph Ellison—with admiration for all of them, including Wright. *Invisible Man* is a truly great novel" (80). Likewise, in her interview with Hazel Arnett Ervin, Petry states: "Ralph Ellison's *Invisible Man* is truly great" (101).

7. For an extensive pictorial account of the violence committed against black bodies through lynching, see James Allen et al., *Without Sanctuary: Lynching Photography in America*. The book documents that while lynching occurred in all parts of the United States, the majority of these crimes took place in the South.

8. Perhaps Petry's rendering of Woodruff's distrust in the white town is partially inspired by the experience of her middle-class father: "When my father opened his store, for example, they told him they were going to run him out of town because they did not want a black druggist in this town. That does not a New Englander make" (Wilson 82).

WORKS CITED

Allen, James, et al. *Without Sanctuary: Lynching Photography in America*. Santa Fe, NM: Twin Palm Publishers, 2000.

Bouson, J. Brooks. *Quiet as It's Kept: Shame, Trauma, and Race in the Novels of Toni Morrison*. Albany: SUNY Press, 2000.

Caruth, Cathy, ed. "Introduction." *Trauma: Explorations in Memory*. Baltimore, MD: Johns Hopkins University Press, 1995. 3–12.

Ellison, Ralph. *Invisible Man*. 1952. New York: Random House, 1982.

Ervin, Hazel Arnett. *Ann Petry: A Bio-Bibliography*. New York: G. K. Hall, 1993.

Garbus, Lisa. "The Unspeakable Stories of *Shoah* and *Beloved*." *College Literature* 26.1 (1999): 52–68.

Hartman, Saidiya V. *Scenes of Subjection: Terror, Slavery, and Self-Making in Nineteenth-Century America*. New York: Oxford University Press, 1997.

Holladay, Hilary. *Ann Petry*. New York: Twayne, 1996.

Horvitz, Deborah M. "Hysteria and Trauma in Pauline Hopkins's *Of One Blood: Or, the Hidden Self*." *African American Review* 33.2 (1999): 245–60.

———. *Literary Trauma: Sadism, Memory, and Sexual Violence in American Women's Fiction*. Albany: SUNY Press, 2000.

Laub, Dori. "Bearing Witness or the Vicissitudes of Listening." *Testimony: Crisis of Witnessing in Literature, Psychoanalysis, and History*. Ed. Shoshana Felman and Dori Laub. New York: Routledge, 1992. 57–74.

Madden, David. "Ann Petry: 'The Witness.'" *Studies in Black Literature* 6.3 (1975): 24–26.

Morgenstern, Naomi. "Mother's Milk and Sister's Blood: Trauma and the Neo-slave Narrative." *Differences: A Journal of Feminist Cultural Studies* 8.2 (1996): 101–26.

O'Brien, John. "Interviews with Black Writers: Ann Petry." *Ann Petry: A Bio-Bibliography*. Ed. Hazel Arnett Ervin. New York: G. K. Hall, 1993, 72–77.

Petry, Ann. "Like a Winding Sheet." 1945. *Miss Muriel and Other Stories.* Boston: Houghton Mifflin, 1971. 198–210.

———. *The Street.* 1946. Boston: Beacon Press, 1985.

———. "The Witness." *Miss Muriel and Other Stories.* Boston: Houghton Mifflin, 1971. 212–34.

Tal, Kali. *Worlds of Hurt, Reading the Literatures of Trauma.* Cambridge: Cambridge University Press, 1996.

Twain, Mark. *The Adventures of Huckleberry Finn.* 1884. New York: Random House, 1996.

Wilson, Mark A. "A MELUS Interview: Ann Petry—The New England Connection." MELUS 15.2 (1988): 71–84.

Woolfork, Lisa. "Trauma and Racial Difference in Twentieth-Century American Literature." Diss. University of Wisconsin, 2000.

Wright, Richard. *Native Son.* 1940. New York: Harper and Row, 1969.

Selected Bibliography

Angelou, Maya. *Black Women Writers at Work*. Ed. Claudia Tate. New York: Continuum, 1983.

"Ann Petry, Acclaimed Author, Dies at 88." *Jet*, 26 May 1997: 57.

"Ann Petry Gets Warm Reception at Book Fair." *Hampton Bulletin*, January 1956: 3.

"Ann Petry Tells Parley of Need for Play Schools." *New York Herald Tribune Book Review*, 14 April 1946: 5.

Baker, Houston A., Jr., ed. "Overview." *Black Literature in America*. New York: McGraw-Hill, 1971. 1–18.

Balliett, Whitney. "Imagining Music." *New Yorker*, June 1990: 93–94.

Bell, Bernard W. "Ann Petry's Demythologizing of American Culture and Afro-American Character." *Conjuring: Black Women, Fiction, and Literary Tradition*. Ed. Marjorie Pryse and Hortense J. Spillers. Bloomington, IN: Indiana University Press, 1985. 105–15.

———. "The Triumph of Naturalism." *The Afro-American Novel and Its Tradition*. Amherst, MA: University of Massachusetts Press, 1987. 167–84.

Bell, Roseann P., Bettye J. Parker, and Beverly Guy-Sheftall, eds. *Sturdy Black Bridges: Visions of Black Women in Literature*. Garden City, NY: Anchor/Doubleday, 1979.

Bone, Robert. "Black Writing in the 1970s." *Nation*, 16 December 1978: 677–79.

———. *Negro Novel in America*. New Haven, CT: Yale University Press, 1965.

Bontemps, Arna. "Tough, Carnal Harlem." *New York Herald Tribune Weekly Book Review*, 10 February 1946: 4.

Brailey, Muriel Wright. "Necessary Knocking: The Short Fiction of Ann Petry." Diss. Miami University, 1997. *DAI* 57.11 (May 1997): 4737.

———. "The Witness." *Issues and Identities in Literature*. Pasadena, CA: Salem Press, 1997. 990–91.

Breton, Marcela. *Hot and Cool: Jazz Short Stories*. New York: Plume, 1990.

Butcher, Margaret Just. "Regional Nationalism in American Culture." *The Negro in American Culture* [based on materials left by Alain Locke]. New York: Knopf, 1968. 241–82.

Cahill, Susan, ed. *Women and Fiction*. New York: New American Library, 1975.

Chambers, Veronica. "Ann Lane Petry 1909–97." *Essence*, August 1997: 148.

Chandler, Zala. "Interview with Toni Cade Bambara and Sonia Sanchez." *Wild Women in the Whirlwind: Afra-American Culture and the Contemporary Literary Renaissance*. Ed. Joanne M. Braxton and Andree Nicola McLaughlin. New Brunswick, NJ: Rutgers University Press, 1990. 342–62.

Chapman, Abraham. *Black Voices: An Anthology of Afro-American Literature*. New York: New American Library, 1968.

Clark, Keith. "A Distaff Dream Deferred? Ann Petry and the Art of Subversion." *African-American Review* 26.3 (Fall 1992): 495–505.

Clarke, Cheryl. "Ann Petry and the Isolation of Being Other." *Belles Lettres* 5 (Fall 1989): 36.

Clarke, John Henrik. *American Negro Short Stories*. New York: Hill and Wang, 1967.

———. *Black American Short Stories: One Hundred Years of the Best*. New York: Hill and Wang, 1993.

Coffey, Michael. "Black Writers Debate 'Being Human in the 20th Century' (5th Annual Celebration of Black Writing)." *Publishers' Weekly*, 17 February 1989: 17.

Condon, Garret. "Profiles in Connecticut Black History: Ann Petry." *Hartford Courant Weekend Magazine*, 8 November 1992: 11.

———. "Street Wise." *Hartford Courant Weekend Magazine*, 8 November 1992: 8–12.

Contributions of Black Women to America (The Arts, Media, Business, Law, Sports). Ed. Marianna W. Davis. Vol. 1. Columbia, SC: Kenday, 1982.

Davis, Arthur P. *From the Dark Tower: Afro-American Writers 1900 to 1960*. Washington, DC: Howard University Press, 1981.

———. "Integrationists and Transitional Writers." *From the Dark Tower: Afro-American Writers, 1900 to 1960*. Washington, DC: Howard University Press, 1974. 193–97.

Davis, Arthur P., J. Saunders Redding, and Joyce Ann Joyce, eds. *Cavalcade: Negro American Writing from 1760 to the Present*. Boston: Houghton Mifflin, 1971.

Davis, Marianna W., ed. *Contributions of Black Women to America (The Arts, Media, Business, Law, Sports)*. Vol. 1. Columbia, SC: Kenday, 1982.

Davis, Thulani. "Family Plots: Black Women Writers Reclaim Their Past." *The Village Voice*, 10 March 1987: 14–17.

Ervin, Hazel Arnett. "Adieu Harlem's Adopted Daughter: Ann Petry (12 October 1908–28 April 1997)." *Langston Hughes Review* 15.1 (1997 Spring): 71–73.

———. *Ann Petry: A Bio-Bibliography*. New York: G. K. Hall, 1993.

———. "Just a Few Questions More, Mrs. Petry." *Ann Petry: A Bio-Bibliography*. Ed. Hazel Arnett Ervin. New York: G. K. Hall, 1993. 101–3.

———. "The Subversion of Cultural Ideology in Ann Petry's *The Street* and *Country Place*." Diss. Howard University, 1993. *DAI* (1993): 3027.

Foley, Martha. *The Best American Short Stories 1946: And the Yearbook of the American Short Story*. Boston: Houghton Mifflin, 1946.

Ford, Nick Aaron. "From Test Tube to Typewriter." *Afro-American* (Baltimore), 11 December 1948: 3.

"From Pestle to Pen." *Headlines and Pictures*, March 1946: 42–43.

Fuller, James E. "Harlem Portrait." *Pittsburgh Courier*, 9 February 1946 [Special Collections, Boston University].

Garvey, Johanna X. "That Old Black Magic? Gender and Music in Ann Petry's Fiction." *Black Orpheus: Music in African American Fiction from the Harlem Renaissance to Toni Morrison*. Ed. Saadi A. Simawe. New York: Garland, 2000. 119–51.

"General Courses." *All the Women Are White, All the Blacks Are Men, But Some of Us Are Brave*. Ed. Gloria T. Hull, Patricia Bell Scott, and Barbara Smith. Old Westbury, NY: Feminist Press, 1982. 337–78.

Gilbert, Sandra M., and Susan Gubar. "Fighting for Life." *No Man's Land: Vol. 1, The War of the Words*. New Haven, CT: Yale University Press, 1988. 65–121.

Green, Marjorie. "Ann Petry Planned to Write." *Opportunity: Journal of Negro Life* 24.2 (April–June 1946): 78–79.

Gross, Theodore L. "Ann Petry: The Novelist as Social Critic." *Black Fiction: New Studies in the Afro-American Novel since 1945*. Ed. A. Robert Lee. New York: Barnes and Nobles, 1980. 41–53.

Hamer, Judith A., and Martin J. Hamer. *Centers of the Self: Stories by Black American Women from the Nineteenth Century to the Present*. New York: Hill and Wang, 1994.

Holladay, Hilary. *Ann Petry*. New York: Twayne, 1996.

———. "Creative Prejudice in Ann Petry's 'Miss Muriel.'" *Studies in Short Fiction* 31.4 (Fall 1994): 667–75.

———. "Holding Together, Breaking Apart: Communities and Relationships in Ann Petry's Fiction." Diss. University of North Carolina–Chapel Hill. *DAI* (1993): 3029–30.

"An Interview with Ann Petry." *Artspectrum* (Windham—Regional Arts Council, Willimantic, CT), September 1988: 3–4.

Issacs, Diana Scharfeld. "Ann Petry's Life and Art: Piercing Stereotypes." Diss. Columbia University Teachers College, 1982. *DAI* 43 (1982): 446A.

Ivey, James. "Ann Petry Talks about First Novel." *Crisis* 53.2 (February 1946): 48–49. Reprinted Hazel Arnett Ervin. *Ann Petry: A Bio-Bibliography*. New York: G. K. Hall, 1993, 69–71.

———. "Mrs. Petry's Harlem." *Crisis* 53.5 (May 1946): 154–55.

Jackson, Blyden. "A Review of J. L. Dillard's 'Black English.'" *Journal of Negro History* 58.1 (January 1973): 90–96. Reprinted Blyden Jackson, ed. *The Waiting Years*. Baton Rouge: Louisiana State University Press, 1976. 146–54.

———. "A Survey Course in Negro Literature." *College English* 35 (March 1973): 631–6. Reprinted *The Waiting Years*. Ed. Blyden Jackson. Baton Rouge: Louisiana State University Press, 1976. 198–208.

James, Charles L., ed. *From the Roots: Short Stories by Black Americans*. New York: Dodd, Mead, 1970.

Jones, Gayl. *Liberating Voices: Oral Tradition in African American Literature*. Cambridge, MA: Harvard University Press, 1991.

Karrer, Wolfgang, and Barbara Puschmann-Nalenz. *The African American Short*

Story, 1970–1990: A Collection of Critical Essays. Trier: Wissenschaftlicher Verlag Trier, 1993.

Kaufmann, Peter S. *Ann Petry Portrait Collection.* New York: Rapid News Photo, 1945.

Kazin, Alfred. "Brothers Crying Out for More Access to Life." *Saturday Review in Literature,* 2 October 1971: 33–35.

Kent, George E. "Struggle for the Image: Selected Books by or about Blacks during 1971." *Phylon* 33.4 (Winter 1972): 304–11.

Kunitz, Stanley, ed. "Ann Petry." *Twentieth Century Authors: A Biographical Dictionary of Modern Literature.* New York: H. W. Wilson, 1955. 776.

"The Lighter Side" (Petry's weekly column). *People's Voice,* 7 March 1942–48 May 1943.

Littlejohn, David. Introduction. *Black on White: A Critical Survey of Writing by American Negroes.* New York: Viking, 1966. 3–20.

Lucy, Robin Jane. "'Now is the Time! Here is the Place!': World War II and the Black Folk in the Writings of Ralph Ellison, Chester Himes, and Ann Petry." Diss. McMaster University, Hamilton, Ontario. *DAI* 59.12 (June 2000): 188.

Madden, David. "Ann Petry: 'The Witness.'" *Studies in Black Literature* 6.3 (1975): 24–26.

———, ed. "Commentary." *The World of Fiction.* Chicago: Holt, Rinehart and Winston, 1990.

Major, Clarence. *Calling the Wind: Twentieth Century African-American Short Stories.* New York: Harper Perennial, 1993.

McMahan, Elizabeth, Susan Day, and Robert Funk. *Nine Short Novels by American Women.* New York: St. Martin's Press, 1993.

Mobley, Marilyn Sanders. "Ann Petry." *African American Writers.* Ed. Valerie Smith. New York: Scribner's, 1991. 347–59.

Moffett, James, and Kenneth R. McElheny. *Points of View: An Anthology of Short Stories.* New York: Mentor, 1966.

Morrison, Allan. "Women in the Arts." *Ebony,* August 1966: 90–94.

Nge, Carmen. *Religion in the Works of Richard Wright and Ann Petry, 1936–1947.* Honors thesis, Department Honors in English, 1994.

Nichols, Charles H. "The Forties: A Decade of Growth." *Phylon* 11.4 (Fourth Quarter 1950): 377–80.

Noble, Jeanne. *Beautiful, Also, Are the Souls of My Black Sisters: A History of the Black Woman in America.* Englewood Cliffs, NJ: Prentice Hall, 1978.

O'Brien, John, ed. "Ann Petry." *Interviews with Black Writers.* New York: Liveright, 1973.

O'Donnell, Heather. "Ann Petry." Voices from the GAPS: Women Writers of Color. <www.voices.cla.umn.edu>.

"On the Author." *New York Herald Tribune Book Review,* 16 August 1953, Section 6, 2.

Page, Ernest R. "Black Literature and Changing Attitudes: Does It Do the Job?" *English Journal* 66.3 (March 1977): 29–33.

Peden, William. "The Black Explosion." *Studies in Short Fiction* 12.3 (Summer 1975): 231–41.

Petry, Ann. "Ann Petry." *Contemporary Authors: Autobiography Series.* Ed. Adele Sarkissian. Vol. 6. Detroit: Gale Research, 1988. 253–69.

————. "The Bones of Louella Brown." *Opportunity: Negro Journal of Life* 25.4 (October–December 1947): 189–92, 226–30. Reprinted *Miss Muriel and Other Stories*. Boston: Houghton Mifflin, 1971; Boston: Beacon Press, 1989. 163–80.

————. "Doby's Gone." *Phylon* 5.4 (Fourth Quarter 1944): 361–66. Reprinted *Miss Muriel and Other Stories*. Boston: Houghton Mifflin, 1971; Boston: Beacon Press, 1989. 296–305.

————. "Has Anybody Seen Miss Dora Dean?" *New Yorker*, October–November 1958 41–48. Reprinted *Miss Muriel and Other Stories*. Boston: Houghton Mifflin, 1971; Boston: Beacon Press, 1989. 89–111.

————. "In Darkness and Confusion." *Cross Section*. Ed. Edwin Seaver. New York: L. B. Fisher, 1947. 98–128. Reprinted *Miss Muriel and Other Stories*. Boston: Houghton Mifflin, 1971; Boston: Beacon Press, 1989. 252–95.

————. "Like a Winding Sheet." *Crisis* 52.11 (November 1945): 317–18, 331–32. Reprinted. *Miss Muriel and Other Stories*. Boston: Houghton Mifflin, 1971; Boston: Beacon Press, 1989. 198–210.

————. "Marie of the Cabin Club." *Afro-American* (Baltimore), 19 August 1939: 14.

————. "The Migraine Workers." *Redbook*, May 1967: 66–67, 125–27. Reprinted *Miss Muriel and Other Stories*. Boston: Houghton Mifflin, 1971; Boston: Beacon Press. 112–25.

————. "Miss Muriel." *Soon One Morning: New Writing by American Negroes, 1940–1962*. Ed. Herbert Hill. New York: Knopf, 1963. 166–209. Reprinted *Miss Muriel and Other Stories*. Boston: Houghton Mifflin, 1971; Boston: Beacon Press, 1989. 1–57.

————. "The Moses Project." *Harbor Review* (English Department, University of Massachusetts) no. 5/6 (1986): 52–61.

————. "Mother Africa." *Miss Muriel and Other Stories*. Boston: Houghton Mifflin, 1971; Boston: Beacon Press, 1989. 126–62.

————. "The Necessary Knocking at the Door." *The Magazine of the Year 1947*, August 1947: 39–44. Reprinted *Miss Muriel and Other Stories*. Boston: Houghton Mifflin, 1971; Boston: Beacon Press, 1989. 243–51.

————. "The New Mirror." *New Yorker*, 29 May 1965: 28–36, 38, 40, 43–44, 46, 49–50, 52, 55. Reprinted *Miss Muriel and Other Stories*. Boston: Houghton Mifflin, 1971; Boston: Beacon Press, 1989. 58–88.

————. "The Novel as Social Criticism." *The Writer's Book*. Ed. Helen Hull. New York: Harper and Brothers, 1950. Reprinted Patricia Liggins Hill, ed. *Call and Response: The Riverside Anthology of the African American Literary Tradition*. Boston: Houghton Mifflin, 1997. 1114–18; Hazel Arnett Ervin, ed. *African American Literary Criticism, 1773 to 2000*. New York: Twayne, 1999. 94–98.

————. "Olaf and His Girl Friend." *Crisis* 52.5 (May 1945): 135–37, 147. Reprinted *Miss Muriel and Other Stories*. Boston: Houghton Mifflin, 1971; Boston: Beacon Press, 1989. 181–97.

————. "On Saturday the Siren Sounds at Noon." *Crisis* 50.12 (December 1943): 368–69.

————. "Solo on the Drums." *The Magazine of the Year 1947*, October 1947: 105–10. Reprinted *Miss Muriel and Other Stories*. Boston: Houghton Mifflin, 1971; Boston: Beacon Press, 1989. 245–42.

————. "The Witness." *Redbook*, February 1971: 80–81, 126–34. Reprinted *Miss Muriel and Other Stories*. Boston: Houghton Mifflin, 1971. Boston: Beacon Press, 1989. 211–34.

Poirier, Suzanne. "From Pharmacist to Novelist." *Pharmacy in History*. Madison, WI: American Institute of the History of Pharmacy, 1986. 27–33.

Pratt, Louis Hill. Review of *Ann Petry: A Bio-Bibliography*. *CLA Journal* 38.2 (December 1994): 261–65.

Puschmann-Nalenz, Barbara. "Ann Petry: 'Mother Africa' (1971)." *The African American Short Story 1970–1990*. Trier: Wissenschaftlicher, 1993. 29–40.

Rayson, Ann. "Ann Petry." *American Women Writers: A Critical Reference Guide from Colonial Times to the Present*, Vol. 2, M to Z. Ed. Langdon Lynne Faust. 1979. New York: Frederick Ungar, 1983. 377–78.

Review of *Miss Muriel and Other Stories*. *Booklist* 68 (15 September 1971): 83.

Review of *Miss Muriel and Other Stories*. *Kirkus* 34.11 (June 1971): 587.

Review of *Miss Muriel and Other Stories*. *Library Journal* 96 (July 1971): 2348.

Review of *Miss Muriel and Other Stories*. *Library Journal* 96 (November 1971): 3915.

Review of *Miss Muriel and Other Stories*. *Publisher's Weekly* (12 July 1971): 66.

Robinson, William H. *Black New England Letters: The Uses of Writings in Black New England*. Boston: Trustees of the Public Library of the City of Boston, 1977.

Roses, Lorraine Elena, and Ruth Elizabeth Randolph, eds. "Ann Petry." *Harlem Renaissance and Beyond*. Boston: G. K. Hall, 1990. 258–64.

Ruffin, Carolyn F. "In All Shades of Black." *Christian Science Monitor*, 19 August 1971: 10.

Shea, J. Vernon. *Strange Barriers*. New York: Pyramid Books, 1961.

Smith, Harrison. "Writers are Unhappy." *Saturday Review of Literature*, 28 December 1946: 16.

Thomas, Robert McGee. "Ann Petry, 88, First to Write a Literary Portrait of Harlem." (Obituary) *New York Times*, 30 April 1997: B9.

Troupe, Quincy. "A Conversation with Terry McMillan." *Emerge*, October 1992: 51–56.

van Gelder, Lawrence. "Events." *New York Times*, 14 December 1998: E1.

Vechten, Carl Van. "A Portfolio of Photographs." *Amistad 2*. Ed. John A. Williams and Charles F. Harris. New York: Random House, 1971. 323.

"Violence against Black Women." *All the Women Are White, All the Blacks Are Men, But Some of Us Are Brave*. Ed. Gloria T. Hull, Patricia Bell Scott, and Barbara Smith. Old Westbury, NY: Feminist Press, 1982. 208–20.

"A Visit with Ann Petry." College of Pharmacy, University of Illinois at Chicago. Deposited in Kremers Reference Files. Madison: University of Wisconsin School of Pharmacy, 1984.

Washington, Gladys J. "Solo on the Drums." *Masterplots II: Short Story Supplement*. New York: Salem Press, 1996. 4057–59.

Washington, Mary Helen. "'Infidelity Becomes Her': The Ambivalent Woman in the Fiction of Ann Petry." *Invented Lives: Narratives of Black Women, 1860–1960*. Ed. Mary Helen Washington. Garden City, NY: Anchor/Doubleday. 1987. 297–306.

Wilson, Mark. "A MELUS Interview: Ann Petry—The New England Connection." *MELUS* 15.2 (Summer 1988): 71–84.

Woolfork, Lisa. "Trauma and Racial Difference in Twentieth-Century American Literature." Diss. University of Wisconsin–Madison, 2000. *DAI* (2000): 22.

Index

About the Editors and Contributors

GEORGE R. ADAMS. In 1972, when Professor Adams published "Riot as Ritual: Ann Petry's 'In Darkness and Confusion,'" he was teaching at Wisconsin State University in Whitewater, Wisconsin.

KEITH CLARK teaches in the Department of English at George Mason University. He is the author of *Black Manhood in Ernest J. Gaines, James Baldwin, and August Wilson* (2002) and editor of *Contemporary Black Men's Fiction and Drama* (2002). His critical essays on Ann Petry, Lorraine Hansberry, and William Faulkner have appeared in journals such as *African American Review, Callaloo,* and the *Faulkner Journal.* He has also contributed to a number of biocritical and pedagogical volumes, including *The Oxford Companion to African American Literature* and *An Ann Petry Encyclopedia.*

HAZEL ARNETT ERVIN is presently an associate professor of English at Morehouse College. Her work on Ann Petry has appeared in the *MAWA Review, Langston Hughes Review,* and *The Oxford Companion to African American Literature.* Her edited works include *Ann Petry: A Bio-Bibliography* (1993), *African American Literary Criticism, 1773 to 2000* (1999), and *The Handbook of African American Literature* (2004). A Fulbright Scholar, 2001–02 and a UNCF-Mellon Fellow 1999–2001, she appears in the *World Who's Who of Women* (Cambridge, England) and *Who's Who of African Americans.*

GENE FENDT teaches philosophy at the University of Nebraska, Kearney, and he has published considerable interdisciplinary works, including *Is*

Hamlet a Religious Drama? An Essay on a Question in Kierkegaard (Marquette University Press) and *Platonic Errors: Plato, a Kind of Poet* (Greenwood Press). He is currently polishing a work on the purpose of comedy from an Aristotelian perspective entitled *Love Song for the Life of the Mind*.

CAROL E. HENDERSON is associate professor of African American literature and American literature at the University of Delaware, Newark campus. Her recent publications include a 7,000-word critical biography of the noted cultural theorist bell hooks in the *Dictionary of Literary Biography* series and an article entitled "In the Shadow of Streetlights: Loss, Restoration, and the Performance of Identity in Black Women's Literature of the City" in *Alizes, Journal of the Universite de la Reunion*, France. She is currently editing a special issue on James Baldwin's *Go Tell It on the Mountain* for *MAWA Review*, and she has published an article on Ann Petry's *The Street* that appeared in the winter 2000 issue of *Modern Fiction Studies*. In November of 2002, she published *Scarring the Black Body: Race and Representation in African American Literature* (University of Missouri Press).

HILARY HOLLADAY is a Professor of English at the University of Massachusetts Lowell, where she teaches African American literature, literature of the Beat Movement, and modern poetry. She is the author of *Ann Petry* (Twayne 1996) and *Wild Blessings: The Poetry of Lucille Clifton* (LSU Press 2004).

GAYL JONES is a novelist, poet, playwright, professor, and literary critic. Her best-selling novels include *Corregidora* and *Eva's Man*. Her acclaimed short story collection is *White Rat*. Jones's criticism of Petry's short story "Solo on the Drums" that is reprinted in this volume first appeared in her book of criticism *Liberating Voices: Oral Tradition in African American Literature* (1991).

SHEIKH UMARR KAMARAH is an assistant professor of English and Linguistics at Virginia State University. He earned his B.A. (Honors) in English from Fourah Bay College, University of Sierra Leone, and an M.A. in Linguistics from Leeds University in England. His Ph.D. in African linguistics was earned at the University of Wisconsin, Madison. The author of several books of poetry and several articles on literature and linguistics in refereed journals, Kamarah teaches English, African literature, and linguistics.

AMY LEE is an assistant professor at the Hong Kong Baptist University. She teaches in the Humanities Programme and in the Department of English Language and Literature. Her research interests include: gender and fiction, contemporary women's fiction, the Chinese diaspora, mother-daughter relationships in contemporary Chinese women's writing, representation of marginal experiences, and fiction of detection. She is a contributor to various reference collections including the *Encyclopedia of the Novel*, *An Ann Petry Encyclopedia*, *Encyclopedia of the Harlem Renaissance*, *The Literary Encyclopedia* and *Literary Dictionary* (online references), and *Black Diaspora Drama* (Electronic Database).

BARBARA LEWIS is an associate professor and chair of the Department of Theatre at the University of Kentucky. She writes about African American cultural and literary history. The essay in this volume was inspired by rereading Petry for a course she taught on the social history of Harlem at New York University's Gallatin School in the summer of 2002.

DEIRDRE RAYNOR is an assistant professor at the University of Washington, Tacoma, where she teaches American Ethnic literature, particularly a number of courses on American women writers, African American writers, and Native American writers. She is finishing a book on teaching about race in American literature, tentatively titled *Navigating the Frontlines of Academia*.

NORA RUTH ROBERTS has published over 40 articles, short stories, and poems. Author of *Three Radical Women Writers: Class and Gender in Meridel El Sueur, Tillie Olsen, and Josephine Herbst*, Roberts is finishing a book on contemporary working-class culture.

EVA TETTENBORN is an assistant professor of English at the New York Institute of Technology, Manhattan campus. Her scholarship and teaching focus on African American literature, multicultural American literature, and trauma and loss in African American literature. She earned her Ph.D. in English from Binghamton University, State University of New York. Her dissertation, "Empowering the Past: Mourning and Melancholia in Twentieth-Century African American Literature," won the 2002 Binghamton University Distinguished Dissertation Award for the Humanities.

GLADYS J. WASHINGTON is a retired professor of English at Texas Southern University. She is author of *Viewpoints from Black America, A Curriculum Approach to College Writing* and numerous articles on Petry that have appeared in the *CLA Journal*, *Masterpieces of African American Literature*, *Masterplot II: African American Literature*, *The African American Encyclopedia*, and *An Ann Petry Encyclopedia*. Her play on Tituba Indian has been performed throughout Texas.

PAUL WIEBE is an associate professor of English at Morehouse College. He is author of *Myth as Genre in British Romantic Poetry* (1999) and a contributor to the *Encyclopedia of Romanticism: Culture in Britain, 1780s–1830s* and to *An Ann Petry Encyclopedia*. He is currently finishing a study of genres in British colonial discourse.